China's Managerial Revolution

STUDIES IN ASIA PACIFIC BUSINESS

1369-7153

Editors: Robert Fitzgerald, Chris Rowley and Paul Stewart

Greater China: Political Economy, Inward Investment and Business Culture
Edited by Chris Rowley and Mark Lewis

Beyond Japanese Management: The End of Modern Times?
Edited by Paul Stewart

Management in China: The Experience of Foreign Businesses
Edited by Roger Strange

Human Resource Management in the Asia Pacific Region: Convergence Questioned
Edited by Chris Rowley

Korean Businesses: Internal and External Industrialization
Edited by Chris Rowley and Johngseok Bae

East Asian Direct Investment in Britain
Edited by Philip Garrahan and John Ritchie

CHINA'S MANAGERIAL REVOLUTION

Editor

Malcolm Warner

FRANK CASS
LONDON • PORTLAND, OR.

First published in 1999 in Great Britain by
FRANK CASS PUBLISHERS
Newbury House, 900 Eastern Avenue, London IG2 7HH

and in the United States of America by
FRANK CASS PUBLISHERS
c/o ISBS, 5804 N.E. Hassalo Street
Portland, Oregon 97213-3644

Website www.frankcass.com

British Library Cataloguing in Publication Data

China's managerial revolution. – (Studies in Asia Pacific business; no. 7)
1. Industrial management – China 2. Organizational change – China 3. China – Economic policy
I. Warner, Malcolm, 1937–
658.4′06′0951

ISBN 0 7146 5025 0 (cloth)
ISBN 0 7146 8081 8 (paper)
ISSN 1369-7153

Library of Congress Cataloging-in-Publication Data:

China's managerial revolution / editor, Malcolm Warner.
p. cm. – (Studies in Asia Pacific business)
Includes bibliographical references and index.
ISBN 0-7146-5025-0 (cloth). – ISBN 0-7146-8081-8 (paper)
I. Industrial management – China. I. Warner, Malcolm.
II. Series.
HD70.C5C4418 1999 99-32400
658′.00951 – dc21 CIP

This group of studies first appeared in a special issue of *Asia Pacific Business Review* [ISSN 1360-2381] Vol. 5, Nos. 3 & 4 (Spring/Summer 1999) published by Frank Cass.

Printed in Great Britain by Antony Rowe Ltd., Chippenham, Wilts.

Contents

1

Introduction: China's Managerial Revolution

MALCOLM WARNER

The People's Republic of China will celebrate its fiftieth birthday this year. It has come a long way since the Liberation in 1949 *vis-à-vis* not only its economic evolution but also the 'managerial revolution' (a term we will elaborate upon in more detail below) experienced since its opening-up to outside influences in the last two decades.

Two years after the death of Mao Zedong in 1976, Deng Xiaoping embarked upon an 'Open Door' policy. But the full impact of the changes in the economy and management were not to be fully felt until well into the 1980s. These were then consolidated in the late 1980s and early 1990s. Deng, according to some, deliberately adopted a wholly pragmatic strategy.

China has accomplished a great deal since Deng's reforms. It is now an 'economic superpower' in waiting (Lardy, 1998). After a decade of rapid economic growth of over 10 per cent per annum, a remarkably sustained achievement, the Chinese economy then went into a slow-down in the latter part of the 1990s. The double-digit growth per annum phase is now held to be over, according the Chinese Academy of Social Sciences Institute of Economics (see *Beijing Review*, 23 November 1998: 16). A more moderate growth-rate is forecast for the end of the century and into the next. Too much was invested, resulting in a surplus of productive capacity; the lack of effective demand has allegedly been a result of over-tight personal credit in recent times. Due to competition from the non-state sector and greater imports, the vast array of state-owned enterprises (SOEs) is now faced with 'downsizing'. Whereas formerly there was 'bottleneck' restraint in the command economy, there now appears to be a 'demand' restraint in the more marketized one.

China is for sure now at a critical juncture in its economic and political development (Ma *et al.*, 1994). It seemed for a while that its progress to economic superpower status might follow a smooth course and entry to the WTO would climax its progress this century. But this was an overly optimistic analysis. Few were to predict the full weight of the Asian economic crisis of 1997–98 and the aftermath of the Embassy bombing in Belgrade in 1999. The magnitude and depth of these crises were not expected. Given the interdependence of those regional economies in the Asia Pacific Rim, a domino-effect of sorts was anticipated.

The Chinese economic policy makers, it is said, have behaved very responsibly under their new leadership in these difficult times but the economic stewardship of Premier Zhu Rongji has been hard-pressed to keep the lid on the political cauldron. The high economic growth rate considered achievable earlier may prove to be too high, given the natural calamities at hand. At least, the grain harvest in 1997 was a bumper one. However, the Asian crisis will just not go away and China's economy has not been untouched by it. Pressure on the Chinese authorities to devalue the yuan has dominated the headlines of the international business press. The prospect of deflation kept consumer spending seriously reined in and interest rates have been cut successively; investment plans have been scaled down; the downsizing of the state-owned enterprises was put on the agenda but then placed 'on hold'.

The roots of the present crisis were essentially external to China, but overly rapid growth in the last decade has also played its part in making China vulnerable. The infrastructure was overstretched. Many problems from the past, like the indebtedness of the SOEs, were to not be decisively resolved. If the PRC is to be the next economic superpower, its leaders must indeed tread more carefully than ever.

STRUCTURAL REFORMS

The fate of China's state-owned enterprises, the true inheritors of the 1950s enthusiasm for Soviet-style everything (the slogan was 'Let's Be Soviet and Modern', for instance), indeed hangs in the balance (see Child, 1994; Warner, 1995). Once, their workers were the 'masters' of the society (or *zhuren*); now, their future is increasingly uncertain (Lu and Perry, 1997). Those employed in SOEs numbered over 77.6 million in the mid-1990s but now are a smaller percentage of the industrial workforce than they were in their heyday. The township and village enterprises, joint ventures, foreign-funded businesses and the like now provide more and more jobs annually, though the rate of growth of such work-creation is decelerating.

The statistical picture, according to official estimate at least, is daunting. Once, state firms made two-thirds of the nation's industrial production; now, this is down to less than a third (Lardy 1998). Numbers of smaller and medium-sized ones have closed or merged. Many are in poor shape, possibly over half of the state sector, and perhaps even more are 'in the red'. Forty per cent were seen as virtually 'bust' for some time; now, the World Bank and others produce even greater estimates in this genre. They have 'inflexible mechanisms, irrational structures, heavy social burdens and weak enterprise managements' (*Beijing Review*, 17 June 1996). The Chinese now want to turn the more robust ones into something like 'chaebols', Korean-style (a little questionable and late in the day, given the recent South Korean economic crisis), and have the strongest hundred firms control the commanding heights of the economy. This leaves the remaining smaller and mid-sized SOEs in a vulnerable condition. Over 110,000 firms are at risk. These are 95 per cent of the total; 80 per cent of this subset are said to be in deficit (*Beijing Review*, 15 September 1997).

Jiang Zemin, the new President of the People's Republic of China, set out to stamp his name on a new reform policy, and Zhu Rongji, the new Premier it is said, wants to be the 'hard man' to lay low the spectre of 'soft loans' and 'triangular debt'. It is the logical progression from Deng's reform legacy. Shanghai, for example, has selected one thousand of its key enterprises for modernization and reform. One hundred conglomerates have been formed there. Of course, unemployment in that city is officially low but may be in reality probably closer to one in twelve workers. Foreign investment there was set to decline (*Financial Times*, 5 December 1997). Given the complexities of bankruptcy in the Chinese system, mergers are favoured. 'Privatization' in all but name looms large for many large SOEs, nationally. A 'revolution' not only in managerial terms but also in corporate governance is in prospect.

Joint ventures between Chinese and foreign firms were once seen as the answer, however the outlook became distinctly 'glum' by early 1999 (see *Financial Times*, 25 March 1999: 19). There are now over 315,000 agreements signed; if only half implemented. But their performance has been a mixed bag. Indeed, there have been many substantial problems in creating a competitive culture in them, as in the case of Beijing Jeep (see Mann, 1997). They were often grafted on to old SOE 'cores'; the old mind-sets persisted as well, in all too many cases. In fact, not all of the apparent 'dinosaurs' were at fault. Some SOEs and collectives have established themselves as path-breakers, like Legend Computers, which has a very strong position in the PC market. Others, like Beijing Founder, have a massive share of the market for hardware and software for newspaper and book publishing. The Haier Group, dating from the mid-1980s in Qingdao, making domestic appliances, is another 'benchmark' company of this kind that has won many awards for quality. It aims to be among the top 500 firms in the world in the next century.

Since 1992, China has allowed many of its SOEs to trade on the Hong Kong stock market, where they are dubbed H-shares. The object was to allow access to foreign investors' funds. Another motive was to give an impetus to their managements to become more efficient. In 1992, Tsingtao Brewery, a top state-owned Chinese brand, was floated and was heavily oversubscribed. Now over 40 or so such firms have floated on the market. Their financial performance has been mixed, but after an initial period when price–earning ratios were excessively high by market standards some of these 'red-chips' are now in a comparable range to many other 'blue chips'.

Other Chinese state-owned industrial giants are well in the black; most of the low-performers or loss-makers were small state firms, a number of whom have been already swallowed up by more robust ones. The profit level of over 300 key SOEs is alleged to 'be better than in general', according to official sources. In many cases, the losses of the SOEs, funded by 'soft loans', have been incurred for basically non-economic reasons, at least in part, to prop up the costly 'iron rice bowl' cradle to grave welfare facilities of those employed there. Those costs would anyway have to be borne by national or local governments, if such facilities were provided outside the enterprise. To create a level playing-field for firms, the new idea is to externalize these costs. Many costs, such as social insurance and medical care, now have to be partly paid for by the individual rather than the enterprise. The 1997 Party Congress announced that the era of life-long free benefits was now officially over.

Whereas the 'big bang' was the favourite route to reform in Eastern Europe and the former Soviet Union, for some Western economists at least, the Chinese way is one of pragmatic prudence, 'by groping for stones across the river'; then, transcending private ownership; last, achieving enterprise reform. If China had pursued the 'big bang' strategy, it would not have won the success it enjoys today. Indeed, 'gradual' does not at all mean 'slow'; pragmatism was the rule.

MANAGERIAL REFORMS

In this volume, we hope to examine the degree to which China has undertaken managerial reforms in order to make the economic changes work. The economic reformers inherited the Soviet-inspired management structures and practices of the 1950s. These were based on the SOE work-unit (*danwei*) model, involving life-time employment and cradle to grave welfare arrangements. There was an 'iron rice bowl', 'iron chair' and 'iron wages'. The first involved jobs for life for workers; the second meant managers were equally sure of their jobs; and the third ensured relative equality of rewards.

The introduction of the economic and management reforms of the 1980s led to substantial changes in how Chinese industry was run. New legislation made enterprises more autonomous in their management practices. Managers could, for example, hire and fire more freely.

In this collection, we have assembled a set of contributions that attempt to describe and analyse the managerial changes which have taken place in the Chinese economic system as a whole as well as in specific enterprises. They range from the general to the specific. All the contributions are based on up-to-date empirical research in the fields of economic and managerial change in the People's Republic of China.

We have used the term 'China's managerial revolution' more as a play on words rather than to strictly refer to the term used in the economics and management literature on the 'managerial revolution' that was supposed to have occurred in Western capitalist economies, with the separation of ownership and control in large corporations, as managers rather than owner-entrepreneurs began to run corporations (see Berle and Means, 1932; Marris, 1996). With the economic reforms in China, there has increasingly occurred a split between ownership and control, at least first at the operational level, then later at a more strategic one, as managers have been given greater powers *vis-à-vis* the state and its officials (as agents of the official owners).

The state-owned sector has been downplayed and downsized; the non-state sector has grown very rapidly. In 1978, four-fifths of industrial output came from the SOEs; now it is down to just over a quarter. There are now more domestic privately owned and foreign-invested firms, especially equity joint ventures. Even more recently, steps have been taken to 'corporatize' Chinese domestic firms and diversify ownership.

We turn now to the batting-order of the specific contributions in this symposium on China's 'managerial revolution'. First, in a broad overview, Ross discusses whether 'communitarian capitalism' is a viable model for China in its transition to market socialism. As between American style 'individualism', European 'statism' and Japanese 'communitarianism', he cogently analyses their systemic characteristics, advantages and disadvantages as well as costs and benefits. He believes that the socio-cultural environment in China poses no substantial hurdles to moving closer to the Japanese model. China is expected to do in just a few years what Japan did in forty. Corporate groupings would thus form a 'mezzo-level' bridge between government agencies and relatively independent business interests. Whether China is taking up a model that has now been superseded by economic events is another matter.

Second, Selmer and colleagues look at how the Chinese management model has been transformed over the last two decades. Unlike in other countries that have set out on the path of modernization, economic transformation in China has been effectively shaped by countless individual managers in business organizations. Within the framework of the economic reforms, the state has encouraged this process of managerial adaptation. Whether by way of their mistakes or successes, managers are now 'active' participants in setting the course of future change. In their contribution the authors clearly emphasize the incremental nature of the Chinese reform process.

Third, Forrester and Porter examine the politics of management in the PRC. They look at the Contract Management Responsibility System (and its antecedents) as it emerged in the wake of the 'Open Door' policy over the last decade. They analyse both the 'state contract system' as well as the 'internal contract system' and their respective features, and then look at the 'Modern Enterprise System' which was introduced after 1993 to replace the CMPS. This addressed itself to the questions of ownership, short-termism, negotiations, tax reforms and corporate responsibilities. Forrester and Porter's data show that it was widely felt that the MES was an improvement on its predecessor. The way it addressed the question of ownership, for example, is interesting in the context of the focus on the 'managerial revolution'. Despite the introduction of management autonomy and discretion, the authors believe that there are differences of opinion on what precisely the current industrial problems are and how to address them. Whatever the lip-service to modern management techniques, many managerial cadres feel they must put the interests of the state as a major 'owner' before those of the enterprises.

Next, Bennett looks at relationships (*guanxi*) and management practices in China. Examining over a hundred foreign enterprises in the PRC, he attempts to see how far *guanxi* are a major factor in sales-force marketing. His main conclusion is that businesses that did not see relationships as important were more likely to employ behaviour-based rather than outcome-based rewards systems. He concludes that is vital for foreign firms operating in the PRC to incorporate *guanxi* into their management systems. In fact, the longer Western firms have operated in China, the more they have used it, partly because of the learning effects and observation of how local firms do business effectively.

Lan then examines management in the Chinese construction industry. He finds that the behaviour of key stakeholders, such as contractors, government and suppliers, as well as new entrants to the market, has changed dramatically as the firms have become more market driven. But the industry is poorly regulated and fragmented. Government intervention is still strong. He concludes that further reforms are needed if international competitive advantage is to be achieved.

This is followed by the Ilari and La Grange case-study discussion on setting up a joint venture in China. It concerns a Sino-Italian JV making motor cycles that tried to replicate the features of the parent company when setting up in the PRC. The company believed that there was a rapidly expanding market for the product in China. A major problem was that suppliers were reluctant to relocate there. It found that there was resistance by core suppliers to enter into joint ventures to manufacture their products in China; they had anxieties about shortages of skilled personnel as well as the high costs and uncertainties of operating in this difficult business environment. Marketing and distributional difficulties also became apparent, as well as those relating to work organization. Euro-motor, the company in the case-study, thought it could create a flexible work structure in its Chinese JV with minimal hierarchical divisions. The local Chinese and expatriate Italian managers had very different perceptions of the required management style. Technology-transfer is often easier than passing on managerial know-how.

Child and Heavens then describe their research on managing corporate networks from America to China. They examine how eight prominent American MNCs handled the process of linking the management of their China joint ventures into their global structures. The study looks at how the MNCs address the tensions that arise between maintaining control in terms of their worldwide standards while attempting simultaneously to adapt to the complex and dynamic environment of China. The reconciliation of these requirements depends on a relatively few focal actors, who are located at critical interfaces within the MNCs' internal networks between the China joint ventures and the corporate level.

After this, Yan discusses managerial and organizational learning in a large set of international JV firms in the Chinese context, 67 enterprises in all. They varied in size between 50 and 2000 employees in the PRC. The companies were Western, Overseas Chinese and Japanese, according to their headquarters base. She highlights the trade-off between the gains of managerial and organizational learning *vis-à-vis* the need for the JV partners (as owners) to keep a level of control appropriate to securing a reasonable returns on their assets. A larger equity share is found to support a greater parent company's influence over the strategy of the Chinese partner firm.

Ebrahami next looks at the applicability of the 'motivation to manage' construct, to provide a new tool for more effective strategic human resource management practices in Chinese organizations. Contrary to expectations, he found that there are no differences between motivation to manage in SOEs and 'for-profit' organizations. There are a number of possible explanations here. First, until recently most PRC for-profit organizations were state-owned enterprises and, as a result, major differences between the two sectors may not be that clear cut. Second, slower job mobility in China may lead to a delay in the mobility of higher-motivated managers from the SOEs to the newly formed private firms. He concludes that Chinese organizations can improve their recruitment, selection, management development and training, promotion, and ultimately their strategic human resource management systems.

The 'myth' of human resource management in China is discussed in the contribution by Warner, Goodall and Ding. In a study of 62 enterprises in China, based on a sample consisting of both SOEs and JV firms, the authors conclude that because of organizational inertia, the transfer of Western-style HRM has proved problematic. The main findings show how difficult it has been to change the 'mind-sets' associated with the 'iron rice bowl' that characterized Chinese state firms first established in the post-1949 period. People-management in JV firms was closely compared with that in SOEs in the sample. They found that in many ways the two sets of firms both retained many old-style employment practices, though JVs had the edge on their SOE counterparts in many diverse ways. Although HRM practices are becoming more de rigueur in JVs, it will be some time before they are the norm for all large firms.

To sum up, we have presented above a range of contributions that relate to the managerial innovations that have been part and parcel of China's economic reforms since 1978. It is clear that there has not been a neat linear progression over the last two decades towards a Western management model, for instance. The reforms have been introduced in an essentially pragmatic way and have affected some sectors and enterprises more dramatically than others. It is clear that much reform in the managerial arena has been achieved in the foreign-invested sector as opposed to the SOEs. Even here, the distinction has not been clear cut. Some JVs have remnants of the older *danwei* system, whereas a number of 'leading-edge' SOEs have been models of change. Much now hinges on the next stage of the economic reforms that China may attempt to implement, as we move into the next century.

REFERENCES

Beijing Review, 17 June 1996.

Beijing Review, 15 Sept. 1997.

Beijing Review, 23 Nov. 1998.

Child, J. (1994), *Management in China in the Age of Reform*. Cambridge: Cambridge University Press.

Financial Times, 15 Dec. 1997.

Lardy, N. (1998), *China's Unfinished Revolution*. Washington, DC: Brookings.

Lockett, M. (1988), 'Culture and the Problem of Chinese Management', *Organization Studies*, Vol. 9, No. 4, 475–496.

Lu, X. and Perry, E.J. (eds) (1997), *Danwei: The Changing Chinese Workplace in Historical and Comparative Perspective*. New York: Armonk / London: M.E. Sharpe.

Ng, S.H. and Warner, M. (1998) *China's Trade Unions and Management*. London: Macmillan / New York: St Martin's Press.

Ma, H. *et al.* (1994), *What Is the Socialist Market Economy?* (In Chinese.) Beijing: China Development Press.

Mann, J. (1997), *Beijing Jeep: A Case Study of Western Business in China*. Boulder, CO/ London: Westview.

Marris, R.L. (1996) 'Managerial Theories of the Firm', in M. Warner (ed.), *International Encyclopedia of Business and Management*. London: International Thomson Business Press, Vol. 4, pp.3117–25.

Warner, M. (1995), *The Management of Human Resources in Chinese Industry*. London: Macmillan.

Warner, M. (ed.) (1999), *Changing Workplace Relations in the Chinese Economy: Beyond the Iron Rice Bowl*. London: Macmillan/New York: St Martin's Press (in preparation).

2

Communitarian Capitalism: A 'Market' Model for China?

DOUGLAS N. ROSS

A China in transition marks a hopeful beginning to the twenty-first century. If China succeeds in its simultaneous move from developing to industrializing country and from command economy to 'market-orientated socialist economy', then one-quarter of the world's population may look forward to economic betterment. Countries are shedding economic systems underpinned by heavy government intervention because these have failed to deliver growth and a better life for their populations (Yergin and Stanislaw, 1998). Faced with global competitive forces, market-orientated socialism attempts to optimize two very different goals: first, the transformation of domestic, state-owned firms into global, competitive firms; and second, the protection of the functions of the state-owned firms – such as the provision of social services (Spence, 1990; Starr, 1997; Westland, 1998). To achieve the goals, Deng Xiaoping set out two basic principles: first, reforms should promote rapid economic growth and not weaken the party's control of the political system; second, everything else is negotiable (Starr, 1997).

North's (1990) hypothesis is germane. Institutions, constrained by economic scarcity, create opportunities in a society. Organizations then emerge to take advantage of those opportunities, which in turn alters the institutions themselves. Some such process is underway in China. The operative question, however, is: Which institutional 'model' of capitalism seems the most suitable to encourage China's economic growth, within the constraining principles?

As capitalist regimes – American-style 'individualistic', European 'statist' and Japanese-style 'communitarian' – of the global triad contend for dominance in the emerging world economic order, China is emerging as a critical battleground. Perhaps that characterization understates the importance and distinctiveness of Asian regimes – in particular, Chinese family business of Hong Kong and Taiwan, *chaebol* conglomerates of South Korea and the *keiretsu* and *kigyo shudan* corporate groupings of Japan. This study examines the utility of the Japanese model for China's transition to 'market-orientated socialism'.

Many scholars, looking to Japan for guides, have focused on the transfer of Japanese management techniques to China (Ma, 1997; Wong and Tjosvold, 1998); Japanese business strategy in China (Ritchie, 1997); similarities of Japanese, US and Chinese 'conglomerates' (Chou, 1997); and the viability of Japanese corporate governance itself (Bostock and Stoney, 1997). This contribution focuses on the applicability to China of the complex, enormously successful, but recently troubled Japanese model of industrial capitalism. The first section very briefly explains the Japanese model; the second assesses the feasibility of the Japanese approach to China's transformation. The concluding section addresses some of its implications for China and foreign firms.

UNDERSTANDING THE JAPANESE CAPITALIST MODEL

Japanese communitarian capitalism operates on three levels: macro-level relationships between national governments and between the Japanese government and business; mezzo- or intermediate level relationships among and within corporate groupings and between business groups and the government; and micro-level relationships between a firm and its corporate grouping and between the firm, its industry and the Japanese government. Figure 1 illustrates these levels of Japanese industrial structure.

At the macro level, a government 'roof' provides domestic markets with some measure of protection from the competitive incursions of foreigners. Macro-level decisions involve consensus-orientated government planning to establish and implement policy (Ouchi, 1984). Second, private-sector corporate groupings both act together through the *zaikai* to establish national direction and compete through their member firms. Government, through industry advisory councils and the *zaikai* (big business groups such

FIGURE 1
JAPANESE INDUSTRIAL STRUCTURE

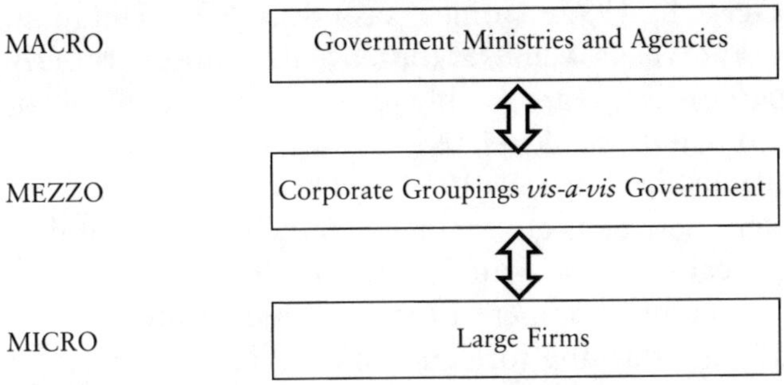

as the Federation of Employers or the Keidanren), interacts to develop agreement upon, and then coordinate the implementation of, national policies. This interface gives government great flexibility to utilize fine-tuning measures to help specific industries while not impairing overall competitiveness (Okimoto, 1989). The Japan model presupposes relatively independent interests apart from government. It also provides big business with a very large say in government policy. In other words, Japanese policies, practices and institutions are the way they are because the various Japanese interests, particularly big business, want them that way.

At work here is not the familiar notion of cooperation between government and business; rather there are 'reciprocal relations'. For example, the Japan Fair Trade Commission (JFTC) may pursue antitrust measures with some flexibility so as to prevent 'overcompetition' in the domestic market. Thus, producer cartels may be formed since Japan's economy favours the 'producer' not the 'consumer'(Thurow, 1992). Government builds an industrial policy by a type of national 'ringi' system – consensual decision making – wherein 'the government is the captain and the Zaikai [big business] the compass of the ship' (Yanaga, 1968: 34). When national priorities are at stake, MITI (the Ministry of International Trade and Industry) may encourage firms to seek efficiencies beyond their corporate groupings. For example, the world's largest steelmaker, New Japan Steel, sells its output to a dozen trading companies. In turn, the trading companies may assist in acquiring iron ore for New Japan, in selling steel, or in selling steel products such as ships domestically and internationally. Abroad, MITI promotes open markets and free trade.

The Critical, Unique Intermediate Level

At the intermediate level, individual firms often group themselves into 'alliances' (Gerlach, 1992; Gomes-Casseres, 1996; Dunning, 1997). Popularly known as *keiretsu* (but usually more properly called *kigyo shudan*) they are a blend of political-financial, strategically coordinated, bank-related, industrially linked and intermarket relationships (Ross, 1991). They form both an institutional bridge between government and business, and a philosophical, strategic and structural context for the Japanese firm. Corporate groupings compete fiercely domestically, yet can also cooperate fully in attacking foreign markets. They represent a stable yet continuously evolving set of political and business structures and relationships which provide member companies with the support to vigorously pursue international market opportunities. This intermediate institution is the hallmark of Japanese-style capitalism.

An integral part of a corporate grouping is its trading company. Most have offices and long-standing connections in China. The largest six *sogo shosha* (trading companies) with assets in excess of $50 billion, both connect their *keiretsu* members to the global market and bring market opportunities to their *keiretsu.* These relationships serve to 'internalize' many intermediate product and labor markets and tie foreign countries and companies into Japanese corporate grouping networks. A trading company's distinctive competence lies in its matching of buyers and sellers of diverse products and the playing of many different roles (Yoshino and Lifson, 1986). For example, Mitsui & Co. helped develop Japan's cotton spinning industry by, first, procuring foreign spinning technology and machinery. As domestic cotton supplies were depleted it found stable foreign sources and then stimulated the weaving industry by buying the products for distribution at home and abroad. Seldom do the *sogo shosha* engage in one-time transactions; more usually they prefer multi-stage involvement in vertically integrated commodity systems and in such products as textiles, steel, metals, chemicals and food. Often, ancillary services such as financing are provided.

At the micro level, a *kaisha*'s (large firm) vertical corporate grouping *(keiretsu)* may be linked to an inter-industry, horizontal *kigyo shudan*. The *keiretsu* system serves as an enabling context for firm strategy. For example, core group banks provide stable sources of long term capital for expansion and continuous upgrading of skills, technology and equipment. Group trading companies may support sales and marketing. Further, members support group member firms as they move to attack foreign markets. To what extent is the Japanese model compatible with changing Chinese economic, social and political environments?

ASSESSING THE ADAPTABILITY OF THE JAPANESE MODEL TO CHINA

Much discussion of market economies seems to be premised on the notion that they are similar. Yet the variety of successful forms suggests that there are a variety of ways for institutions to adapt to business environments. In order to analyse the 'fit' between Japanese approach and Chinese circumstances, we illustrate North's hypothesis with examples from political-economic and socio-cultural institutions. The aim is to develop more appropriate policy and strategy responses for both government and business leaders.

Political-economic Institutions and Environment

An institutional link between freedom of economic choice and freedom of political choice has yet to be forged in China. Chinese leaders are walking a tightrope. To one side lies stasis, as falling back on the old planning system could simply add new layers to the ranks of intermediaries; to the other lies turmoil. Party and military elites and families jockey for position as they work out their roles in a market economy while China struggles to build a post-Marxian rationale for individual political and property rights. Now, however, there exists a clear alternative capitalist structure that may provide some balance, and it is one with which China's leaders have great familiarity.

Much Japanese experience is relevant to China. Soon after the Second World War Japan saw the need to: utilize industrial policy measures to get resources to critical areas; abolish many economic controls and liberalize trade and capital flows; develop a base for competition; create a market for corporate stock ownership and improve managerial skills; convert military industries to civilian uses; encourage capital formation in business, for example through generous depreciation allowances; enhance industrial technology (for example, establishing subsidies and favourable tax treatment for R&D activities and checking increases in royalties to conserve foreign exchange); promote exports (for example, the government established the Export-Import Bank of Japan in 1951 for export financing and the Japan External Trade Organization (JETRO) in 1954 to carry out overseas market research); and encourage the 'soft' infrastructure of the economy (such as the promotion of industrial standards and the creation of laws on patents and trademarks). This same list could belong to China.

Major differences exist between China and Japan. According to the China Statistical Yearbook (1996) over 75 per cent of China's people live in rural areas, with agriculture providing over two-thirds of the employment. About 25 per cent, or 300 million people, live in urban areas. About 100,000 state-owned industrial enterprises (as well as two-thirds of the wholesale distributors, two-fifths of the retail outlets, and virtually all the banks, schools and hospitals) form the core of the economy. Noteworthy is that the military 'own' a significant percentage of these enterprises. State-owned enterprises account for 18 per cent of employment and 36 per cent of output. There are approximately 33,000 townships in China each with about 750 collective enterprises. Of this 750, 300 are production sector, 300 service sector, 10 are agricultural, and the rest are construction and transportation. Additionally, over 2 million industrial and 2 million service collectives are in the major cities. All told, collectives employ 76 per cent of Chinese workers and produce 49 per cent of the output. While still a relatively small proportion of the Chinese economy, the over 500,000 private enterprises (this includes 200,000 foreign joint ventures) represent its fastest growing segment. Private enterprise accounts for 6 per cent of employment and 15 per cent of output. Overall, GNP per capita amounts to $620, purchasing power parity estimates of GNP per capita raise that to $2,920, and the growth rate is 8.3 per cent (World Bank, 1997).

Various structural reforms are needed to improve the chances for success of the high growth private segment. These include a price mechanism to enable realistic prices and a financial system to facilitate commerce and international transactions. Rational decisions could then be made about resource use, privatization and incentives (for example, wages tied to productivity and competition from other firms), all of which require a strong currency (Lipton and Sachs, 1992).

The weather difficulties of August 1998 have brought to light endemic PRC corruption. To illustrate, billions have been poured into dams and other large scale infrastructure projects by both the central government of the PRC and the International Monetary Fund ($30 billion in the period 1980–97). Many dams and dikes supposedly built to contain flooding are failing because of improper construction. Billions were siphoned off into individual pockets.

China and Japan are similar in that their economies are highly protected and export driven. China's trade surpluses have created US$121 billion currency reserves, and attracted $42 billion investments. The bilateral trade surplus with the USA was running at $49 billion. Economic reforms began in China in the mid-1970s with four Special Economic Zones in the southern coastal region. Much early capital, technology and know-how came in small to medium scale ventures from overseas Chinese. Their foreign investments also began to provide links between global markets and the collectives of the townships and villages. This growth of private and semi-private business created market pressure on state-owned enterprise. At the macro level, government sets policy and organizes economic activity. While this contravenes official International Monetary Fund (IMF) policy, to a considerable degree eminent Chinese agree with Japan's MITI that 'the IMF first seeks macro-economic stability. After that they think the market will decide. From our thinking, this is not enough. Some kind of industrial policy is needed to supplement' (Schlesinger, 1992: A9).

An 'Intermediate' Level in China

The National Peoples' Congress is responding to global pressures by creating clusters of formerly state-owned enterprise. Their rationale appears to have several facets: first is the attempt to restore state companies to health so that some outstanding loans can be repaid. The primary means employed is through rationalizing state-owned enterprise. As stronger companies take over weaker ventures, chronically unprofitable companies will be absorbed. An example is Sinochem, which began in the petrochemicals industry and is diversifying into industrial projects, maritime shipping, retail, theatres and other areas. By 1995, it was 26th in Fortune's ranking of international companies. A less sanguine example is the Baoshan Group's takeover of Shanghai

Metallurgical Holdings and Wuhan Iron and Steel. As the Asian crisis grows, China's steel industry faces declining demand, declining prices and excess labour. Baoshan, profitable and with an excellent credit rating, must absorb unprofitable firms with over ten times its employees (Chang, 1998).

Selected companies get preferential treatment in loans and research and development funding in order to assist them to become competitive. A prime example is the government-owned China International Trust and Investment Company (CITIC), a development bank modelled on the Japan Development Bank. CITIC provides capital to enterprises, and equity participation through holding companies and through joint venture links to foreign capital, technology and markets (Leung, 1996). Yet clustering may obscure the need to nurture new, small firms. Smaller firms typically grow due to product and market innovations rather than cost reductions and rationalization. Thus longer term economic growth comes from helping small firms expand. Both the emerging groups and the state via CITIC may have a role in this, but only if the need is clearly recognized and met with an appropriate response.

The second facet is the attempt to shield enterprise from political interference and, further, to counteract political interference in economic reform. In the former instance, a state-owned holding company is formed to oversee the activities of a group. For example, the China Aerospace Corporation located in Beijing, acting on a directive from the Aerospace Ministry, instructs XiAn Aerospace to consolidate aerospace parts manufacturers. Additionally, joint ventures and multinational, multi-product trading arrangements may be encouraged. XiAn, for example, has a joint venture with McDonnell-Douglas. Obviously, government still retains control of the group and over whatever arrangements are made.

Forward and backward integration of activities is meant to affect not only the economies of production but also the politics. For example, in aircraft manufacturing, creating integrated clusters of enterprises cuts across both ministerial jurisdictions (under the Ministry of Aerospace Industry and the Ministry of Machinery and Electronics) and administrative authorities (such as provincial councils). Table 1 sets out seven industry groups established in the early 1990s.

TABLE 1
CHINESE 'INTERMEDIATE' GROUPINGS

Group	*Industry*	*Total Assets*
Baoshan Iron & Steel Group	Steelmaking	$9.2 billion
Haier Group	Appliances	$4.1 billion
Shanghai Automotive Group	Automobiles	$4.0 billion
Sichuan Changhong Group	Televisions	$1.7 billion
North China Pharmaceutical Group	Drugs	$866 million
Jiangnan Shipyard Group	Shipbuilding	$658 million
Peking University Founder Group	Software	NA

Source: Adapted from *Wall Street Journal*, 30 April 1998, p.R9; and Chou, 1997.

This type of integration is roughly akin to earlier Japanese *zaibatsu* – pre Second World War, family owned, diversified holding companies, which were disbanded by SCAP (Supreme Command Asia Pacific). They had quickly reformulated themselves into vertical *keiretsu* and horizontal *kigyo shudan*. The *zaibatsu* model is closer to the one followed by South Korea's chaebols, and most Asian country conglomerates.

Third, is the attempt to develop functioning groups of enterprise as being more viable and attractive to foreign investors. Walder (1995) observes that the Chinese have tended to avoid Western economic advice. One such example is privatization. Fearful of repeating Russian experience with the sell-off of state assets – rigged auctions, military ownership of business, and contracts for a politician's own company (Brooks, 1993) – China's approach to privatization has been indirect. Two stock markets – Shanghai and Shenzhen – sell four classes of equity shares: A shares for PRC citizens, B shares for foreigners, H shares for selected Hong Kong listed securities, and N shares for selected securities also listed in New York. Typically, only some of the equity of an enterprise is available for sale (Rawski, 1995). About 10,000 state-owned companies are slated to become publicly traded companies (currently some 750 companies have shares listed on Shanghai and Shenzen exchanges) which also creates a need for stronger financial reporting requirements (Westland, 1998).

Mergers and acquisitions, which serve both as a kind of capital market and a means of privatization, may occur through Asset Transfer Centres. Although theoretically it is possible for a private firm to acquire a state-owned firm, this is very difficult because of their quasi-governmental functions – providing social services, health care, housing, education and employment. Usually, however, either a state-owned firm acquires another state-owned firm or a state-owned firm partners with a private firm and forms a new enterprise. Further, it is not likely that so-called backbone industries – energy, communication, transportation – will be fully privatized (Dong and Hu, 1995).

An alternative to indigenous groupings are direct links with Japanese corporate groupings. Such links could provide the Chinese government with a model for financial intermediation as well as Chinese business with access to capital and complete development packages. On the Japanese side, political-business leaders are clear in their aims. Claims Koichiro Ejiri, former head of Mitsui & Co. and the Japan Foreign Trade Council, 'the development of the Asian economy with Japan at its center will be beneficial to everyone' (Fortune, 1992: S-12).

Socio-cultural Institutions and Environment

Is there a demonstrable connection between culture and industrial structure? Table 2 sets out cultural dimensions for China, including Hong Kong, and Japan based upon values that incorporate the Chinese Value Survey (CVS). The dimensions are: power distance, individualist/collectivist, masculinity/femininity, uncertainty avoidance and, added by the CVS, long term orientation. L, M, H reference relevant locations within the range of values for a specific dimension (Hofstede, 1980, 1991, 1993). We note that 'national' cultural dimension scores may be too broad, and effort should be made to include regional, ethnic and language variations. For illustrative purposes, however, national dimensions may assist in assessing the applicability of the Japanese model to China.

China has a relatively high power distance (PD) – that is, the extent to which a society accepts the unequal distribution of power within its institutions. Its score places it among the top ten countries (50 countries in the Hofstede (1980) studies, 23 in the CVS (Hofstede, 1991), but these countries mostly overlap). PRC Chinese, based upon Hofstede scores, tend to prefer formalized organization, authority from the top and centralized power, as well as a relatively high level of formalism in relationships and communications. Shenkar and Ronen (1985) note that Chinese negotiators are influenced greatly by their emphasis on social obligations and notions of politeness and emotional restraint. Thus,

TABLE 2
CULTURAL DIMENSION SCORES AND STRUCTURAL 'FIT'

Dimensions/Countries	*PD*	*IND/COLL.*	*M/F*	*UA*	*LTO (CVS)*
China (PRC)	80H	20L	50M	60M	118H
Hong Kong	68H	25L	57H	29L	86H
Japan	54M	46M	95H	92H	80H
Culture/ Structure 'fit'	neutral/ negative	neutral/ negative	neutral/ negative	neutral/ neg active	positive

Source: Based on Hofstede, G. (1993) 'Cultural Constraints in Management Theories', *Academy of Management Executive*, Vol.7, p.91.

the cultural bias is towards a formal, centralized organization with control from the top.

On the other hand, the Japanese power distance score places it 33rd of 53 (Hofstede, 1991: 26), meaning that there is a preference for consultation over authoritarian rule, but organizations are still not prone to be organic, flexible or with decentralized power. Other things being equal, then, the greater a country's power distance scores, the greater the preference for centralized, relatively authoritarian organizations. Thus, we rate this factor as having an essentially 'neutral' but slightly negative influence on the adaptability of the Japan model to China.

The individualist dimension relates to societies in which connections between individuals are essentially 'each person for himself/ herself'. Individualist cultures see the self as autonomous and independent. At the polar extreme, a collectivist culture describes societies in which people are part of cohesive groups, with individual loyalty offered in exchange for protection by the group. In collectivist cultures, a conception of the 'self' develops as an individual learns connectedness to others and acquires deeper discernment about others' expectations of correct and incorrect behaviours (Kitayama *et al.*, 1997). Individuals then are seen as part of an interconnected social web whose focus is to correct shortcomings (Bailey *et al.*, 1997). Hofstede (1991) notes a correlation between power distance and collectivist scores: in cultures where individuals depend upon ingroups, often there is also relatively large power distance. We would rate this dimension too as 'neutral-negative' in terms of 'fit'.

On these two dimensions, Hong Kong is closely aligned with China. In Hong Kong, Chinese family business (CFB) tends to be either family members only or a 'clan' consisting of a core of family members, plus relatives and outsiders. CFB may be summarized as paternal, familial, hierarchical, personal, and subject to mutual obligations and connections (Redding, 1990; Chou, 1997). Thus, the 'clustering' tendency is similar in China and Hong Kong, but the nature of the cluster differs.

China has a medium uncertainty avoidance (UA) score – that is, a preference for stability, order and predictability – while Japan is in the 'high' category. Since many strategic problems are unstructured, their solution involves innovation, and tolerance for ambiguity. Uncertainty avoidance suggests less tolerance and less flexibility in dealing with different-from-the-norm ideas and a greater belief in experts. On the other hand, it also suggests that where implementation requires attention to procedures, precision and stability, then it may be a strong positive. This again suggests a proclivity for centralized organizations. Hofstede (1991) notes a correlation between strong uncertainty avoidance and high collectivist scores: in such cultures, rules tend to be formal, implicit and traditional. Communications tend to be high context. Hall (1976: 79) explains: 'a high context communication . . . is one in which most of the information is either in the physical context or internalized in the person, while very little is coded, explicit, transmitted as part of the message. A low context message is just the opposite; i.e. the mass of the message is vested in the explicit code.' High context countries include Japan and China; low context countries include Germany and the United States. We thus conclude that, other things being equal, the greater the power distance, the greater the collectivist, and the greater the uncertainty avoidance scores, the greater the prevalence of centralized, bureaucratic organizations. We rate this dimension as neutral-negative as well.

On the masculinity/femininity (M/F) dimension, masculinity is associated with earnings, recognition, opportunities for advancement and distinct gender roles. Production efficiency is an important value. The femininity score is associated with relationships, cooperation, employment security and overlapping gender roles. Assertive behaviour may be fostered by masculine cultures but tempered in feminine ones. Performance and success may be important goals in masculine cultures, whereas welfare and happiness tend to be more important in feminine cultures. China's M/F score is mid-range. Japan's score is highest, at 95, of all countries studied. By way of comparison, Sweden's is lowest at 5, and the USA's is 62 (Hofstede, 1991: 84). We rate this dimension as neutral-negative.

On the long term orientation (LTO) dimension, the top five countries are China (118), Hong Kong, Taiwan, Japan (80), and South Korea (of the 23 countries in the study). Long term orientation is associated with a concern for the future, persistence, perseverance in pursuing goals, having a sense of shame, and thrift. These values relate to other dimensions. For example, 'having a sense of shame' underpins the notion of self in a collectivist society as being connected to others in a group and encouraging the keeping of commitments. Thrift provides savings for investment. Persistence is a fundamental trait of any entrepreneur. Further, a strong correlation exists between LTO scores and economic development for the period 1965–87 (Hofstede, 1991:166–7). These scores also have implications for would-be partners. Park and Ungson (1997) note that international joint venture longevity decreases with the cultural distance between partners (cultural distance means the degree to which cultural norms in one country differ from those in another country (Kogut and Singh, 1988)).

Short term orientation was associated with respect for tradition, saving 'face', and reciprocal favours. For example, a too-traditional approach may slow innovation. Or, for example, the Chinese notion of *guanxi,* or connections, is more a reciprocal obligation to respond to requests for assistance than a simple interpersonal relationship (Tsang, 1998). Historically, many Chinese have lived in hierarchically organized, closed communities with ruling elites controlling and allocating resources. The only way for most Chinese to gain access to resources has been through connections. Whitley (1992) shows how primarily family-based relationships underpin many of the extensive networks of Chinese business. The LT/ST mix of values, taken with PD scores relating to acceptance of unequal power, may lead to an emphasis on stable, harmonious relations within hierarchical organizations.

On balance, the socio-cultural environment seems to pose few insurmountable hurdles to the Japan model.

CONCLUSIONS

The new reality for the Chinese people is a growing exposure to global economic forces. Two main needs emerge: first, weave new patterns of efficiency-inducing competition from the old fabric of bureaucratic bargaining; and, second, deliver growth. Just as countries reject the excesses of government intervention, so also 'free market' capitalism will be rejected unless it delivers economic growth, employment and improved living standards. Can the Japanese model deliver for China? Stated differently, which model of capitalism has been followed by virtually every East Asian industrializing country since 1960? If we examine these now-tarnished countries, their failings come down to some variation of 'corruption'. US experience with securities markets just after the Crash of 1929 may be instructive. A bank examining committee report on bad loans noted that often they had been made to friends and relatives of bank directors, judges and politicians (Wigmore, 1985: 121–2).

Implications of the Japanese Model for Chinese Leaders

Japan has successfully exported its political-business model to many areas of the world. Hollerman (1988) documents Japan's movement of its older 'smokestack' industrial base to offshore, lower wage areas in order to reduce costs and increase 'imports'. Headquarters remain in Japan, along with most high value added manufacturing. Products serve the local market and may be reimported to Japan. It is in this context that much development has occurred in newly industrializing countries. The economies of Malaysia and Thailand, for example, have been integrated into Japan due to supply chain and investment ties with Japanese corporate groupings. The effects on the developing country are mixed – on one hand it gets much-needed industry and jobs, yet on the other it may also get locked into smokestack industries and the low end of the value chain.

Chinese products are expected to compete head-on in the world economy. China is expected to do in a few years what took Japan forty. For China, the challenge is to open a path to institutional change. This entails proper incentives to ensure appropriate institution–organization interaction and feedback (North, 1990) and the increasingly efficient use of scarce resources. As noted,

Japanese groupings are not merely conglomerates. A critical political-financial function of corporate groupings is to form a mezzo-level bridge between government agencies and relatively independent business interests that assists in the development and vetting of national policy. It is this area in which adapters of the Japanese model are most deficient.

Implications of the Japanese Model for Foreign Firms

Three main implications emerge: the importance of working with China to meet China's goals; the need to overcome many obstacles in the China environment; and the importance of political backing to business negotiations.

Meeting China's goals. The international competitive implications are striking. Many advantages could flow to Chinese firms linked to trading companies. The *sogo shosha*, for example, can package mammoth deals including hardware, software, personnel, infrastructure (transportation, power, communications), financing and markets (Cutts, 1993). The components in the package are drawn primarily from firms within a corporate grouping and often can include special Japanese government dispensations as well. Increasingly, competition is waged between corporate groupings on a scale beyond the capability of even the largest single firm.

Even strategic alliances and international joint ventures may fall short of *sogo shosha* clout. To the extent that this situation obtains, international managers may suffer barriers to access similar to those into the Japanese market. One response is to create more custom-tailored deals.

From the Chinese perspective, however, both Japanese and Western firms are still foreign firms. Thus large turnkey companies, such as Fluor or Bechtel, and service companies which create and enhance indigenous capabilities should find opportunity.

Overcoming market obstacles. Getting paid presents a special challenge. Since only the highest priority items will be bought for hard currency, most foreign firms will have to learn to deal with the intricacies and variations of countertrade. In the commodity countertrade model Western firms accept local currencies for products and services, purchase local goods with local currencies, and then sell these goods through international commodity exchanges. Or, in what may be called the 'McDonald's variation', Western firms may choose to reinvest in China, with repatriation of proceeds well into the future.

All foreigners face similar obstacles to doing business in China. The challenge for the foreign firm is to clearly delineate a business strategy for dealing systematically with institutional environments, which includes meeting China's need for job creation. On balance, effective Chinese demand rests with about 150 million people. China's leaders need to improve the economic lot of one billion, two hundred million people.

Negotiating deals in a political-business context. China's choice of direction is by no means preordained. Business deal making will be within the political context of China's interests. Western firms are seen as representatives of their countries and thus may be subject to other than economic considerations. For example, just as developing countries once sought aid and military assistance by playing off Soviet and US interests against each other, so also China may seek economic benefits by counterbalancing Japanese and Western interests. Clearly, this has already been the case with respect to Taiwan. Foreign governments, then, are at least implicit partners, along with foreign and Chinese firms, in most large deals.

Dramatic redefinition of the role of the state and the market appears to be assisting the rise in Chinese living standards. Globalization and technological change, however, also bring anxiety, job dislocations and economic crises. The challenge to China's leaders is to ameliorate the insecurities and deliver the growth.

REFERENCES

Bailey, J., Chen, C. and Dou, S. (1997), 'Conceptions of Self and Performance-related Feedback in the US, Japan and China', *Journal of International Business Studies*, Vol. 28, No. 3, pp. 605–25.

Bostock, R. and Stoney, C. (1997), 'Japanese Corporate Governance: Governance for the Twenty-First Century or Model in Decline?', *Asia Pacific Business Review,* Vol. 4, No. 1, pp. 63–82.

Brooks, D. (1993), *Wall Street Journal*, 23 April, p. A12.

Chang, L. (1998), 'Big Is Beautiful', *Wall Street Journal*, 30 April, p. R9.

Chen, M. (1997), *Asian Management Systems*. New York: Routledge.

China Statistical Yearbook (1996).

Chou, Y. (1997), 'Some PRC Perspectives on Conglomeration of Enterprises', *Advances in Chinese Industrial Studies*, Vol. 5, pp. 331–341.

Cutts, R. (1993), 'Eastern Europe's Troubles Open Door for Japanese Expansion', *California Management Review*, Vol. 33, No. 3, pp. 58–72.

Dong, J. and Hu, J. (1995), 'Mergers and Acquisitions in China', *Economic Review*, No. 6. pp. 15–29.

Dunning, J. (1997), *Alliance Capitalism and Global Business*. New York: Routledge.

Fortune (1992), 'New Corporate Alliances Accelerating Trend toward Global Economic Integration', *Fortune*, 24 Aug., p. S12.

Gerlach,M. (1992), *Alliance Capitalism: The Social Organization of Japanese Business*. Berkeley, CA: University of California Press.

Gomes-Casseres, B. (1996), *The Alliance Revolution: The New Shape of Business Rivalry*. Cambridge MA: Harvard University Press.

Hall, E. (1976), *Beyond Culture*. New York: Doubleday.

Hofstede, G. (1980), *Cultures Consequences: International Differences in Work-Related Values*. Beverly Hills, CA: Sage.

Hofstede, G. (1991), *Cultures and Organizations: Software of the Mind*. London: McGraw-Hill.

Hofstede, G. (1993), 'Cultural Constraints in Management theories', *Academy of Management Executive*, Vol. 7, pp. 91.

Hollerman, L. (1988), *Japan's Economic Strategy in Brazil: Challenge for the United States*. Lexington, MA: Lexington Books.

Kitayama, S., Matsumoto, H., Markus, H. and Norasakkunit, V. (1997), 'Individual and Collective Processes in the Construction of the Self: Self-enhancement in the United States and Self-criticism in Japan', *Journal of Personality and Social Psychology*, Vol. 72, No. 6, pp. 1245–1267.

Kogut, B. and Singh, H. (1988), 'The Effect of National Culture on the Choice of Entry Mode', *Journal of International Business Studies*, Vol. 19, No. 3, pp. 411–432.

Leung, J. (1996), 'Firm Hand Steers China's Thriving Hong', *Asian Business*, Vol. 32, No. 4, pp. 26–34.

Lipton, D. and Sachs, J. (1992), 'The Strategy of Transition', in D. Kennett and M. Lieberman (eds), *The Road to Capitalism*. New York: Dryden, pp. 350–353.

Ma, Z. (1997), 'What To Learn from the Japanese: The Process of Japan-style Management Transfer', *Asia Pacific Business Review*, Vol. 3, No. 1, pp. 118–131.

North, D. (1990), *Institutions, Institutional Change and Economic Performance*. New York: Cambridge University Press.

Okimoto, D. (1989), *Between MITI and the Market: Japanese Industrial Policy for High Technology*. Stanford: Stanford University Press.

Ouchi, W. (1984), *The M-Form Society: How American Team Work Can Recapture the Competitive Edge*. Reading, MA: Addison-Wesley.

Park, S. and Ungson, G. (1997), 'The Effect of National Culture, Organizational Complementarity and Economic Motivation on Joint Venture Dissolution', *Academy of Management Journal*, Vol. 40, No. 2, pp. 279–307.

Rawski, T. (1995), 'Implications of China's Reform Experience', *The China Quarterly*, Vol. 144, pp. 1150–1173.

Redding, G. (1990), *The Spirit of Chinese Capitalism*. New York: Walter de Gruyter.

Ritchie, J. (1997), 'Evolving China Strategy: How Japan Compares', *Asia Pacific Business Review* ,Vol. 3, No. 3, pp. 132–147.

Ross, D. (1991), 'Keiretsu: Global Managers' Unseen Competitors', *Advances in International Comparative Management*, Vol. 6, pp. 205–223.

Spence, J. (1990), *The Search for Modern China*. New York: W.W. Norton.

Starr, J. (1997), *Understanding China*. New York: Hill and Wang.

Thurow, L. (1992), 'Who Owns the Twenty-first Century?', *Sloan Management Review*, Vol. 33, No. 3, pp. 5–17.

Tsang, E. (1998), 'Can Guanxi Be a Source of Sustained Competitive Advantage for Doing Business in China?' *Academy of Management Executive*, Vol. 12, No. 2. pp. 64–73.

Walder, A. (1995), 'China's Transitional Economy: Interpreting Its Significance', *China Quarterly*, Vol. 144, pp. 963–979.

Westland, J.(1998), 'A Comparative Study of the Role of Information Technology in State Sector Privatization in China and Russia', *China International Business Symposium Proceedings*, Vol. 2, pp. 490–499.

Whitley, R. (1992), *Business Systems in East Asia: Firms, Markets and Societies*. London: Sage.

Wigmore, B. (1985), *The Crash and Its Aftermath*. Westport CT: Greenwood Press.

Wong, M. and Tjosvold, D. (1998), 'Transferring Japanese Management Competence to a Sino-Japanese Joint Venture in China', *China International Business Symposium Proceedings*,Vol. 2, pp. 392–397.

World Bank (1997), *World Development Report, 1997: The State in a Changing World*. New York: Oxford University Press.

Yanaga, C. (1968), *Big Business in Japanese Politics*. New Haven: Yale University Press.

Yergin, D. and Stanislaw, J. (1998), *The Commanding Heights: The Battle between Government and the Marketplace That Is Remaking the Modern World*. New York: Simon & Schuster.

Yoshino, M. and Lifson, T. (1986), *The Invisible Link: Japan's Sogo Shosha and the Organization of Trade*. Cambridge, MA: MIT Press.

3

Managerial Adaptation in a Transitional Economy: China

JAN SELMER, CAROLYN ERDENER, ROSALIE L. TUNG, VERNER WORM and DENIS F. SIMON

One of the major factors that is shaping the structure and process of international business in the last decade of the twentieth century has been the opening up of the China market. The emergence of China, with its population of over 1.2 billion people, promises to alter the dynamics of international business competition in the next century in fundamental ways (Child, 1994).

For two decades, China has been one of the world's fastest growing economies. By the early 1990s, China ranked tenth in the world in exports, rising from $9.8 billion in 1978 to $85.0 billion in 1992; foreign direct investment (FDI) rose in this period from around $600 million to $11.3 billion, then accelerated to $25.7 billion in 1993 and to $33.8 billion in 1994 (Lardy, 1994; Garnaut, 1996). By 1997, total FDI was $42.2 billion (Far Eastern Economic Review, 1999). In terms of actual purchasing power, the World Bank and International Monetary Fund ranked China's economy third in the world after the USA and Japan. Even after the economic downturn of 1998, as other Asian countries experienced negative economic growth and collapse of their currencies, China maintained an overall positive trend in economic growth, albeit at a somewhat slower pace.

The magnitude of China's achievement stands out in comparison with the European and former Soviet centrally planned economies, where economic dislocations and disruption have been widespread. China has experienced a relatively smooth and gradual transition, characterized by rapid growth of the private sector, for 20 years. To place this in perspective, however, it must also be noted that 'China is not a coherent "system"' (Pye, 1993: 13), and that the lack of a detailed master plan for carrying out the economic transition has been viewed by many as a weakness (Broadman, 1995).

Some of the changes made at the outset of the reform process were designed to open up the system to ad hoc innovations and experimentation in business organizations. As a result, the process of economic reform has benefited from the cumulative effects of a wide variety of managerial initiatives and adaptations (Naughton, 1995).

> [E]ven the Chinese are not exactly sure what they mean by 'capitalism, central planning' or what they want to achieve in the long run. The definitions are constantly being redefined; new ideas are tried out and abandoned if they do not produce the expected results relatively quickly (Murphy, 1994: 23).

Throughout this process of experimentation, China's leaders remain firmly committed to the course of economic reform, expansion, and integration into the world's economy. While rejecting capitalism as a system, they recognize the need to selectively adopt certain practices in order for the market to function. Among these are a number of practices associated with Western management.

Socialist Market Economy

For 14 years following the introduction of economic reforms in 1978, China attempted to create a functioning market economy within the framework of state-owned enterprises and state management of industry.

> The [Chinese] leaders and elite are now committed to building a socialist society based neither on state-run planning nor on a capitalist market economy but rather on a mixture called socialist market economy with Chinese characteristics. No communist-controlled society in this century has successfully established such an economy that could produce high economic growth through high factor productivity, promote a fairly equal distribution of wealth and income while avoiding swings of inflation and deflation, and increase material living standards while not degrading the environment. The Chinese leadership,

> however, now seems determined to establish such an economy which it hopes will outperform both the capitalist and the centrally-planned economy (Myer, 1995: 66).

Following the inflation of 1988 and ensuing Tiananmen incident of 1989, as well as the example of the former Soviet Union, by the early 1990s it was becoming increasingly clear that new approaches were needed. This marked the onset of a renewed effort to implement economic reforms. The change was signalled in early 1992 by Deng Xiaoping's tour of the economically advanced regions in south east China adjacent to Hong Kong, during which he spoke out strongly in support of similar economic advances for the rest of China. By the summer of 1992, plans were underway for a major proclamation at the upcoming 14th Party Congress. On 12 October 1992, the Congress opened with a statement by Jiang Zemin in which he called for establishment of a socialist market economy in China (Myer, 1995).

Since then, the implications of the socialist market economy continue to be clarified. This includes such undertakings as developing commodity markets, reforming the property rights of state enterprises, establishing factor markets for labour and capital, and gradually converting state-owned enterprises to 'a corporate enterprise system of mixed property rights within the context of new macroeconomic regulations and controls' (*Zhongguo tongxun she*, 1994, in Myer, 1995: 56).

FOCAL AREAS FOR MANAGERIAL ADAPTATION

Economic transition in China is being enacted through a process of incremental learning and adjustment, rather than through centralized advance planning. The process is designed to encourage managerial initiative and adaptation (Naughton, 1995), thus enabling decision makers to benefit from the experience and experimentation of countless individual managers and organizations. For those at the top, it is a logical approach to planning long term radical system change while minimizing the potential for disruption that is inherent to transformation of such magnitude.

From the perspective of individual managers, however, the result is an environment fraught with uncertainty. The managerial response to these conditions is best captured in a colloquial

Mandarin expression as 'getting across the river by groping [with your toes] for stones' (Huang, 1998:1).

In the following sections, some characteristic areas requiring managerial adjustment during this process of economic transition are examined in greater detail. Clearly, there are many such areas. The focus here is on several that are especially relevant for Western firms doing business in China: workforce, culture, and technology. Following a brief overview of the context and significance of each of these topics, three empirical studies are summarized in the next section to illustrate the process and some of the problems of managerial adjustment in China.

Workforce

In the new world of market competition, securing a workforce that can consistently maintain the necessary level of performance is a major responsibility for managers in China. Under the old system of guaranteed full employment (the 'iron rice bowl'), workers were paid irrespective of performance. Terminations were relatively rare.

However, new technologies require skills and experience that may not be available in the local workforce. Competitive pressures, especially in export markets, require levels of efficiency, productivity and quality on the part of workers that may conflict with previous experience. Some assignments may require a knowledge of international operations that is not readily available.

It is therefore not surprising that many of the dilemmas faced by foreign companies in China involve staffing. Foreign firms with some experience in China generally tend to learn on their own that hiring ethnic Chinese from outside China to manage operations in the mainland may not be the most effective approach to staffing problems. What has generally not been recognized, however, is that sending managers from Hong Kong to the mainland can be even more problematic for the firm (Selmer and Shiu, 1999).

Culture

Another focal area of managerial adjustment involves culture and work-related values. While selectively borrowing and adapting management and technology from the West, the Chinese authorities continue to reject Western cultural values. 'They want advanced technology, finance and managerial experience . . . but not the West's cultural values – dollars, not democracy; profits, not political pluralism' (Murphy, 1994: 7).

At the same time, however, there is evidence of some assimilation of values associated with individualism, materialism and capitalism (Erdener, 1998; Whitcomb *et al.*, 1998). It is not clear to what extent the values of the marketplace can be unravelled from those of capitalist societies. Some studies of values in Chinese cultural contexts suggest that the process of modernization may foster some Chinese cultural characteristics at the expense of others (Yang, 1996).

Interpersonal relationships are one example of a core element of Chinese culture that is central to the process of social and economic change. Success in business depends to a great extent on having the right connections *(guanxi)*. Technological expertise, which can appear critical from the perspective of the Western firm entering China, may actually be less essential for getting things done than having personal connections with key government officials. Even such basic factors as the price and quality of the foreign firm's product may not be decisive. This topic has been addressed in the work of a number of management scholars including Rosalie Tung, and is reviewed in her empirical study with Vernor Worm, set out later.

Technology

To reach their goal of transforming China into a major industrial power during the early part of the next century, Chinese leaders have placed a very high priority on the upgrading of their country's technological and management capabilities. Realizing that the country's ambitious goals could not be achieved through a policy of self-reliance, the current, reform-oriented leaders have placed an important emphasis on the acquisition and assimilation of foreign technology and management expertise.

From the Chinese perspective, the technology and management know-how that are required to sustain and support overall economic modernization are to be secured either through the direct licensing of technology or through the vehicle of foreign investment.

While the level of national spending on R&D and education has continued to increase, however, the overall availability of funds remains constrained by the other competing priorities that Chinese officials must address. Thus the reality facing many Western firms operating in China is that technology transfer is encouraged to help in upgrading the knowledge and skills of the indigenous workforce. The responses of Western firms to this situation have been explored in research efforts led by Denis Simon, noted below.

THREE EMPIRICAL STUDIES

In this section, three recent empirical studies involving managers in China are summarized as representative examples of managerial adaptation in the context of economic transition in China. These studies deal with a range of issues, including the workforce, Chinese culture, and technology transfer.

Adjustment Issues Managers Face between Hong Kong and the Mainland

Foreign firms operating in China often assign managers from Hong Kong to their China operations in the belief that their common Chinese heritage will make it easy for them to adjust to living and working on the mainland. Failing to recognize the need for adjustment, they do not provide the necessary support, and do not take the difficulties of cross-cultural adjustment into consideration in evaluating managerial performance. Despite a common Chinese cultural heritage, firms cannot assume that managers can be readily transferred between Hong Kong and the mainland with minimal adjustment. Contrary to common wisdom and popular belief about the benefits of cultural similarity, managerial adjustment between Hong Kong and the PRC mainland can be as difficult as anything identified in the literature on expatriate management (Black and Porter, 1991; Selmer, 1995).

Sending managers from Hong Kong to cities like Beijing and Shanghai, or vice versa, is therefore best regarded not as a domestic transfer, but as an expatriate-type assignment. The difference is in the consciousness of dissimilarity. When an expatriate is assigned to a foreign culture, problems are generally attributed to the difficulties of cross-cultural adjustment. But when managers are posted to another city in the same country, cultural differences are typically overlooked, and so the need for cultural adjustment is not recognized. Lacking conscious awareness of cultural dissimilarity, managers may blame their subordinates or themselves for problems which in reality are manifestations of the stress of culture clash (Brewster, 1995; Selmer and Shiu, 1996). This contradicts conventional wisdom, which states that managerial adjustment is facilitated by reducing the cultural distance between the manager's home culture and that of the transfer assignment (cf. Church, 1982).

The purpose of this study is to analyse the experiences of Hong Kong managers who have been transferred to Beijing and Shanghai, and of managers from Beijing and Shanghai who have been transferred to Hong Kong. It is a two-way mirrored comparison of adjustment issues in the transfer of managers between locations in the mainland and in Hong Kong. Building on a recent study of Hong Kong managers assigned to Beijing and Shanghai (Selmer and Shiu, 1996), it is the first known research to test the assumption of easy managerial adjustment between Hong Kong and mainland China.

From the growing literature on business management practices and policies in China (Warner, 1987, 1992, 1993; Tung, 1991; Shenkar, 1993), one could speculate that Western expatriate managers assigned there would have to make considerable work role adjustment. However, there have been very few empirical studies of work role adjustment of expatriate managers in the PRC. Bjorkman and Schaap (1994) highlight some problems encountered by foreign expatriates in China and suggest practical remedies. No published research was found focusing on the subject of adjustment of managers transferred within China in general, or between Hong Kong and other locations in China. The only known research along these lines is a recent study of the adjustment of Hong Kong managers working in Beijing and Shanghai (Selmer and Shiu, 1996).

The unfamiliar setting of a new host country creates psychological uncertainty which the individual tries to reduce, especially with regard to expected new behaviours and unacceptable or inappropriate old behaviours. This can create unanticipated difficulties for the firm (Erdener and Torbiorn, 1999a, 1999b).

Making information about these issues available prior to departure facilitates anticipatory adjustments, and thus the actual adjustment processes in the new context will be easier and faster. Anticipatory adjustment in the Black, Mendenhall and Oddou

(1991) model is affected by both individual and organizational factors. In-country adjustment is affected by individual, job, organizational and non-work factors. Mendenhall and Oddou (1985) also supported the significance of non-work roles. In the present study, the model developed by Black, Mendenhall and Oddou (1991) is used to frame the analysis of interview data.

Personal interviews were conducted with managers from Hong Kong stationed in Beijing and Shanghai, followed by a similar set of interviews carried out with managers from Beijing and Shanghai who are now located in Hong Kong. To avoid industry bias, subjects were drawn from a wide range of industries including manufacturing, construction, food and beverage, services, and trading. All had been working in their current locations for at least two years. Of the companies involved, about half are based in Western countries.

A culturally appropriate approach had to be developed to gain access to prospective interviewees. This was necessary because the issue of trust, a core element in Chinese culture, greatly affects interpersonal relations and information sharing (Zhang and Bond, 1993). Chinese managers typically will not agree to an interview without personally knowing the interviewer very well or being introduced to him by a trusted intermediary, or *guanxi* (see Hwang, 1987; Chang and Holt, 1991; King, 1991). Even with *guanxi*, contacting the potential respondents by fax or letter and inviting them to participate in an interview invariably produced a negative response. Therefore, the initial interviews were conducted with a small number of managers who had solid business connections with one of the researchers, and then expanded into a snowball sample by using interviewee referrals. Such expanding networks of relationships are common in Chinese cultures, in which intermediaries are used to 'pull' or 'climb' *guanxi* with other people (Chang and Holt, 1991).

The results of this study clearly indicate that the assumption of easy adjustment for managers moving between Hong Kong and mainland cities like Beijing and Shanghai is an illusion. The somewhat inaccurate perception of cultural closeness builds up expectations that, when not met, result in frustration, resentment and withdrawal; this seriously impairs the performance of many managers, with adverse implications for firm performance.

This is significant for the selection, training, and performance evaluation of international managers on assignment with multinational firms engaged in China.

Guanxi *and Business Performance in China*

In her latest book, *World Class: Thriving Locally in a Global Economy* (1995), Kanter identified the three intangible assets, referred to as the three 'Cs', for surviving in the global economy. The three 'Cs' are: *concepts* ('the best and latest knowledge and ideas'), *competence* ('the ability to operate at the highest standards anywhere') and *connections* ('the best relationships which provide access to the resources of other people and organizations around the world').

In this section, we focus on the third intangible asset, connections. Specifically, we will discuss the significant role that connections can play in the context of doing business with the Chinese.

In China (as elsewhere), there is a popular saying that 'Who you know is more important than what you know'. 'Who you know' refers to social connections with the appropriate authorities or individuals, commonly referred to as *guanxi*. 'What you know' refers to technological expertise, including price and quality of tendered product and/or service. In other words, there is a widespread belief among Asians and non-Asians alike that in order to succeed in doing business in Confucian societies, *guanxi* (proper connections) are often more important than the price and quality of the product/service which the foreign investor has to offer.

Some people have speculated that as China modernizes, the role of *guanxi* would diminish since greater emphasis should be placed on institutional law. A cursory review of the situations in other advanced or more developed Confucian societies, such as Hong Kong and South Korea, shows that modernization and the establishment of institutional law did not displace completely the reliance upon relationships and connections. Relationships and connections are among the core values upheld by these societies.

In fact, in a survey of 2,000 Chinese from Shanghai and an adjoining rural county in the early 1990s, Chu and Ju (1993) found that over 90 per cent of those polled confirmed the importance of *guanxi* in their daily lives. In addition, they found that the younger generation tended to place greater emphasis on *guanxi* than the older people.

The significance of *guanxi* in attaining business success in present day China was documented by Yeung and Tung (1996). In their study of 19 Hong Kong and non-Hong Kong firms doing business in China, Yeung and Tung found that there was a correlation between a firm's possession of the 'right' and 'strong' connections and its long term financial performance. The Yeung and Tung study represents the first systematic attempt to operationalize the *guanxi* construct and examine its relationship to financial performance.

In a study which builds upon Yeung and Tung's work, interviews were conducted with 30 large multinationals, primarily from Western Europe, which were involved in business in China. These multinationals were engaged in a diverse range of industries, including chemicals, pharmaceuticals, transportation and financial services, and employed an average of 70,000 employees worldwide.

These multinationals perceived *guanxi* to be of critical importance to success in doing business in China, though to a lesser extent than those firms surveyed in the Yeung and Tung (1996) study. This difference may be due, in part, to the fact that large multinationals can generally wield more bargaining power *vis-à-vis* their Chinese partners. Furthermore, the Western European multinationals are more diversified in their operations geographically than the Hong Kong firms. In the Yeung and Tung (1996) study, the majority of companies surveyed were from Hong Kong. Most Hong Kong firms derived 100 per cent of their revenues from China. In contrast, for the non-Hong Kong firms, between 5 and 45 per cent of their revenues from the Asia-Pacific region came from China.

Technology Transfer to China: A Corporate Perspective

Since the launching of the open door policy in the early 1980s, the PRC government has made strenuous efforts to attract foreign investment and technology imports. Unfortunately, throughout most of the 1980s, confronted with an immature legal and regulatory system and uncertain political risks, many foreign firms decided to take a wait-and-see attitude; while many firms were indeed willing to commit to one two joint ventures, there was a high degree of hesitancy to make a major commitment of resources and technology to China. The political events of 1989 only seemed to make things more unsettled.

Ironically, however, within twenty-four months after the Tiananmen incident, foreign investment by the world's major firms started to grow rapidly, and quickly surpassed the levels of the first decade in a few short years (Schroath *et al.*, 1993). For the first time, Chinese officials were in a position to utilize the growing purchasing power of their industrial enterprises and individual consumers as a form of leverage and bargaining power. In return for access to the expanding Chinese domestic market, PRC government officials began to press their demands for stepped up transfers of technology. In other words, the quid pro quo for gaining access to the Chinese domestic market was measured in terms of the quantity and composition of technology to be transferred.

With so much emphasis being placed on the transfer of technology, in summer 1996 Andersen Consulting embarked on a study of the technology transfer practices and attitudes of MNCs in China (Simon, 1997). The Chinese case provides an excellent vantage point from which to gain an overall better understanding of the strategic management of technology by MNCs because of the centrality of the issue to business success in the PRC. MNCs have been the principal purveyors of technology transfer around the world and primarily have been responsible for the rapid diffusion of advanced technology since the end of the Second World War. Yet, on the whole, the record of MNCs abroad insofar as technology transfer is concerned has not been a stellar one, especially when American and European firms have ventured beyond their Western comfort zones. Interestingly, the pressures for enhanced transfers of technology by MNCs to host countries have become even greater today. This suggests that without an effective, well designed approach to the transborder management of technology, MNCs will lack one of the critical success factors for doing business in new strategic locations that include India, Brazil, Mexico, Indonesia and Russia as well as China.

The Andersen study team, which was based in the Beijing office, surveyed via questionnaires approximately 75 multinational firms operating in China to ascertain how they were approaching the issue of technology transfer to China, and to identify some of the critical success factors associated with the effective leveraging of technology. The survey examined firms operating in four major cities: Beijing, Shanghai, Tianjin and Dalian. It also concentrated on five key industries: consumer electronics, telecommunications, food processing, pharmaceuticals and automotive components. In addition to the questionnaires that were sent out, site interviews were conducted with 20 of the foreign firms to flush out some of the details pertaining to their China experiences. Moreover, a series of interviews was conducted with PRC officials to determine their perspective on the strategies and tactics of MNCs regarding technology transfer.

The results of the survey brought to light a variety of interesting and at times surprising findings. These findings must be looked at in the context of the prevailing atmosphere regarding technology transfer to China. Over the last year or so, a number of complaints have been raised by foreign corporate executives about the pressures Chinese officials have placed on multinational firms to open up further regarding technology transfer, often playing one firm against several others to extract the most favourable benefits during intensive commercial negotiations. Yet, despite these concerns, 63% of the firms surveyed reported that they were involved in rather extensive technology transfer activities in China. The main motivation for these firms (80%) was to gain market access. Most important, 76% of these same companies indicated that they saw their technology transfer activities as being beneficial in terms of achieving their business goals in the PRC.

One of the more revealing findings of the survey was the fact that 60% of the firms reported that the underlying motivation for technology transfer to China was to achieve a better alignment between their PRC-based operations and their global or regional business strategies. This finding is consistent with the transition that has taken place within many corporate boardrooms regarding China business. Whereas China was a small blip on the computer screen of many corporate executives just a few years ago, it has now moved to centre stage in terms of strategic importance, especially as the locus of competition has shifted from the Atlantic to the Pacific over the last decade. In addition to viewing the Chinese domestic market as a major business opportunity, more and more MNCs are interested in integrating their China operations for manufacturing, sourcing or R&D with their global plans and activities. A transition has begun to occur in their attitude towards China – no longer is the PRC simply seen as a low-cost labour export platform, but rather it is gradually, albeit steadily, being viewed as a site for more higher-value-added manufacturing.

Another significant impetus for engaging in technology transfer for these firms has been the imperatives of cost reduction and localization. In the past, many Japanese firms, in particular, had reported a reluctance to expand their operations in China due to the absence of adequate numbers of competent local subcontractors and component producers. Today, according to the findings of Andersen researchers, many of these same firms are now building their own production networks in China, especially in the electronics and automotive components sectors. Moreover, while some of these newly architected production networks are localized in cities such as Dalian and Tianjin, a growing number of them are increasingly integrated into the regional production structure of Japanese firms in the Pacific Rim.

These findings shed light on another provocative finding from the survey. Approximately 57% of the firms surveyed indicated that their technology transfer activities were self-initiated, with only 7% reporting that the PRC government was the primary initiator. This seems to contradict the general impression noted above, namely that the PRC government is asserting excessive pressure on foreign firms to transfer technology. In addition, only 20% of the firms reported that their Chinese partner, joint venture or otherwise, had initiated the original discussions about technology transfer.

One of the reasons for this situation may be that the Chinese side frequently lacks a tangible perspective on the content of the technology transfer package in the up-front portion of the negotiating process. The Chinese side often utilizes the discussions regarding technology transfer across several competing firms as a learning process. Information revealed during negotiations with one firm is often leveraged to acquire concessions from other firms. The data also seems to indicate that an increasing number of firms have moved away from a project-by-project or opportunistic approach to adopting a more strategic, longer term vision. Companies such as Motorola and Siemens, for example, have begun to make substantial investments in China, apparently with an eye towards addressing future competitive requirements in their respective industries.

Among the reasons cited by firms in the survey regarding their degree of success *vis-à-vis* technology transfer, 40% suggested that their key success factor was adequate preparation. Another 40% suggested that their key success factor was an ability to communicate and share their goals with their Chinese partner; and

18% pointed to effective training as a key ingredient. Unlike the situation in the 1980s, when many firms came to China largely unprepared to handle the complexities of the PRC business environment, more and more companies have climbed up the learning curve and now seem to enter China with their eyes wide open and their strategic goals much clearer. In addition, the increased normalization of the Chinese business environment also seems to be a key factor, as there is now a more comprehensive body of laws and regulations regarding the treatment of foreign firms in China. At the same time, however, a majority of the firms stressed, in retrospect, that they need to have more flexibility regarding doing business in China. In particular, foreign firms cited the ongoing process of economic reform as one of the reasons for the continued shifts in operating environment in China.

In terms of the content of the technology transfer package being offered, 71% of the firms reported that the transfer of management know-how and systems was one of the most significant elements in almost all cases. Again, in contrast to the earlier periods of China's open door, there has been a shift that now emphasizes securing more soft technology rather than hard technology. Increasing emphasis is being placed on the transfer of design and process know-how rather than just on equipment purchases by the Chinese side. Over 52% of the firms surveyed indicated that training also was a critical element in their approach to technology transfer. Of these, over 50% indicated that they had sent significant numbers of Chinese employees abroad for training to ensure that their business developed in a fashion consistent with their strategic goals inside and outside China. The big issue, however, is getting the Chinese to pay for these intangible aspects of technology transfer. In spite of the policy changes noted above, a sizeable number of foreign companies reported that many of their PRC counterparts continue to be reluctant to provide compensation for the conveyance of management know-how or training programmes.

Finally, a number of major concerns were expressed regarding technology transfer to China. Ironically, while 72% of the firms noted that they had strong concerns about adequate protection of their technology, very few of the firms in the survey indicated actually experiencing specific problems involving intellectual property rights. At the same time, 88% of the firms indicated that they had engaged in some form of renegotiation regarding the provisions of their technology transfer agreement, with 62% reporting that they had to approach the local government for assistance in resolving the disputes. To protect their technology in China, 47% indicated that they had adopted an incremental approach that involved reciprocal performance-related requirements; continuous transfers of technology were contingent upon both sides fulfilling their contractual obligations, financial and otherwise. These findings suggest that many of the agreements signed by foreign firms are, in fact, self-obsolescing agreements. The moment the ink is dry on the contract, the rationales that brought the Chinese and foreign company together begin to dissipate, often overtaken by larger business or economic developments inside and outside China. Under such circumstances, the foreign firm coming to China must be prepared to reconstitute their agreements and to nurture their relationships with their Chinese partners in order to sustain their presence in the market and to retain the support of a local sponsor or champion.

In summary, the survey reinforced the growing notion that China is becoming increasingly integrated into the fabric of global business. In global industries ranging from petrochemicals to telecommunications, the world's leading MNCs frequently line up five or six deep to compete for projects and market share in China. In contrast to the situation in the 1970s and 1980s, China has also become much more sophisticated with respect to the acquisition of foreign technology. In essence, the situation regarding China has shifted from a seller's to a buyer's market, with the Chinese side becoming ever more effective at leveraging access to its domestic market as a means to secure technology from foreign firms.

Finally, to achieve technology transfer success in China as well as longer term strategic goals, adequate emphasis must be placed on the transfer of management know-how and systems. These technologies are often even more critical to building a long term presence in China than simply the sale of equipment and other pieces of hardware.

CONCLUSIONS

Unlike that in other countries engaging in similar processes, economic transformation in China is being shaped by the innovations and initiatives of countless individual managers in business organizations. Within the framework of certain basic parameters, the state has encouraged this process of managerial adaptation. Through their mistakes and successes, managers actively participate in charting the course of future reforms.

Through the socialist market economy, Chinese leaders aim to create a third alternative to the old dichotomy of capitalism versus communism. Whether or not they succeed in outperforming both of those systems, they are creating a new synthesis of socialist ideals and market discipline which is unprecedented. As Western countries also continue to evolve towards post-capitalist social systems, there may be a lessening of some of the differences that now divide Western economies and businesses so sharply from those of China. These are developments that the rest of the world will want to follow closely in the years to come.

China's leaders are firmly committed to economic reform, expansion, and integration into the world's economy. While rejecting capitalism, they recognize the need to adapt certain managerial practices from the West in order for the market to function. Their objective is to develop an economy and society uniquely suited to China, 'based neither on state-run planning nor on a capitalist market economy but rather on a mixture called socialist market economy with Chinese characteristics' (Myer, 1995: 66).

For two decades, China has experienced a relatively smooth and gradual transition characterized by rapid growth of the private sector. This impressive achievement is attributable in no small part to the Chinese leadership's relatively cautious approach to system change. Economic reform measures are not planned in detail by those at the top in a highly centralized decision making process, and then imposed downwards through the system. Instead, those at the top identify problem areas, set general guidelines, and then allow small scale experimentation to flourish at the grassroots level. The objective is to test a wide variety of possible alternatives for solving problems, weeding out those that are ineffective, and stimulate new ideas and solutions. Ultimately, decisions are informed by the outcomes of these experiments. Economic transition is thereby enacted incrementally, rather than according to a detailed master plan. China stands out among the former centrally planned economies in this regard.

Internationally, China is well on its way to becoming a dominant force in international business and the global economy. Western and especially American businesses and managers must respond effectively to this new reality, or risk missing out on one of the most important economic developments of the new century.

ACKNOWLEDGEMENTS

This contribution is based on a symposium sponsored by the International Management and Social Issues in Management divisions of the Academy of Management and presented at the 1997 meetings of the Academy in Boston, Massachusetts.

Participating in the symposium were: Rosalie L. Tung, Ming and Stella Wong Professor of International Business, Simon Fraser University (Symposium Chair and Presenter of First Paper); Jan Selmer, Professor and Management Department Chair, Hong Kong Baptist University (Presenter of Second Paper); Verner Worm, Assistant Professor, Copenhagen Business School (Co-presenter of First Paper); Denis F. Simon, Head of China Strategy Group, Andersen Consulting (Author of Third Paper); Thomas W. Dunfee, Professor of Social Responsibility, The Wharton School (Discussant); Chen Xiao Yue, Associate Dean, School of Economics and Management, Qinghua University (Discussant); and Paul Beamish, Professor of International Business, University of Western Ontario (Discussant). The symposium was planned and coordinated by Carolyn Erdener, Associate Professor, Hong Kong Baptist University, in consultation with Jan Selmer and Rosalie L. Tung.

REFERENCES

Bjorkman, I. and Schaap, A. (1994), 'Outsiders in the Middle Kingdom: Expatriate Managers in Chinese–Western Joint Ventures', *European Management Journal*, Vol.12, No.2, pp. 147–53.

Black, J.S. and Porter, L.W. (1991), 'Managerial Behaviors and Job Performance: A Successful Manager in Los Angeles May Not Succeed in Hong Kong', *Journal of International Business Studies*, Vol.22, No.1, pp.99–113.

Black, J.S., Mendenhall, M. and Oddou, G. (1991), 'Toward a Comprehensive Model of International Adjustment: An Integration of Multiple Theoretical Perspectives', *Academy of Management Review*, Vol.16, No.2, pp.291–317.

Brewster, C. (1995), 'The Paradox of Expatriate Adjustment', in J. Selmer (ed.), *Expatriate Management: New Ideas for International Business*. Westport, CT: Quorum Books.

Broadman, H.G. (1995) *Meeting the Challenge of Chinese Enterprise Reform*, Discussion Paper No. 283. Washington, DC: World Bank.

Chang, H. and Holt, G.R. (1991), 'More Than Relationship: Chinese Interaction and the Principle of Kuan-Shi', *Communication Quarterly*, Vol. 39, pp.251–71.

Child, J. (1994), *Management in China During the Age of Reform*. Cambridge: Cambridge University Press.

Chu, G.C. and Ju, Y. (1993), *The Great Walls in Ruins*. Albany, NY: State University of New York Press.

Church, A. (1982), 'Sojourner Adjustment', *Psychological Bulletin*, Vol.91, pp.540–72.

Erdener, C.B. (1998) 'Confucianism and Business Ethical Decisions in China', *International Journal of Management*, Vol.15, No.1, pp.72–8.

Erdener, C.B. and Torbiorn, I. (1999), 'A Transaction Costs Perspective on International Staffing Patterns: Implications for Firm Performance', *Management International Review*, Special Issue on International Human Resource Management, in press.

Far Eastern Economic Review (1999), *Asia 1999 Yearbook: A Review of the Events of 1998*. Hong Kong: Review Publishing Co. Ltd, p.108.

Garnaut, Ross (1996), 'Economic Reform in India and China: An Essay in Honor of Heinz Wolfgang Arndt', *Journal of Asian Economics*, Vol.7, No.1, pp.29–47.

Huang, Y. (1998), 'Reform of State-Owned Enterprises in China: Autonomy, Incentives and Competition'. Paper presented in a Department of Economics seminar, Hong Kong Baptist University, 28 April.

Hwang, K.K. (1987), 'Face and Favor: The Chinese Power Game', *American Journal of Sociology*, Vol.92, pp.944–74.

Kanter, R.M. (1995), *World Class: Thriving Locally in the Global Economy*. New York: Simon & Schuster.

King, A.Y.C. (1991), 'Kuan Hsi and Network Building: A Sociological Interpretation', *Daedalus*, 120, 63–84.

Lardy, Nicholas R. (1994), *China in the World Economy*. Washington, DC: Institute for International Economics.

Lincoln, Y. and Guba, E. (1985), *Naturalistic Inquiry*, Beverly Hills, CA: Sage.

Mendenhall, M. and Oddou, G. (1985), 'The Dimensions of Expatriate Acculturation: A Review', *Academy of Management Review*, Vol.10, No.1, pp.39–47.

Murphy, Geoffrey (1994), *Doing Business in China: The Last Great Market*. Kent, UK: China Library.

Myer, Ramon H. (1995), 'Chinese Debate on Economic Reform: Can China Create a Socialist Market Economy?', *Asian-Pacific Economic Literature*, Vol.9, No.2, pp. 5–68.

Naughton, Barry (1995), *Growing Out of the Plan: Chinese Economic Reform, 1978–1993*. Cambridge: Cambridge University Press.

Pye, Lucien W. (1993), 'China's Search for Political Stability', US–China Business Council 20th Anniversary, pp.12–13.

Schroath, F.W., Hu, M.Y. and Chen, H. (1993), 'Country-of-Origin Effects of Foreign Investment in the People's Republic of China', *Journal of International Business Studies*, Vol.24, No.2, pp.277–90.

Selmer, J. (1995), *Expatriate Management: New Ideas for International Business*. Westport, CT: Quorum Books.

Selmer, J. and Shiu, L.S.C. (1999), 'Coming Home? Adjustment of Hong Kong Chinese Expatriate Business Managers Assigned to the People's Republic of China', *International Journal of Intercultural Relations*, in press.

Shenkar, O. (1993), 'People's Republic of China', in R.B. Peterson (ed.), *Managers and National Culture: A Global Approach*. Westport, CT: Quorum Books.

Simon, D.F. (1997), *Technology Transfer Practices of MNCs in China*. San Francisco: Andersen Consulting.

Tung, R.L. (1991), 'Corporate Executives and Their Families in China: The Need for Cross-Cultural Understanding in Business', *Columbia Journal of World Business*, Vol.21, No.1, pp.21–5.

Warner, M. (ed.) (1987), *Management Reforms in China*. London: Pinter, pp.113–26.

Warner, M. (1992), *How Chinese Managers Learn: Management and Industrial Training in the PRC*. London: Macmillan.

Warner, M. (1993), 'Human Resource Management with Chinese Characteristics', *International Journal of Human Resource Management*, Vol.4, No.1, pp.45–65.

Whitcomb, L.L., Erdener, C.B. and Li, C. (1998), 'Business Ethical Values in China and the US', *Journal of Business Ethics*, Vol. 17, pp.839–52.

Yang, Kuo-Shu (1996), 'The Psychological Transformation of the Chinese People as a Result of Societal Modernization', in M.H. Bond (ed.), *The Handbook of Chinese Psychology*. Hong Kong: Oxford University Press, pp.479–98.

Yeung, I.Y.M. and Tung, R.L. (1996), 'Achieving Business Success in Confucian Societies: the Importance of *Guanxi* (Connections)', *Organizational Dynamics*, Autumn, pp.54–65.

Zhang, J.X. and Bond, M.H (1993), 'Target-Based Interpersonal Trust: Cross-Cultural Comparison and Its Cognitive Model' (in Chinese), *Acta Psychologica Sinica*, Vol.2, pp.164–72.

4

The Politics of Management in People's China: From CMRS to Modern Enterprise and Beyond

PAUL L. FORRESTER and ROBIN S. PORTER

China commenced a programme of wholesale modernization of its economy in the late 1970s. The so-called *Four Modernizations* programme (for industry, agriculture, science and technology, and national defence) relied to some considerable extent on the import of technology from the West and Japan. This *Open Door* policy was ultimately bound to open up a debate on how the economy, at both the macro and micro levels, should be run. The decades of separate development, and the primacy of social goals achieved by political means, had left China still technologically and managerially backward in a comparative global sense. Such modernization was always going to be a radical and complex programme of events, especially given the time scales for change.

The logic of rapid modernization involved a sequence of imperatives. Fundamentally, the import of foreign technology could only be achieved by payment in hard currency (which was extremely scarce in China in the late 1970s), or through a variety of forms of foreign investment. In either case the export of goods to world markets on a scale hitherto unknown in China was likely to be involved. There was a major barrier to the increase in international trade: the quality of products produced for and consumed in the domestic market was not comparable with the quality of those produced in other countries and currently traded on world markets. So, to increase export trade, standards in design and manufacture needed to take a giant step forward within Chinese enterprises (Forrester, 1996). As a consequence of this, management techniques which had been in force for thirty years under the command economy needed to be thoroughly reviewed, as both the concept of commercial competition and the practice of profit and loss accounting were introduced in the People's Republic for the first time.

It was in this climate of discussion, and of challenge to long held beliefs about the economy, that the Contract Management Responsibility System (CMRS) was born. This sought not only to provide greater independence for the firm at the enterprise level, but also to install contemporary market-orientated management practices within the organization. In so doing, the content of contracts extended to more than just profit sharing: it encompassed mechanisms for technical improvement investments and grants, and introduced a link between wage levels and company performance. Some contracts guaranteed an expansion of assets, whilst others were incorporated under an input–output system that laid down mechanisms for payments and deliveries between contracted parties.

This contribution will therefore review the CMRS – its origins, objectives, main provisions and impact – before then analysing the Modern Enterprise System which is now seen as a replacement for the CMRS, though it has significant differences in substance and a number of broader provisions.

THE CONTRACT MANAGEMENT RESPONSIBILITY SYSTEM

The Antecedents

It has often been suggested in accounts published in the West that the contract system in enterprise management was inspired by the Household Responsibility System in agriculture (Dong, 1992; Fan and Nolan, 1994; Chen, 1995). However, we argue here that the objectives in introducing the two systems were in many ways distinct, as were also the outcomes. The HRS in agriculture was introduced in Sichuan in 1978, and subsequently in stages throughout China. It was intended to address the motivation of the individual farmer, increasing and diversifying output by giving each household responsibility for the management of a piece of land, and obliging it to pay tax to the government on the profits obtained. The positive consequences have been noted in terms of increased production, a wider variety of crops made available through free markets and, for a time and in some parts of the country, a significantly increased standard of living. There have, however, been significant negative outcomes (White, 1993; Blecher, 1995).[1] These include the serious threat to staple grain production from the shift in attention to other, more profitable crops, the loss of topsoil, and ploughing for profit of land not suitable for cultivation. Another consequence was the age-old tendency to neglect essential rural public works that can only be maintained by common effort within the collectivist society that characterizes China. For our purpose, however, it is necessary to note that the basic activity HRS sought to address was that of the individual farmer labouring to cultivate the land, not the activity of collective groups of people working within business organizations.

The decision in principle to apply the CMRS to industry appears also to have been taken as part of China's overall economic reform programme as long ago as 1979. The main purpose was to better integrate government administration and enterprise management whilst also developing a sense of *enterprise* on the part of managers and workers within the companies (Bond and Huang, 1986). Elements of the contract system were introduced to industry, including the important iron and steel industry, during the course of the Sixth Five Year Plan (1980–85). By the end of this period, experiments had been undertaken by 85 per cent of state-owned companies in the iron and steel industry, as well as in many other heavy and light industries. Reports from within China suggest some favourable results, though also some not insignificant problems (Warner, 1987; Child and Lockett, 1990).

The situation with industry would inevitably be very different to peasant agriculture, and much more complex. The wide variety of interconnected activities within a factory, differing from one factory to the next according to the product manufactured, defied straightforward regulation. The motivation of the individual was always going to be of far less concern than was the case in agriculture. Issues of corporate strategy, organization, finance, procurement, marketing, technical innovation and human resource management would all need to be addressed in any reform of the way industry, or specifically the large-scale, state-owned enterprise, was run (cf. Brown and Porter, 1996).[2] It is therefore necessary to consider carefully the objectives of the programme of reform as perceived by the Chinese government when it introduced the CMRS into industry in the 1980s (Boisot and Child, 1996). Moreover, we should assess the extent to which these objectives were realized in order to set the context to the changes that began to take place in 1993 with the introduction of the modern enterprise system.

Objectives of the Contract Management Responsibility System

The various objectives of the CMRS emerged as part of the process of formulating the policy itself. It is noteworthy that the new contract system was never likely to offer a comprehensive set of strategic solutions to the felt needs of Chinese industry (see Morris, 1995). There was, and there continues to be, underlying disagreement over what those needs might be, and over the political costs of satisfying them. Thus within the Chinese Communist party even more than within most political institutions, ideological differences and factional strife may blight the formation and implementation of policy. This said, one objective certainly had to do with performance – a desire to see industry achieve higher output targets through the inducement of retained profits. Discussion of the possible reintroduction of material incentives in industry in some form followed in the wake of the Eleventh Party Congress in 1978, and experiments were tried in the early 1980s.

Another important objective was to increase the independence of state-owned enterprises (SOEs) with respect to operational decisions on a range of matters of concern to them (Porter, 1996; Wedley, 1992). These included: what to produce and how; sales; pricing; purchasing; the spending of company funds; disposal of assets; organizational matters; personnel; wages and bonuses for individual employees; and links with other enterprises (Wu, 1989, cited in Chen, 1995). The intention to extend greater autonomy in these areas to SOEs was stated explicitly by the government in 1984, and confirmed in the Enterprise Law of 1988, though there was a wide variation in practice even in the pace and nature of implementation of this policy. Local circumstances, including the size and type of enterprise and the attitudes of its leaders, played a very large part.

Finally, the desire of the government to maximize its revenue from SOEs led to fiscal measures. These included the progressive application of a regime of income tax to all enterprises in place of the requirement to hand over all profits to the state. It was assumed that performance inducements, and the new autonomy to be given to enterprises, would be sufficient to ensure that, in the long term at least, the state would benefit from the new arrangements.

The government appears to have been in pursuit of these three main objectives, therefore: improved performance in terms of output; progressive devolution of autonomy to SOEs; and increased income for the state. Experimentation with the CMRS commenced in the early 1980s (Lee, 1988; Nee, 1992). The 'factory director system', which placed the factory director's right to manage above the right of the party secretary to intervene, was evident in places from around 1984 (Tidrick and Chen, 1987; Walder, 1989). The change from profit transfers to taxation of enterprises began around the same time. But it was really in 1987 that China began to see the widespread application of the CMRS to industrial enterprises. For most SOEs, the requirements of the contract provided that:

1. Enterprises must hand over to the state a fixed target of profit, negotiated with the enterprise, as 'income tax', shortfalls to be made up by the company from its own funds, and additional profits to be shared between government and enterprise in a prescribed way. The enterprise would usually also be subject to a variety of indirect taxes, which would vary according to the nature of its activity and circumstances.
2. The growth of total wages and bonuses paid by the enterprise should be linked to any growth in profits and taxes paid.
3. Targets should be agreed for technological upgrading and for investment in this.

There were some minor variations in detail in these requirements as they were imposed on different enterprises. These were the basic principles of the CMRS, as they were applied in both its first (1987–90) and second (1990–93) phases.[3]

The Provisions of the Contract Management Responsibility System

The CMRS usually operated at two distinct levels:

1. the *state contract system*, which covered enterprise-level contracting with the state;
2. the *internal contract system*, which dealt with contracting within the enterprise's own business activities.

At both levels, issues noted above of profit-sharing, investment in technology, the link between performance and wages and other matters might arise.

The state contract system. Broadly speaking, there were two types of state-enterprise contract, defined by their profit-sharing character, under the CMRS. An enterprise would either:

1. turn over a fixed percentage of its annual profits to the state throughout the duration of the contract; or
2. turn over an amount, which would be increased each year at a fixed rate.

Typically, under both schemes, the percentage would average somewhere between 5 and 20 per cent. Any surplus profits where then in theory available for use by the enterprise for new investment, acquisitions, restructuring, etc. In some sectors, however, such as light industry and textiles, enterprises were obliged in addition to pass over a share of surplus profits to the state. Enterprises became for the first time what is commonly known as 'legal persons', able to conduct business and, in theory, even to sue and be sued. Thus, under the CMRS, enterprises had some scope to act on their own initiation, overturning the policy whereby only the state, through government agencies, could represent SOEs. Most contracts ran for three to five years, but there were exceptions: one enterprise negotiated a 14-year contract with the state.

The internal contract system. The internal contract system was, in effect, a target-setting cascade similar to those adopted by firms in capitalist economies. The targets encompassed a broad range of criteria including operational efficiencies, use of raw materials and consumables, the maintenance of facilities, and conformance to regulations. Internal contracting was, and continues to be, adopted by many enterprises in China, and can be both vertical (i.e. top-down) and horizontal (across functions and through the supply chain). Financial incentives in some instances have been developed whereby production workers' pay was linked to their performance *vis-à-vis* the achievement of targets. However, whereas workers' bonuses have been retained in many enterprises beyond the CMRS experiments, the linking of managers' pay to profit has been largely abandoned. This was chiefly due to the fact that managers began to adopt short termist perspectives to improve profit figures in the near term rather than tackle the major problems requiring extensive restructuring and longer term expenditure.

THE CONTRACT MANAGEMENT RESPONSIBILITY SYSTEM IN PRACTICE

The CMRS, while in operation, was judged by many, both within enterprises and by external analysts, as successful in bringing about a degree of enterprise and management reform in the state-owned sector of Chinese industry (Byrd, 1991; Hay *et al.*, 1994; Nolan, 1993). Individual enterprises developed more autonomy and were more responsive to change, as they could exercise a degree of discretion in terms of investment decisions and organizational change (Campbell and Henley, 1990; Child, 1994). Staff commitment to the enterprises increased, especially managers' commitment (Child and Lu, 1990). However, a number of 'difficulties' were identified and these were deemed sufficiently serious to result in the gradual phasing-out of the CMRS. It is therefore appropriate to consider the broad issues arising from this system in practice.

Chen Derong's Analysis

Perhaps the most comprehensive study of the workings of the CMRS to have appeared since it was superseded by the modern enterprise system in 1993 is that of Chen Derong, *Chinese Firms between Hierarchy and Market* (Chen, 1995). Chen's work incorporates a close analysis of the experience of four representative SOEs throughout the official six-year period of the CMRS (summarized in Tables 1 to 4). Chen follows Byrd in asserting that implementation of the system varied widely, and that a proper understanding of its successes and failures may only be gained by looking at actual cases. The issues raised by Chen have been summarized and recategorized in Tables 1 to 4 to take into account the range of recurring themes.[4]

A number of observations relating to these points follow from this brief summary. First, it is apparent that the great majority of 'issues' arising from implementation of the CMRS are conditioned or caused directly by the state, or by the regulatory position of enterprises – as Chen puts it, 'between hierarchy and market'. State-owned enterprises no longer benefit from the structural certainties of the old command economy, yet are not free to respond autonomously to market pressures in a whole variety of ways. Indeed, it can be further argued that in many respects, and

TABLE 1
ENTERPRISE AUTONOMY (HOW MUCH? WHAT CONSTRAINTS?)

Relations with customers:
- Prices that enterprises can charge for finished product are too low, either because they are fixed or because the market won't bear a higher price.
- Protectionism for local goods undermines the wider market.
- Export prices usually determined by the government import/export company.

Relations with suppliers:
- Enterprises cannot prevent rising costs – partly determined by government prices, and partly by the market.
- Government may supply raw materials for goods for export.

Investment:
- Government constraints on certain investment decisions (i.e. construction of new buildings).
- New projects may depend on government funds, which the government may have no commitment to providing.
- Government support needed to obtain bank loans.
- Enterprises constrained by the commercial climate for loans.

Organizational matters:
- Constraints over the appointment of the enterprise deputy director, especially.
- Conflict over who should have final authority – the enterprise director or the party secretary.
- Bureaucratic and 'social' stakeholders prevent the streamlining of the organization.
- No freedom to dismiss workers.

Financial matters:
- Need to borrow 'circulation' funds from the banks.
- Enterprises are not free to access funds; they are dependent on the Bureau and the banks.
- Shortage of hard currency with which to fund inward technology transfer from overseas.

for many of the products of SOEs, the market itself is not a proper market in the unrestricted way that term would be understood in the West. This is so whether one speaks of the domestic market, subject to constraints and interventions, or the international market, where in the period in question Chinese state-controlled import/export corporations often largely determined the terms of trade.

In some cases, the issues raised as problems clearly signal a failure on the part of managers to understand the way a market economy functions. Thus, complaints about rising costs, or the inability of the market to bear higher prices for finished products (Table 1), disagreements among managers over strategy, inability to attract joint venture capital (Table 3), and the drain of talent abroad

TABLE 2
CONTRACT TARGETS

Profit targets:
- While production is increasing, profitability is decreasing, because of the cost of inputs, price controls, lack of work capital rising wages, and intracompany debt.
- CMRS does not provide for sustained growth, because of continual shifts in policy.
- Targets may be fulfilled, but have been set too low.
- Taxes are too high: 55% 'income tax', plus as many as 18 other taxes.
- Frequent changes in tax policy.

The wage bill:
- Wages outstrip productivity.
- Staff shift to office work to avoid piece rates and performance checks.
- Enterprises unable to make employees redundant.
- Very difficult to determine what piece rates for workers should be.
- Government imposes maximum wages, reducing ability to reward high skill levels and hard work.
- The 'inside contract system' within firms leads to decentralized control over wages and lack of responsibility.
- The 'inside contract system' makes accounting much more difficult.

Targets for investment in technology:
- Investment targets often achieved, where actual technological targets have not been.
- Long term investment strategy often brings conflict within enterprises and between enterprises and government.
- Investment opportunities are determined by government; all enterprises can do is to respond quickly.
- Where investment in technology depends on the government, it may lack the will to carry this through or may have other priority areas for investment.
- Less spent on investment in technology by enterprises during CMRS than before it was introduced.

(Table 4), all illustrate the difficulty some managers had in coming to terms with the new situation.

It is also the case that the CMRS caused confusion. This was because it tried to embody often conflicting goals of encouraging increased output from industry, giving enterprises a greater measure of independence, and reaping a bigger financial return for central government through a variety of taxes. As one manager remarked, ' Managing a company is like sailing a boat with much wind. The most important thing is to find out how the wind blows' (cited in Chen, 1995). Many observers close to the CMRS experiment comment on the short term behaviour it induced in managers (see respondents Y, 1995, and Z, 1996).[5] Given the wide variations in the productive activity and special circumstances of the different enterprises, and the sometimes conflicting objectives and changes in policy of the government, this is scarcely surprising.

TABLE 3
CONSTRAINTS ON STRATEGIC DECISIONS

Constraints from government:
- Price controls fixed by government: prices too high for some raw materials, too low for certainproducts of some enterprises.
- Some enterprises have been obliged against their better judgement to diversify their product mix.

Gaining autonomy:
- Disagreements among senior managers over what to produce; no clear responsibility.
- Resort to a joint venture just to avoid government interference.

Industrial policy:
- Long term strategy impossible because government policy is constantly changing.
- Only chosen 'key companies' get consistent support from government.
- Government sometimes compels enterprises to merge; obliges enterprises to take on additional workers whom they cannot dismiss, and lame duck enterprises in which they must invest.
- Difficult for some enterprises to achieve a joint venture with a foreign partner; they cannot export products of poor quality while they are prevented from selling the upgraded products of a joint venture on the domestic market.

Flexibility in decision making:
- Political clampdowns, such as after Tiananmen, discourage enterprises from developing independent strategy under which the enterprise might be seen to be trying to 'escape government control'.
- Flexibility may only be achieved in some enterprises by 'doing deals' with subcontractors and licensees.
- Scope for international expansion depends in part on the import/export company, controlled by the government.
- Where joint ventures are struck, control over foreign markets may be handed to the foreign partner.

In implementing the CMRS, the government had believed that it would facilitate technological upgrading through progressive investment and inward transfer of technology from overseas. The evidence from Chen's study suggests that, if anything, technological upgrading may have slowed down in many enterprises under the CMRS. This impression was supported by comments made to the present authors on the difficulty encountered in obtaining and paying for new technology, and the stark choices it posed, even at relatively wealthy plants such as Yanshan Petrochemicals. Although the government, except in the case of 'key' enterprises, by and large no longer provided funding for new technology, it still set the parameters for investment. It had to approve all major building projects, its support was needed for critical bank loans, and it might hold things up by disagreeing with enterprises on long term investment strategy. Even where investment targets were met, technical targets may not have been.

TABLE 4
MEASUREMENT AND ENFORCEMENT MECHANISMS

Directors' financial rewards and penalties:
- Some contracts do not specify directors' bonuses; it is claimed that the real reward for directors lies in their power and the progress of their careers.
- Even as the system matured, directors' bonuses remained far too low; it was claimed that young talent was all leaving for joint venture companies or for jobs abroad.
- Bonus arrangements were changed too frequently.
- In 'higher collectives', where directors may see their career path as being primarily in business and not in government, directors could be rewarded through titles negotiated as part of joint venture arrangements; this option was not available to most directors of SOEs.

Measurement:
- 'Financial residents' (observers) were placed in companies to monitor finances. However: some feared they had 'too much power'; some said they had no grip on finances at the 'lower levels' of the enterprise; and some noted that they tended to 'get on well' with the directors whose firms they were supposed to be monitoring. There were no financial residents in the 'higher collective' enterprises.
- Performance measurement of workers is difficult; attitudes opposing it prevail, both among workers, and among many managers.

Appraisal and inspection:
- The view frequently expressed that inspections and appraisal have little effect on performance.
- Some directors dismissive of the procedures.
- Inspections of financial records, quality control, maintenance levels, and safety standards, etc., may bring prizes, but this mentality is from the command economy; some managers feel that market forces and customer choice are the real proof of enterprise achievement.

One way around this problem was to form a joint venture with a foreign company, but in this case managers stood to lose their overall control over the enterprise. Moreover, over all investment decisions hung the ever-present cloud of political uncertainty. On top of all this, the major advantage of the planned approach to the import of new technology from overseas, that unnecessary duplication would be avoided, was lost (Porter, 1990; Chen, 1995).

On the financial side, while Chen found that state-owned firms generally benefited from the opportunities presented by the CMRS (notably among our own subjects the Shougang Corporation, which nevertheless enjoyed certain special conditions), some firms showed decreasing profitability or contrived to make a loss under the system. Many firms appear to have found that wages outstripped productivity over the six years or so of the CMRS. The application of income tax, along with a host of indirect taxes, to enterprises failed to yield the hoped-for windfall of revenue for the government, while the widespread variations and exceptions granted to many well connected enterprises only served to engender jealousy in others (respondents Y, 1995, and Z, 1996). Many managers were unhappy with the complicated taxation regime and with the generally high levels of taxation.

Further Observed Effects

Our own empirical analysis of both the Contract Management Responsibility System and the Modern Enterprise System (MES) is based on interviews and observations during site visits over the years 1987 to 1997. The observations that follow are derived from discussions with managers at steel plants in Beijing and Baotou, the petrochemical works at Yanshan, a textile plant in Beijing, a brewery in Hangzhou, a refrigerator plant in Shanghai, a components factory in rural Zhejiang, and automotive plants in Changchun and Shiyan. Moreover, in 1995 and 1996 the authors were able to interview a number of leading officials in Beijing concerned at the macro level with forming and monitoring policy for both the CMRS and its successor the MES.[6] Interviews were in general conducted through an interpreter, with follow-up questions put to the respondents by the authors directly in Chinese.

These interviews bring out a number of other, associated, effects in organizations that have adopted the Contract Management Responsibility System.

Disparities between enterprises. Contracts were established and agreed bilaterally between individual enterprises and the state. There was therefore considerable variation in the contracts agreed between enterprises, as there were no definitive regulations regarding the terms and conditions of these contracts (such as the level of profit quotas, which varied in practice between 5 and 20 per cent). Contracts varied according to such factors as the type and nature of the enterprise, the industrial sector, geographic location, the degree of obsolescence of plant and equipment, and past levels of investment. Enterprises deemed to be in need of capital investment were allowed relatively generous contract terms, including low depreciation rates and set rates of value added tax. These discrepancies were considered necessary because standardized targets and contract terms would have resulted in many enterprises not achieving the goals set – if targets were unattainable, there would be little motivation on the part of enterprise managers to reform and improve operations. There was also a real fear among policy makers of enterprises facing bankruptcy, simply not a feasible option given the scale of large enterprises and the economic, political and social consequences of reported failure. The latter consideration meant that an efficient (some would say equitable) allocation of scarce resources did not, in reality, result, despite this being one of the primary aims of the enterprise reform programme. Indeed, the lack of clear, transparent, standardized and definitive regulations relating particularly to profit distribution was a fundamental flaw in the CMRS as it created considerable dissatisfaction, both at the state and enterprise level. Disputes over profit quotas meant that renegotiation of contracts became commonplace, especially when enterprises believed that other firms had negotiated a better deal than they had. The system was open to abuse, especially when politically well connected enterprises used influential networks to their own advantage.[7]

Short-termism. As noted above, this was a recurrent topic in our research and was a particular effect in those enterprises where a three-year contract was agreed. There was a clear tendency for managers to concentrate on the time-phased quantitative targets, mostly near term, to the detriment of longer term, more qualitative objectives such as improving management practices. Such short-termism inevitably leads to a lack of investment in the infrastructure of the enterprise (such as new plant, machinery, product development, etc.). There also continued to be a concentration on quantity of output, rather than quality, and this continues to be a major deficiency in Chinese SOEs generally (Forrester, 1996). This situation is particularly acute where the enterprise has the aim of improving quality of production to the standard demanded by export markets.

Impact on government revenue raising. There is general confusion within Chinese enterprises concerning the taxation system. In the mid-1980s the former system of complete remittance of profits to the state from enterprises was replaced by a system of percentage taxation of profits, only to be replaced by a fixed-rate profit remittance scheme. In 1992, the Communist Party of China took the decision to implement the 'socialist market economy' to wholly replace the planned economy. Under this approach it was reported that there should be equal competition between enterprises whatever their type of ownership (whether state owned, collective, joint venture or other). This included, in principle, the establishment of a uniform and equitable taxation system. This was intended to remove any suspicion of special treatment for certain SOEs (Sino-foreign joint ventures continued to receive special terms), but discrepancies persisted and confusion still reigns in the minds of many enterprise managers. It is clear that the state also has concerns as it seeks to maintain the inflow of funds to the government through taxation.

Enterprise autonomy. There was conflicting evidence with respect to the actual or desirable level of enterprise autonomy. There persisted a lack of responsibility, and therefore autonomy, in many SOEs. This stemmed from the fact that, while enterprises were to a large extent responsible for their own profit generation, the state remained responsible for losses, and as a large number of Chinese SOEs continued to make losses there was a lack of incentive among managers to assume responsibility and create increased autonomy. However, in some enterprises there was another effect. In some cases, enterprise autonomy in decision making had been excessive with some managers having almost unbridled scope and discretion. Such newly acquired power was not always used in the wider interests of the enterprise, its employees or the state.

Little improvement in the quality of management. The problems highlighted above of short-termism and autonomy have been compounded by variable quality of management. There was a general failure to invest in the training and awareness programmes necessary to raise the standard of management in order to adjust to the market economy, and decidedly little impact on the quality of management at the operational level of enterprises.

Social provision. In one other respect, the CMRS failed to address the pressing problems of China's industry. Since 1949, the larger SOEs especially have been required to provide for their workers and their families in a variety of ways, some of which are not normally associated with the practice of firms in the West. Large corporations have therefore run subsidized restaurants, built and operated schools and hospitals, provided very cheap housing, laid out parks and playgrounds, set up old people's homes, run pension schemes, and in other ways borne a very substantial burden of social provision. The financial cost of performing these functions has become all too apparent as market pressures and the withdrawal of automatic central government support have affected the SOEs. Yet the potential cost in political stability of any sudden withdrawal of these services on a grand scale is also recognized by the central government.

For many of the SOEs continuing to register losses at the end of the CMRS period, the cost of social provision was clearly a far from negligible factor. The failure to address this problem under the CMRS would need to be remedied if any future scheme were to be successful.

Now that we have analysed the provisions and impact of the CMRS in some detail, let us now turn our attention to the later model of enterprise reform introduced to Chinese SOEs: the *Modern Enterprise System.*

THE MODERN ENTERPRISE SYSTEM

Following a discussion in the press and among high party officials and senior managers of industrial reform, initiated in 1990 (respondent Y, 1995), the new modern enterprise system (MES) was introduced to replace the CMRS in 1993. While this is now the principal system in force, vestiges of the CMRS remain in some firms (respondent W, 1995), and are still evident at the time of writing in 1998. Moreover, the MES itself is still in a process of evolution.

Objectives of the Modern Enterprise System

Among the reasons cited by informed Chinese observers for transition to the new system are:

1. the need to address the question of ownership of enterprises (respondents X, 1996, Y, 1995, and Z, 1996);
2. the need to combat short-termism among enterprise managers (respondents Y, 1995, and Z, 1996);
3. the need to modify the very complex and fraught system of

separate negotiations over contract terms with 'nearly ten thousand enterprises' (respondents Y, 1995, and Z, 1996);

4. the need to correct the negative impact of earlier tax reforms (respondent Y, 1995); and
5. the need to clarify the separate responsibilities of enterprise, state and party, 'enabling enterprises to be managed scientifically' (respondent X, 1996).

The Provisions of the Modern Enterprise System

The MES is best understood by considering the three principles quoted by the state in their definition: reform, reconstruction and restructuring. It was intended to tackle a number of issues not adequately addressed by the CMRS and other previous enterprise models. In so doing it sought to clarify the position on property rights, provides a clearer definition of rights and responsibilities generally, distinguishes between the role of the state and management functions, and introduces so-called 'scientific' enterprise management. The reform element (*gaige*) refers to the adoption of new management mechanisms and practices, reconstruction (*gaizao*) comprises technical transformation and facilities improvement, whilst restructuring (*gaizu*) involves the reorganization and establishment of a legal framework for property rights and assets. The brief discussion that follows reflects the perceptions of senior officials closely involved in monitoring implementation of the new system.

The MES has been implemented progressively since 1993 and has hinged on a division of enterprises into three groups, identified primarily by characteristics of current or potential ownership and the means of governance. The first group have been 'state-owned, limited liability corporations' (respondent Y, 1995). These are exclusively funded, and wholly owned, by the state directly, and include most large SOEs such as the Shougang Corporation, Yanshan Petrochemical Corporation, and most enterprises in the metallurgical, mining and heavy manufacturing industries, as well as the railways, airlines and other capital-intensive enterprises of an infrastructural kind (respondent Z, 1996). It was estimated in 1996 that some ten thousand enterprises fell into this group. These enterprises are intended to have a board of directors, a supervisory committee and a management committee, which 'all watch and control one another' (respondent Y, 1995). These firms have an obligation to increase their asset value, while responding to government policy; frequently, managers and government representatives may not agree on how this is to be achieved. These corporations may not engage in joint ventures.

Secondly there are 'shareholder corporations'. These enterprises are owned by their shareholders, who may be employees of the company – both managers and workers. Alternatively, the enterprises may have issued shares on the stock exchanges in Shanghai or Shenzhen. Management frequently consists of senior managers and a board of directors. While the management enjoys much greater autonomy with respect to government, it is nonetheless responsible to its shareholders. Such firms have been subject to a variety of regulations and forms of governance, and to overall supervision by the State Assets Administration Bureau (respondent Z, 1996).

The third group comprises smaller enterprises designated 'shareholder partner companies', in which the government has actively invited individuals to invest money. This approach appears to have been inspired by the success since 1987 of the shareholding cooperative system in agriculture. Their employees now own some firms in this group, while others belong to one or more outside private investors. Others are still collectives, waiting for a buyer. Management may vary considerably in such enterprises, and the state plays little role in it. It was believed that, particularly where enterprises are owned by their staff, the problem of motivation would have been solved; no evidence has been adduced for this, however.

According to the officials we interviewed, the injunction under the MES to invite investment in enterprises from a variety of sources applies only to enterprises in the second and third groups above. In addition to these three groups, there are also around one thousand non-state-owned limited liability corporations, most of which are foreign owned.

The Modern Enterprise System in Practice

It is widely felt that the MES has been a substantial improvement over the CMRS. It has gone some way towards addressing the problems of ownership, short-termism, the complex negotiating environment, and the negative impact of earlier tax reforms. But, as of 1998, other matters remain to be resolved. In particular, there are issues of governance (in the Western sense) which still need to be clarified further. These include the separate responsibilities of enterprise, state and party. However, it is important to note that Western and Chinese conceptions of corporate governance differ, most markedly in relation to the residual power of the state and the interlocking relationships and lines of responsibility that persist in many enterprises (see, for example, the contribution of Child, 1994). There are also management issues at the micro level concerning the respective roles of the party secretary and the factory director. Different views have existed on the priority here, with some asserting the need for clear-cut mechanisms to represent the interests of the state and party (respondent X, 1996), and others arguing for greater managerial autonomy (respondent Z, 1996).

The new system has not resolved the financial difficulties faced by many enterprises. It has been recognized that around one-third of all SOEs are loss making. Moreover, they are likely to go on being loss making and in need of continuing government subsidy (respondent Y, 1995). Part of the problem is pricing of their products which, in certain cases (and for one reason or another), continues to be fixed by the state.

A related issue is the ongoing cost of social provision by larger enterprises, noted above. The MES does not address this, though some limited experiments have been undertaken, with commercial provision of these services at certain enterprises in Shanghai and Wuhan (respondent Y, 1995), and provision by the local organs of the state in some other cases. Some experts believe that the state should take over this function from enterprises (respondents X, 1996, and Y, 1995), while one observer suggests that employees are now 'more able to cope with the loss of subsidized provision' (respondent Z, 1996).

While it is generally felt that the exposure of enterprises to market pressures is a good thing, there continues to be controversy over the employment consequences of heightened competition. One suggestion has been that surplus staff could be encouraged to leave enterprises by reducing their pay to 'perhaps 60 per cent of normal' (respondent Y, 1995). Another view holds that bankruptcy of firms, or widespread unemployment induced by free market conditions, would give rise to political instability and would be unacceptable (respondent X, 1996).

A similar dichotomy of view exists on the matter of rewards and bonuses for managers in SOEs. Some commentators have expressed the view that many managers feel a continuing sense of grievance over the fact that their earnings under the MES still in no way reflect the burden of responsibility that they bear (respondent Z, 1996). A contrasting opinion holds that what really concerns managers is the loss of clear delineation of managerial ranks of the old command economy, which often leaves staff in enterprises confused as to who is in charge (respondent X, 1996).

The Implications of the Modern Enterprise System

In summarizing the improvements brought about by the MES, China analysts can be excused for harbouring continuing scepticism that the reforms are truly improving the efficacy of Chinese SOEs. Indeed, although improvements are widely cited, and managers and politicians alike are keen to indicate that change for the better is taking place, experience urges caution. As one system falls from grace, new models are introduced, praised and widely publicized as a change for the better. Later, however, a host of complex and intractable problems are reported. This tends to cast doubt over any claims for success in the case of the MES. While it seems likely that the MES will provide SOEs with access to much needed capital in order to fund change at their own discretion, government interference continues to be an issue.

Moreover, the present authors have found, in agreement with Pan and Parker (1997), that the state continues to exercise a high degree of influence over management decisions of all kinds. The role of the Communist party of China, and the extent to which it is willing to relinquish even part of its power over industrial activity, is of paramount importance. Reducing the role of the state would need a profound change in China's political culture which, it would appear, is unlikely in the near term. Keun Lee (1996) has argued that, rather than consider the changes in China as a move towards Western style capitalism, they are best viewed as moves in the direction of 'capitalism with Chinese characteristics' under the auspices of what he terms 'legal-person socialism'.

Undoubtedly, the most significant issues faced in the transition of large SOEs in China are the issues of surplus labour and social provision of welfare. As noted previously there is as yet no social security system to act as a safety net for workers made redundant.

Although the service sector is growing in certain areas of China, this is centred within the major cities and, even there, will be unlikely to expand anywhere near sufficiently to absorb mass redundancies from heavy industries. The plain truth is that Chinese SOEs are massively overmanned and uncompetitive in world market terms. There is a conflict between the need to streamline industry and boost productivity by reducing headcount, and the fear of widespread unemployment where individuals and families drop out of the firms' social provision with no state welfare to fall back upon. The latter scenario would surely be a precursor to social unrest, something the Chinese government fears above all else. It is not clear how the provisions of the MES would seek to tackle this vexed problem. It is therefore important to analyse more recent statements regarding industry reform from Chinese leaders so as to understand how these issues may be addressed into the future.

POLICY FOR REFORM IN THE LATE 1990s

It is clear that as China approaches the millennium the reform of the SOEs, and therefore of the foundations of the economy, is regarded as an absolute priority. Attempts at management reform over the last decade and a half have led almost inexorably to recognition of a need for root and branch restructuring, and a need to address the question of ownership.

At the 15th National Congress of the Communist party in September 1997, President Jiang Zemin announced further plans to adjust the ownership of SOEs to bring about a new MES, introducing the concept of 'public ownership' in the 'primary stage of socialism' (China Daily Information, 1997b; BBC News, 1997; China–Britain Trade Group, 1997). Under the new arrangement enterprises deemed to be in public ownership would include those which will continue to be directly state owned, and those which come to be collectively owned, along with state and collectively owned elements of enterprises under mixed public and private ownership.

Those enterprises in the first group, which will remain directly under state ownership, are those which constitute what Jiang called the 'life-blood' of the national economy, including steel, armaments, communications and transport, banking, finance, and some major national resources. These are felt to be of critical importance to China's prosperity and security.

Those in the second group, which will be regarded as collectively owned, are being progressively sold off to investors as joint stock companies. This group, it is anticipated, will include a very large number of all present SOEs, large, medium and small. Some such companies may have both state and private shareholders. Of the collectively owned enterprises, Jiang observed that 'what should be specially advocated and encouraged is the kind of collective economy that features, in the main, the association of labourers in labour and capital' (China Daily Information, 1997c).

Finally, in what Jiang referred to as the 'non-public sector', are what are envisaged as the self-employed and private businesses. Apart from wholly foreign owned and joint venture enterprises, most of these businesses would be smaller in scale.

It will be apparent that these three groups may have been derived from, but do not precisely correspond to, those described earlier for the period after 1993. It is clear that under the new plan the state is set to sell shares in most of the current SOEs to what outside China would be called private interests, though the extent of the sale – whether minority, majority or total sell-offs – is undetermined and remains to be resolved in each individual case. The joint stock system is now regarded as the most favoured form of capital organization for enterprises because it separates ownership from management, and so is deemed to raise the efficiency of the operation. However, the term 'privatization' has not been used in reference to this process, in contrast to experience in other countries, whether established market economies or those in transition from centrally planned administration.

At the National People's Congress in March 1998, newly appointed Premier Zhu Rongji, who is personally responsible for restructuring the economy, further clarified the government's intentions (Inside China Today, 1998). Giving his own assessment of the present situation, Zhu indicated that of the current total (according to him) of 79,000 SOEs, there are some five hundred 'extremely large' enterprises accounting for 85 per cent of profits and taxes, and of these only 10 per cent are suffering from losses (South China Morning Post, 1998; BBC News, 1998). These SOEs would be turned around within three years. The party Central Committee has recently decided that teams of five independent government 'inspectors' – officials above the rank of Vice Minister – will be appointed to conduct financial supervision of enterprise operations on behalf of the state, targeting especially the most financially troubled enterprises (China Daily Information, 1998b).

With regard to the 40 per cent of enterprises presently considered as loss making (of the total number of 79,000 SOEs), many were said to be 'very small'. Those that can issue shares and raise capital apparently have some chance of survival, though it is equally clear that Zhu sees a process of attrition as inevitable (Zhu Rongji, Guildhall speech, London, 1 April 1998).

As of the beginning of 1999, the Chinese government is still committed to its pronouncements of 1997 and 1998 on enterprise reform. However, reports indicate that the Asian crisis, and the prospect of widespread unrest attendant on the prospective abandonment of unprofitable enterprises, with all their social provision, has put a damper for the time being on the process of disinvestment by the state.

CONCLUSIONS

In the context of the imperatives of modernization and the integration of China into the global economy, noted in our introduction, various attempts have been made to implement management reform. The Contract System of the late 1980s and early 1990s in its different dimensions sought to address issues of enterprise management – especially the question of autonomy, improvement of performance and output, and the raising of profits which could then be subject to the new system of taxation. In most respects the Contract System was only partially successful.

The MES has, since 1993, focused on ownership and governance more than on issues of management *per se*, taking diversification of investment in SOEs and the divestment of loss makers as the twin keys to generating capital and offloading costs.

Taken as a whole, the recent pronouncements on enterprise reform have served to clarify matters to some extent from a structural point of view, but still leave some of the most critical problems facing Chinese enterprises unresolved. In particular, the complete integration in the past of the SOEs into the economic and social provision for China's population, and the state's guarantees of employment to its citizens – legacies of China's political system – have prevented any easy transition to a market environment for very many SOEs. The introduction of policies to enforce such a transition has so far proved politically impossible.

As noted above, outstanding problems include the provision of employment opportunities (and necessary retraining) for the very many workers made redundant by the process of slimming down. They also include the establishment of effective alternative institutions to make up for the social provision being stripped away from the SOEs – pensions, housing, medical care and educational facilities, among others. Moreover, there is no obvious reason to believe that the 'collectivization' and the floating of shares in loss making enterprises is likely to be an effective means of raising necessary capital for those organizations.

Finally, it is not clear that there are any policies in the pipeline that will address the many practical issues of day to day management thrown up at the time of the failure of the Contract System. Many of these relate to the continued direct or indirect role of the state in the Chinese market. In part this may be because, despite assurances to the contrary, there is as yet no clear agreement among China's leaders on what should be done.

Significantly one observer, with final responsibility for the current national programme to expose up-and-coming Communist party cadres to modern management techniques, insists that whatever happens the interests of the state must come before those of the enterprises, and that the party controls the state. 'Most managers are party members, and must follow orders' (respondent X, 1996). There would ultimately seem to be no way to reconcile this view with that of those who hold that 'the trend to a market economy is irreversible; in time, the mechanism of competition will spread to the political sphere, leading China toward a democratic system' (respondent Z, 1996). In this context, the MES, like the CMRS before it, may turn out to be no more than transitional.[8]

NOTES

1. There is consensus that the benefits of rural reform began to diminish after the bumper harvest of 1984, especially as agriculture ceased to be a priority and investment in it declined. See White, 1993: 109–110.
2. The complexity of the challenge in the reform of industry was all the greater because of the party's need simultaneously to engender loyalty following a long period of political

instability, and to bring about an improvement in the standard of living. See 'Introduction' to Brown and Porter, 1996: 1–9.

3. This contribution focuses on reform of enterprises at the macro level. Experience suggests, however, that many of the problems facing Chinese industry existed at the micro level, within the individual enterprise. Among important micro-level issues not addressed by the CMRS was whether or not Chinese managers were equipped through their skills and experience to achieve the objectives set for them. See for example Warner, 1992, on management training in China in the 1980s. Exposure to the varieties of Western management practice has not always proved to be the panacea that some might have expected. In the course of involvement in one major UN-funded programme of management training in China in the late 1980s and early 1990s, one of the present authors found the Western message to be neither always consistent nor always appropriate to China's needs and circumstances.
4. Chen's four case studies related to the following enterprises: The Beijing Electric Power Generator Company, the Beijing Transformer Company, the Beijing Dahua Shirt Company, and the Beijing Leather Shoe Company. These enterprises were chosen to illustrate a range of problems typically faced by China's state-owned industries.
5. In 1995 and 1996 the authors were able to interview in Beijing a number of leading officials concerned with forming and monitoring policy on both the Contract Management Responsibility System and its successor Modern Enterprise System.
6. The respondents were: Professor W, Institute of International Trade and Economics, Beijing; Professor X, Centre of Management Studies, Central Party University, Beijing; Professor Y, Research Institute on Economic Systems and Management, State Commission for Economic Re-structuring, Beijing; Professor Z, China Enterprise Management Association, Chinese Academy of Management Science, Beijing.
7. For example, Shougang Corporation was widely reported in the press in 1995 for having used its connections with high party officials to negotiate special terms. The practice of *guanxi*, the cultivation of a 'special relationship', especially with people in authority, is of long standing in China.
8. Evolving approaches to management, as we have suggested here, are clearly linked to the success or failure of plans to restructure the whole state-owned sector of the economy. Given Premier Zhu's recent assertion in London (Guildhall speech, 1 April 1998) that the state-owned industries would be reformed within three years, further dramatic developments may be expected.

REFERENCES

BBC News (1997), '1997 – 'Important and Extraordinary Year for China' – Jiang Zemin', BBC News Internet Edition, http://www.monitor.bbc.co.uk, 31 December.

BBC News (1998), 'Zhu Promises to Blaze Trail on Reforms', BBC News Internet Edition, 19 March.

Blecher, M. (1995), 'Collectivism, Contractualism and Crisis in the Chinese Countryside', in R. Benewick and P. Wingrove (eds), *China in the 1990s*. London and Basingstoke: Macmillan.

Boisot, M. and Child, J. (1996), 'The Institutional Nature of China's Emerging Economic Order', in D. Brown and R. Porter (eds), *Management Issues in China*, Vol.1: *Domestic Enterprises*. London: Routledge.

Bond, M.H. and Hwang, K.K. (eds) (1986), *The Psychology of the Chinese People*. Hong Kong: Oxford University Press.

Brown, D. and Porter, R.S. (eds) (1996), *Management Issues in China*, Vol. 1: *Domestic Enterprises*. London: Routledge.

Byrd, W.A. (1991), 'Contractual Responsibility Systems in Chinese State-Owned Industry: A Preliminary Assessment', in N. Campbell, S. Plaschaert and D. Brown (eds), *The Changing Nature of Management in China*. Greenwich, CT: JAI Press.

Campbell, N. and Henley J. (1990), *Joint Ventures and Industrial Change in China*. London: JAI Press.

Chen, Derong (1995), *Chinese Firms between Hierarchy and Market: The Contract Management Responsibility System in China*. London and New York: Macmillan/St Martin's Press.

Child, J. (1994), *Management in China in the Age of Reform*. Cambridge: Cambridge University Press.

Child, J. and Lockett, M. (1990), *Reform Policy and the Chinese Enterprise*. London: JAI Press.

Child, J. and Lu, Yuan (1990), 'Industrial Decision-making under China's Reform, 1985–88', *Organization Studies*, Vol.11, No.3, pp.321–51.

China–Britain Trade Review (1997), 'President Jiang and Public Ownership', *China–Britain Trade Review*, 19 November.

China Daily Information (1997a), 'Ownership Form and Democracy Should Accord with National' [sic], *China Daily Information*, Cbnet, http://chinadaily.com.cn.net/cndy/history, 13 September.

China Daily Information (1997b), 'Jiang Zemin on China's Ownership Structure', Cbnet, 24 September.

China Daily Information (1997c), 'Jiang Zemin on Economic Restructuring and Development Strategy', Cbnet, 24 September.

China Daily Information (1998a), 'Breakthroughs Urged in Reform', Cbnet, 6 March.

China Daily Information (1998b), 'Premier Highlights Role of New System: Inspectors to Assist Reform', Cbnet, 11 May.

Dong, Fureng (1992), *Industrialization and China's Rural Modernization*. London and New York: Macmillan / St Martin's Press.

Fan, Qimiao and Nolan, P. (eds) (1994), *China's Economic Reforms*. London and New York: Macmillan / St Martin's Press.

Forrester, P.L. (1996), 'The Challenges Facing Manufacturing Managers in Chinese Factories', in D. Brown and R. Porter (eds), *Management Issues in China*, Vol.1: *Domestic Enterprises*. London: Routledge.

Hay, D.A., Morris, D.J., Liu, G. and Yao, Shujie (1994), *Economic Reform and State-owned Enterprises in China, 1979–1987*. Oxford: Clarendon Press.

Inside China Today (1998), 'How to Understand the Strategy of Market Pluralism', Inside China Today, European Internet Network Inc. (from *Renmin Ribao / People's Daily*), 7 May.

Lee, Keun (1996), 'An Assessment of the State Sector Reform in China: Viability of "Legal Person Socialism"', *Journal of the Asia Pacific Economy*, Vol.1, No.1, pp.105–21.

Lee, P.K. (1988), *Industrial Management and Economic Reform in China, 1949–1984*. Oxford: Oxford University Press.

Morris, D. (1995), 'The Reform of State-Owned Enterprises in China: The Art of the Possible', *Oxford Review of Economic Policy*, Vol.2, No.4, pp.54–69.

Nee, V. (1992), 'Organizational Dynamics of Market Transition: Hybrid Forms, Property Rights, and Mixed Economy in China', *Administrative Science Quarterly*, Vol.37, No.1, pp.1–27.

Nolan, P. (1993), *State and Market in the Chinese Economy: Essays on Controversial Issues*. London and Basingstoke: Macmillan.

Pan, W. and Parker, D. (1997), 'A Study of Management Attitudes in Chinese State Owned Enterprises, Collectives and Joint Ventures', *Asia Pacific Business Review*, Vol.3, No.3, pp.38–63.

Porter, R.S. (1990), 'Centralization, De-centralization and Development in China: The Automotive Industry', in N. Campbell and J. Henley (eds), *Joint Ventures and Industrial Change in China*. Greenwich, CT: JAI Press.

Porter, R.S. (1996), 'Politics, Culture and Decision-making in China', in D. Brown and R. Porter (eds), *Management Issues in China*, Vol. 1: *Domestic Enterprises*. London: Routledge.

South China Morning Post (1998), 'Zhu's Press Conference: "I Will Blaze My Trail"', *South China Morning Post*, Internet Edition, http://www.scmp.com, 20 March.

Tidrick, G. and Chen, J. (eds) (1987), *China's Industrial Reforms*. Oxford: Oxford University Press.

Walder, A.G. (1989), 'Factory and Manager in an Era of Reform', *The China Quarterly*, Vol.118. No.2, pp.242–64.

Warner, M. (ed.) (1987), *Management Reforms in China*. London : Pinter.

Warner, M. (1992), *How Chinese Managers Learn: Management and Industrial Training in China*. London and Basingstoke: Macmillan.

Wedley, W.C. (ed.) (1992), *Changes in the Iron Rice Bowl: The Reformation of Chinese Management*. Greenwich, CT: JAI Press.

White, G. (1993), *Riding the Tiger: The Politics of Economic Reform in Post-Mao China*. London and Basingstoke: Macmillan.

Wu, J. (1989), 'The Review and Re-thinking of the Ten Years' Development and Reform', *The Reference for the Economist*, Vol.59, No.1, pp.1–10.

5

Guanxi and Salesforce Management Practices in China

ROGER BENNETT

Numerous empirical studies have examined the problems and prospects confronting foreign businesses seeking to market goods within the People's Republic of China (PRC), and the special considerations that selling within the PRC involves (see for example Shenkar, 1990; Boisot and Xing, 1992; Child and Maroczy, 1993; Bjorkman, 1995; Martinsons and Tseng, 1995; Shao and Herbig, 1995; Luo, 1997; Wong and Chan, 1997). Such widespread interest is hardly surprising considering the rapid expansion of the Chinese economy in recent years (see Luo, 1997, and Reuvid, 1997, for details of the extent of growth); the fact that China (after the USA) is the second largest recipient of foreign direct investment in the world; and the steadily increasing affluence of tens of millions of urban Chinese consumers who, according to Chan and Leng (1995: 128) have become 'materialistic, fashion, image and quality-conscious and wish to purchase premium (Western) branded goods'. Since the early 1990s, more than two-thirds of all internal sales of Western brands within China have been locally produced and marketed rather than being imported from abroad (Martinsons and Tseng, 1995). China's annual retail sales are forecast to reach US$6,000 billion by the year 2000, and the number of 'affluent' consumers to have risen to 200 million by that date (Davies, 1995).

Most investigations into Chinese business practices have been based on case-studies and interviews with Chinese executives, often while the latter were attending training courses in Western countries. The present study contributes to the literature in the field by examining (via a reasonably extensive mail survey) the salesforce remuneration policies of a sample of foreign companies active – either through joint ventures (JVs) or wholly owned subsidiaries – in the Chinese market. In line with several previous analyses (such as Campbell, 1987; Shenkar, 1990; Roehrig, 1994; Martinsons and Tseng, 1995; Bjorkman, 1995; Luo, 1997; Wong and Chan, 1997) the study focuses on the role played by close personal relationships (*guanxi*) and the use of networks of connections to expedite business transactions within China. This is an important topic worthy of serious academic investigation in view of the large volume of foreign investments in the PRC (258,444 had been approved by the end of 1995 [Luo, 1997: 52] and the number continues to rise steadily) and the need for foreign investors to understand at least some of the special characteristics of salesforce management within this nation.

GUANXI

Guanxi is a Chinese word used to describe the practice of exploiting networks of personal connections and relationships in order to secure preferential treatment. It has been called the 'second currency' of the Chinese economy (Luo, 1997), and is known to pervade numerous dimensions of China's business and social life (Campbell, 1987; Shenkar, 1990; Ambler, 1994; Chen, 1994; Luo, 1997). *Guanxi* relationships are governed by an implicit code of equity and reciprocity (Hwang, 1987; Kao, 1993), the violation of which can lead to a humiliating 'loss of face' (*mianzi*). Although the Chinese customer is known to be increasingly discerning when confronted with alternative offers of goods, it has been alleged by a number of authorities (for reviews of relevant literature see for example Ambler, 1994; Chen, 1994; Bjorkman and Koch, 1995; Luo, 1997; Arias, 1998) that, in the words of Buttery and Leung (1998: 382) 'nothing much happens in China other than through the *guanxi* network, and certainly little is sustainable without it'. The Chinese market is evolving and becoming more competitive, but *still* requires the 'right personal connections to open the right doors in order to facilitate and smooth business transactions' (Arias, 1998: 154).

Guanxi itself has been described as a manifestation of historical Chinese approaches to communal order which unify the individual, family and societal ties that define a person's role and position in his or her wider social *milieu* (Luo, 1997). People sharing a *guanxi* relationship are committed to each other by an unspoken code of mutual respect, equity and reciprocity. Ignoring the commitment damages the individual's social reputation and causes a humbling loss of prestige. A *guanxi* network also involves the recognition and assumption of reciprocal obligations (*renqing*) with strong expectations that all favours will eventually be repaid. *Renqing* is 'social capital' that provides leverage during interpersonal exchanges and, together with the 'giving of face' (that is, enhancing someone else's social position), creates access to the influence necessary to make things happen (Buttery and Leung, 1998). *Guanxi* is said to reflect the Confucian principles of harmony in interpersonal relations and the maintenance of a conflict-free society wherein every person knows and stays in their proper place (Shenkar, 1990; Arias, 1998). This implies that organizations as well as individuals need to become part of a business circle and contribute to the 'mutual orientations' within it (Buttery and Leung, 1998: 384). Indeed, Bjorkman and Koch (1995) insist that within the PRC, *guanxi* connections have to be developed prior to and are a *prerequisite* for a meaningful business relationship. One reason for this has of course been the implementation of highly complex, bureaucratic and centralized state administrative systems from 1949 onwards, consequent to which 'the use of personal connections has frequently been the only way to get things done' (Arias, 1998: 147).

More generally, the cultural and social origins of *guanxi* are founded, perhaps, on close family loyalties within Chinese society, clan-like networks, in-groups, and personal ties. Note how the concept of the 'family' in this connection extends far beyond its biological meaning, embracing persons who are in some way connected with blood relatives: friends, colleagues, people from the same area, classmates, and so on. A practical consequence of *guanxi* is that personal loyalties and connections can be far more important in business than formal rules, government regulations or organizational affiliations. Rules can be circumvented via *guanxi*, so that the development and cultivation of personal relations becomes vital for commercial success (Shenkar, 1990). Chen (1994), Luo (1997), Buttery and Leung (1998) and others have argued that *guanxi* has become even more important since China's economic reforms, as it gives firms the ability to claim preferential treatment regardless of current market conditions and trends, leading to superior performance and a long run competitive edge.

Within the business context, *guanxi* has been found to exercise especially powerful influences in the field of salesforce marketing, even to the extent of its utilization significantly affecting market performance (Luo, 1997). Salesforce marketing directly involves people and organizations outside the firm, and is a major vehicle for marketing goods in China (Tai, 1988; US Department of Commerce, 1990; Ambler, 1994; Reuvid, 1997). *Guanxi* permeates all primary aspects of salesforce marketing: direct sales negotiations between marketing and purchasing personnel; the establishment and operation of regional sales offices; the engagement of commission agents and other representatives, etc. It is not about obtaining a single sale; rather, *guanxi* involves building up lifelong relationships based on the knowledge that when a reasonable favour is asked it will be given. Thus, sales people can use their own and their colleagues' social networks to promote products and hence generate impressive long term results *irrespective* of the objective competitive worth of the goods (Luo, 1997). This can of course be critical for foreign enterprises entering the Chinese market, as it enables market growth in the absence of pre-existing distribution contacts. Indeed, a potential buyer who does *not* buy from someone with whom he or she has a *guanxi* relationship could lose face. It follows that entry to the (difficult) Chinese market can be greatly facilitated by the cultivation of local *guanxi* relationships, operationalized by finding the 'right Chinese partner with the right network, preferably going through Hong Kong companies with good track records in China' (Wong and Chan, 1997: 1106).

A major consequence of *guanxi* for Western firms entering the Chinese market is that within the PRC scarce resources might be allocated mainly via personal connections and loyalties rather than through bureaucratic rules (Alston, 1989), so they need to participate in the numerous devices for circumventing official procedures that can be activated. This is crucial within an economy frequently criticized for the sparsity of its commercial infrastructure (Bjorkman, 1995) and 'bewildering bureaucracy' (Shao and Herbig, 1995: 65) involving numerous ministries and levels of government, and hence the need for Chinese managers to devote time and effort to bargaining with state bureaucrats at the expense of addressing customer requirements (Boisot and Xing, 1992). It is hardly surprising, therefore, that *guanxi* networks have been characterized as representing 'the most effective (market growth) and efficient (low cost) market tool' available to Chinese enterprises (Ambler, 1994: 51; see also Wong and Chan, 1997), and as binding together 'literally millions of Chinese firms into a social and business web that can be particularly useful for market access and growth' (Luo, 1997: 66). Allegedly, Chinese businesses frequently seek to maintain *guanxi* relationships with certain favoured enterprises (*guanxihu*) to which they extend preferential treatment regardless of commercial rationality (Chen, 1994; Ambler, 1994; Hu and Chen, 1996). It follows that foreign firms doing business within China are likely to need to build their own *guanxi* networks in order to access and expand local markets (Punnett and Yu, 1990; Luo, 1997).

GUANXI AND SALESFORCE MANAGEMENT

The academic literature on salesforce management typically distinguishes between outcome-based (OB) and behaviour-based (BB) control systems (see Anderson and Oliver, 1987; Barker, 1995). Outcome-based approaches evaluate salespeople quantitatively (for example, by sales volume achieved, sales growth, sales revenue, new accounts obtained, and/or unit sales profitabilities); whereas BB techniques utilize input measures such as the number of calls made, distances travelled, reports completed, displays set up, etc. According to Anderson and Oliver (1987), BB systems are more subjective and complex than their OB counterparts, as they require evaluations of 'what salespeople bring to the selling task' (p.76), rather than sales outcomes. The authors noted (p.76) the role of the 'invisible hand of the marketplace', which supposedly optimizes the performances of sales personnel under an OB system. Thus, within a competitive market situation the salesforce can be viewed as a market contractor that can be left alone to maximize its reward via normal market mechanisms, so that objective measures of results (such as sales values or volumes) can be used to evaluate and compensate salespeople. In a BB system, conversely, the firm typically possesses a substantial management-information gathering staff to back up the salesforce's efforts, and the senior management knows exactly what it wants salespeople to do. Sales results, Anderson and Oliver alleged, were *presumed* to follow in the longer period, so that short term salesforce compensation systems would involve more complex and subjective assessments of salespeople's *inputs* to the selling process rather than immediate outcomes.

The effects of *guanxi* on the salesforce management practices of companies operating within the PRC has been noted by a number of studies (such as Campbell, 1987; Bjorkman and Koch, 1995; Luo, 1997), though its operational consequences have not been investigated extensively (Luo, 1997). Selling in China is known to rely heavily on personal relationships between individuals in partner firms (*guanxihu*), with *guanxi* representing the 'fertile soil where direct personal selling can flourish . . . even when the product's attributes are not competitive' (Luo, 1997: 55). Arias (1998), moreover, argues that 'social networks are also relevant for the marketing of consumer products and services' (p.152) in that although Chinese buyers tend to be brand loyal, 'once their neighbours have tried the product they follow suit promptly' (1998: 152; see also Yau, 1988).

Such considerations imply that enterprises which recognize the critical importance of *guanxi* for salesforce marketing within China will tend to select BB rather than OB salesforce reward systems. The BB approach suggests that a salesperson's behaviour performance *vis-à-vis* such matters as the planning of sales calls, making presentations, team-based selling, cultivating relationships, etc., are highly significant contributors to salesforce effectiveness (Piercy *et al.*, 1998). In particular it recognizes the importance of environmental factors that impact on outcomes but which (like *guanxi*) lie outside an individual salesperson's control (Churchill *et al.*, 1993). Hence the existence of *guanxi* implies a heavier reliance on call planning, support and advisory activities, extensive customer liaison, and a higher proportion of time spent on non-selling duties; all of which are conventionally associated with BB control systems (see Piercy *et al.*, 1998: 82). This, in turn, suggests that salesforce management systems should emphasize the monitoring, direction and evaluation of sales personnel, rather than simply measure outcomes. Also the prevalence of *guanxi* is likely to engender within salespeople *attitudes* compatible with behaviour control in relation to commitment to the organization, acceptance of direction, team cooperation, enthusiasm for performance reviews, and so on.

Hypotheses

The first hypothesis to emerge from the above mentioned considerations is as follows.

H1 Firms that recognize the crucial role of *guanxi* in salesforce marketing within the PRC will tend to opt for BB salesforce remuneration systems.

A major justification for this hypothesis is that *guanxi*-related personal selling can produce excellent results *even when* a product's attributes are not competitive. And since sales levels will not then relate to product characteristics, sales might be unnaturally high so that a commission linked system becomes inappropriate. Moreover, the existence of active *guanxi* networks means there is no 'invisible hand' to guide a competitive marketplace towards optimum outcomes. Rather, management needs (1) to intervene and *direct* the salesforce in order to exploit *guanxi* networks as extensively as possible, and hence (2) to monitor and evaluate salespeople on their abilities to contribute to various stages in the processes of relationship building. Thus it is reasonable to regard the use of *guanxi* by a salesforce as a critical *input* leading to long term customer loyalty, enhanced goodwill and eventually therefore to higher sales. Time and effort must be devoted to planning and organizing network development, so that it is sensible to suppose that senior management will evaluate the methods and behaviours applied during the course of *guanxi* building activities when determining salespeople's remunerations; as opposed to final sales outcomes. Arguably, the lack of attention to long term customer satisfaction and overemphasis on immediate payoffs implied by outcome-based reward systems (cf. Anderson and Oliver, 1987: 78) are not compatible with *guanxi* development.

Further hypotheses examined in the course of the present investigation are as follows.

H2 Western firms engaged in joint ventures with local enterprises are more likely to incorporate *guanxi* considerations into their salesforce management policies than are wholly owned subsidiary businesses.

Around 70% of all foreign (including Hong Kong) companies operating in China do so *via* JVs with Chinese organizations. The local partner ought to be fully familiar with the Chinese business culture, possess a stock of *guanxihu* contacts, and be able to access more general *guanxi* networks. If the operation is a wholly-owned Western enterprise then it is hypothesized that (H2a) Western companies that delegate major salesforce management decisions in a wholly owned subsidiary to locally recruited Chinese executives will be more *guanxi*-orientated in their salesforce management practices than firms wherein Western managers take such decisions.

H3 Joint ventures in which the foreign partner is a firm from a Chinese commonwealth country (such as Hong Kong, Taiwan, Singapore and Macau) will incorporate *guanxi* considerations into their salesforce management policies more than JVs with non-Chinese-commonwealth partners.

Hypothesis H3 derives from the suggestion of Bjorkman (1995) and Hu and Chen (1996) that the country of origin of the foreign company is a reliable index of its 'socio-cultural' distance from its Chinese partner, and that socio-culturally close firms (especially those from Hong Kong) have significantly different perspectives on Chinese business compared to companies based in countries that are socio-culturally distant. Thus, Chinese commonwealth foreign partners should understand the importance of *guanxi* when doing business in China, and will want to use it intensely.

H4 The longer a foreign firm has been operating in China the more likely it is to recognize the importance of *guanxi*.

Arguably, time is needed for a foreign business to learn about the role of *guanxi* and to build up networks.

H5 Foreign enterprises that recognize the importance of *guanxi* experience significantly greater sales growth than others.

THE INVESTIGATION

In order to investigate these matters, a questionnaire was developed consequent to (1) an examination of the academic literature in the fields of *guanxi* and Chinese enterprise management, and (2) in-depth interviews with four senior managers in three companies with wide-ranging experience of Chinese business. A mail questionnaire approach to the research was adopted because the sample companies were distributed across four continents, so visits to a representative spread of enterprises was neither financially nor logistically feasible. The questionnaire was pre-tested on a subsample of 75 enterprises drawn at random from the sampling frame used for the survey (see below). Twenty-four replies were received (32 per cent), enabling the refinement and clarification of particular items.

The Appendix to this chapter summarizes the final questionnaire, which begins with questions concerning the nationality of the people within the enterprise who take salesforce management decisions, the importance of commission payments, and the criteria used to reward salespeople. The item about commission does not include 'commission only' systems as a separate option because of the particular wage payment legislation that prevails within China. Wholly owned subsidiaries of foreign companies and JVs containing a foreign partner may establish specific individual contracts of employment with locally recruited staff, and the 'basic wage' paid to an employee can be based on commission. However, Chinese law requires that *all* enterprises pay into funds for employees' housing subsidies; pensions; and medical, educational, transport and other allowances that subsequently make up a substantial part (possibly most) of an employee's total remuneration (Tseng and Martinsons, 1995; Reuvid, 1997). Nevertheless, incentive and commission payments are common among enterprises with foreign participation (Luo, 1997) and might account for up to two-thirds of an individual's aggregate income. Section 2 of the questionnaire starts with a couple of innocuous items, followed by five *guanxi*-related questions central to the study. The third section concerns matters identified by previous literature as potential determinants of whether an organization adopts an OB or BB approach to salesforce remuneration, such as demand and environmental uncertainty, how easily salespeople's performances can be measured, and how readily the firm can recruit fresh sales staff. Finally the questionnaire asks for the nationality of the person filling in the form and for his or her assessment of the rate of growth of the enterprise's Chinese sales during recent years. Evidence that subjective evaluations of this type represent reliable sources of information is presented by Pearce *et al.* (1987).

The construction of a sampling frame for the study required the assembly of a list of foreign companies operating in China (via subsidiaries or JVs with local enterprises) and engaging in salesforce marketing. Decisions concerning salesforce management might be taken either by foreign or by locally recruited Chinese executives. The 1993 edition of Reuvid, 1997, lists details of 898 major JVs between foreign and Chinese organizations, while the 1997 version gives information on the (1996) top 500 foreign investments in China. Additionally, details of companies completing JV arrangements with Chinese enterprises are reported in the 'Industry Monitor: Joint Ventures' pages of the EIU newsletter *Business China,* and in MAID Profound. These sources were examined for foreign investments undertaking lines of business likely to involve salesforce marketing (such as clothing, foodstuffs, white goods, personal electronics, etc.).

Note how the rapid expansion of the Chinese market has induced foreign firms to want to develop *domestic* Chinese sales and not just to produce within China and then export (Forestier and Abdoolcarim, 1994; Chan and Leng, 1995). Regulations restricting foreign companies to export-orientated activities were lifted from 1986 onwards. And even an export-orientated operation benefits from domestic sales, the revenues from which can be used to purchase local materials, premises, equipment and labour.

Eventually, a list of 677 candidate companies across a variety of product sectors was extracted, the largest representations occurring in the areas of clothing, shoes and textiles (22%); foodstuffs (11%); and consumer durables (11%). Half of the foreign firms had a Hong Kong address; 97 had offices in the USA or Canada, 49 in Europe, 31 in Japan, 17 in Singapore and 17 in Australia; the remainder were based in a wide range of countries. Contact and other details of all Sino-foreign JVs are in the public domain and available from a variety of sources, notably the 'statement of Sino-Foreign Joint Ventures' published annually in the *Almanac of China's Foreign Economic Relations and Trade* (Ministry of Foreign Trade and Economic Cooperation) and listing JVs by region, scope, duration in years, nationality of the foreign partner, and the ratio of foreign to total investment in the venture. Note that the Chinese authorities treat Hong Kong firms as 'foreign' enterprises under the 'one country two systems' concept that has been in place since July 1997.

The questionnaire was mailed to the 'Head of Marketing (China)' at the registered domicile address of the subsidiary or joint venture (typically in the home country of the foreign partner), accompanied by a letter explaining the nature of the research and asking the recipient to pass the questionnaire on to the person in charge of the subsidiary or JV's Chinese marketing if he or she was not personally responsible for relevant matters. It also asked the recipient to return the questionnaire uncompleted if the business did not engage in salesforce marketing within China. Letters were addressed to Heads of Marketing because such personnel are key informants where a firm's international operations are concerned and may be reasonably expected to possess expert knowledge of an enterprise's international marketing activities. Even if Heads of Marketing are not totally familiar with the intricate details of day-to-day on-site functions, they nevertheless exercise authority over important decisions concerning salesforce management and remuneration policies.

Sixty-one uncompleted and 111 completed questionnaires were returned, collectively representing 26% of the 677 enterprises canvassed. Although modest, this response is considered reasonable in view of the difficult circumstances in which the research was undertaken – namely, having to send a questionnaire in English to a number of executives for whom English was not their first language (no budget was available to translate the questionnaire into other languages); the absence of telephone follow-ups; constraints on postage expenditures; and not being able to offer financial incentives to encourage questionnaire completion. A letter was sent to companies failing to respond to the second mailing, enclosing a slip that asked for the reason (using prompts) for non-response. Forty-one companies returned these slips. 'Company policy not to answer questionnaires' was the commonest response (31%), followed by 'too busy' (21%), 'lost the questionnaire' (11%) and 'passed to another department' (11%). No significant biases in non-response patterns could be discerned. Forty-nine of the 111 respondents were based in Hong Kong, 23 in the USA or Canada, and 17 in Western Europe. The remainder were located in Australasia, Singapore and a variety of other countries.

RESULTS AND DISCUSSION

Breakdowns of the response patterns for the all-sample data are given in the Appendix. The overwhelming majority of enterprises (72%) reported (see Q1.1) that foreign rather than local managers assumed ultimate responsibility for critical decisions concerning the management of the local salesforce. This outcome is unsurprising, perhaps, considering the numerous studies that have reported a general lack of confidence among Western managers in the marketing abilities of their Chinese counterparts (see for example de Bruijn and Jai, 1993; Child and Maroczy, 1993; Forestier and Abdoolcarim, 1994; Martinsons and Tseng, 1995). Specific criticisms have focused on Chinese managers' (alleged) lack of experience of competitive market situations; the paucity of qualified marketing personnel; absence of appraisal, accountability and responsibility systems; scant regard for product quality; lack of concern for delivery deadlines; and failure to understand the relationships between profits and sales.

Possibly, therefore, it is generally considered best for Chinese partners to concentrate on other aspects of operations where they can more usefully employ their local knowledge and expertise. The replies to Q1.2 about the use of commission to reward salespeople indicated a 60/40 split in favour of systems relying mainly on a flat rate salary. It may be that within this country fixed salary incomes continue to be seen as more prestigious than commissions, a belief fostered by decades of governmental 'iron rice bowl' policies whereby all Chinese people have enjoyed a variety of welfare benefits and a guaranteed basic wage. Nevertheless, 73% of sample enterprises paid at least some commission to their sales staff. The factors considered when determining salespeople's remuneration (Q1.3) suggest, by Western standards, a generally unsophisticated approach to these issues (cf. Anderson and Oliver, 1987; Barker, 1995). Why this should be so is a matter for further research, though it clearly implies a need for training within the sample enterprises. 'Value of sales achieved' registered the highest score among the outcome-related measures (mean = 4.1), followed by the number of calls made and sales volume. However, *both* the behaviour based criteria (Q1.3(ix) and (x)) attained a slightly greater value (4.2) than any of the outcome indicators, implying an essentially behaviour-orientated approach to remuneration management within the majority of the sample firms. The high average score for value of sales achieved lends support to the proposition that salesperson behaviour performance is a major contributor to salesforce effectiveness (cf. Piercy *et al.*, 1998), leading to discernible linkages between behaviour and outcomes (Churchill *et al.*, 1993). Organizational objectives might be better served by BB approaches, causing the firm to be able to reward its selling staff more generously.

Guanxi issues are dealt with in Q2.2(i) to (v). Cronbach's alpha was calculated for these items, the result (0.79) indicating sound reliability. Accordingly, the raw scores for the five scales were combined into a single measure (mean = 2.84). Although the all-sample responses to these items were relatively evenly divided (see the Appendix), significant differences emerged when the data were split with respect to Hong Kong and other Chinese commonwealth respondents on the one hand, and replies from non-Chinese-commonwealth companies on the other. The mean for the combined scales for the former was 3.07, and the latter 2.21; this difference being significant at the 0.01 level. A significant difference ($p < .01$) also arose when the replies for the *guanxi* composite were dichotomized into categories for ethnic Chinese and non-Chinese respondents (see Q3.9). It seems, therefore, that Chinese business people were far more aware of and concerned with the *guanxi* variable than their non-Chinese counterparts. This result was expected, given that the concept of *guanxi* cannot be divorced from so many aspects of a Chinese person's social life. Equally it implies the need for training and/or awareness programmes in the subject for non-Chinese executive staff.

Next, the *guanxi* composite was used, together with relevant items from questionnaire section 3, as an independent variable in logistic regressions containing the state variable 1 = 'The enterprise uses commission to reward its salespeople to a large or extremely large extent' (see Q1.2); 0 = 'The enterprise uses commission payments to a small extent or not at all' as the variable to be explained. The regressions were computed first for the all-sample data and then for Chinese commonwealth based companies only. Although it is technically feasible to employ as a regressor a dummy variable with value 1 if a firm is based in the Chinese commonwealth and 0 otherwise in order to test for significant differences between groups, the use of one state variable to explain

TABLE 1
LOGISTIC REGRESSION ANALYSIS

Variable	*Beta coefficients (Chi-square values in parentheses)* All-sample data		*Chinese-commonwealth*	
Guanxi composite	–0.112	(4.013)*	–0.125	(4.938)*
Uncertainty composite	0.104	(3.694)*	0.101	(3.911)*
Salespeople's activities easy to measure	0.098	(3.889)*	0.066	(2.924)*
Period the enterprise has operated in China	–0.104	(2.992)*	–0.019	(3.102)*
Ease with which new salespeople can be recruited	0.106	(1.316)	0.107	(3.142)*
Intrinsic motivation of salespeople	–0.017	(0.724)	0.020	(0.515)
Product complexity	0.009	(0.801)	–0.022	(0.437)
Regression Chi-square	71.44		88.34	
Hosmer-Lemeshow statistic	19.17		21.96	
Somer's D index	5.98		6.63	
2LL statistic	274.77		312.12	

*Denotes statistical significance at the 0.05 level or less.

another is not generally recommended as a regression procedure (see Menard, 1995: 88–91) and, in the present case, further econometric difficulties would be created by the multicollinearity of the dummy variable with both the *guanxi* composite and the variable for the 'period the enterprise has operated in China'. (Multicollinearity among independent variables results in severe upward biases in the significance levels of regression coefficients.) Items 3.1 and 3.2 were highly correlated (R = 0.82), and hence were aggregated into a single 'environmental uncertainty' variable. The results are shown in Table 1, from which it is evident that the *guanxi* composite is highly significant ($p < .001$) in both regressions, and that the influence of this variable exerts a more powerful effect among the Chinese-commonwealth companies. Recognition of the importance of *guanxi* clearly discourages the practice of rewarding salespeople mainly by commission payments. This finding underscores the idea that network integration, the banking and recall of favours, willingness to rely on network partners, and other *guanxi*-related characteristics can result in sales outcomes for which OB reward systems might not be appropriate. The other significant variables were uncertainty and the measurability of salespeople's activities (cf. Anderson and Oliver,

1987) and the period during which an enterprise has done business in the PRC. Volatility in the business environment in which a company operates seemingly impels its management to adopt a more market-led approach to remuneration. The ease with which an enterprise can recruit fresh sales staff is significant only for Chinese-commonwealth companies, reflecting perhaps a greater familiarity among the latter with local Chinese employee recruiting practices. The sign on the coefficient for this variable for the all-sample data is positive, in accordance with a priori expectations. Neither of the remaining variables (intrinsic motivation and product complexity) is significant.

CONCLUSIONS

Overall, the results generally conform to the outcomes of previous academic research in relevant fields. Key variables suggested by the seminal work of Anderson and Oliver (1987) did in fact significantly contribute to the determination of the mode of salesforce compensation, as did the *guanxi* composite. Also the results support the conclusions of previous literature which has argued that it is essential for foreign firms operating in China to understand *guanxi* and incorporate it into their management systems. The first hypothesis (H1), which supposes that firms recognizing the critical importance of *guanxi* tend to opt for BB reward systems, is accepted as far as this particular sample is concerned. Hypotheses H2 and H2(a) were tested by rerunning the regression using data for JVs only (N = 75); wholly owned subsidiaries only (N = 36); and then for firms which delegated major salesforce management decisions to local Chinese executives (N = 32). No significant differences between the outcomes for JVs and subsidiaries could be discerned, so that H2 is rejected. However, the coefficient on the *guanxi* variable was greater when Chinese managers were in charge (Beta = –0.129, Chi-square = 5.121), and the mean value for the *guanxi* composite was higher (M = 3.11) than for any other subsample. Hence H2(a) is accepted. Hypothesis 3 is also accepted in accordance with the earlier discussion. The correlation between the *guanxi* composite and the period of enterprise's operation within China was positive and significant (R = 0.59, p <.001). Moreover the *guanxi* composite also correlated significantly (R = 0.55, $p < 0.001$) with respondents' perceptions of the rates of growth of their sales relative to competitors over the previous five years (Q3.7). The latter result was not sensitive to whether respondents' firms were based in the Chinese commonwealth (N = 57, R = 0.565) or in Western nations (N = 54, R = 0.547), the difference being insignificant at the 0.25 level thus implying that Western as well as Chinese-commonwealth enterprises can employ *guanxi* networks to facilitate rapid sales expansion. Hence H4 and H5 are accepted. The regression results also support acceptance of H4.

The essential conclusion to emerge from the present investigation is that recognition of the role of *guanxi* in Chinese business did influence the manner in which firms rewarded their salesforces. Companies from the Chinese commonwealth appreciated the importance of *guanxi* more than their Western counterparts when operating in the PRC; and within Chinese-commonwealth businesses the greater the extent of their recognition of the role of *guanxi* the more they employed behaviour-based salesforce remuneration systems. It seems, moreover, that the longer a company has operated in China the more it incorporates *guanxi* considerations into its management systems, presumably in consequence of learning effects and observation of the successful activities of local firms with more extensive *guanxi* connections. The results of this study are compatible with the outcomes to Luo's (1997) empirical analysis of the relative performances of 156 foreign-invested enterprises in Jiangsu Province – that firms using *guanxi* frequently and intensely in the course of their salesforce marketing experienced significantly ($p <.0001$) higher levels of profitability, market growth and 'asset efficiency' (that is, ratio of sales to assets). Also the utilization of *guanxi* networks was more prevalent in foreign firms (including Hong Kong enterprises) from Chinese-commonwealth countries (as in the present study). In contrast to the findings of the current investigation, however, Luo concluded that JVs employed *guanxi* to a greater degree than wholly owned subsidiaries, implying that the possession of an appropriate local partner greatly facilitated the acquisition of the benefits of *guanxi*. Longer-established foreign operations had more extensive *guanxi* networks than recently founded businesses, with consequent effects on profitability, suggesting that foreign firms *learned* how to use *guanxi*. Large firms employed and benefited from *guanxi* just as much as smaller establishments.

Note that heavy reliance on networks of personal contacts is by no means unique to China. Yet this phenomenon has received scant attention from scholars in the field other than those mainly concerned with Chinese businesses. Further research is needed into the possible role of *guanxi*-related variables in various cultures and business situations.

APPENDIX
THE QUESTIONNAIRE

Section 1: Management of the Salesforce

1. Who takes the really major decisions concerning the management of the local Chinese salesforce (*please tick*):
   (i) foreign managers (with or without the advice and assistance of local staff) 72%
   (ii) locally recruited Chinese managers? 28%

2. Many enterprises motivate their salespeople by paying them commission. So far as your Chinese operations are concerned, how large a proportion of a typical salesperson's total remuneration is attributable to commission? (*Please tick*)

An extremely large proportion	19%
A large proportion	23%
A small proportion	31%
Our salespeople do not receive any commission	27%

3. To what extent do you base your Chinese salespeople's remunerations (salaries or commission) on each of the following? (*Please tick*)

		5	4	3	2	1	M
(i)	Financial value of sales achieved in a given period	26%	33%	34%	7%	0%	4.1
(ii)	Number of units sold in a given period (regardless of their financial value)	20%	24%	32%	14%	10%	3.3
(iii)	Number of customer calls made in a given period	18%	26%	34%	12%	10%	3.4
(iv)	Distance travelled	9%	10%	19%	33%	29%	1.9
(v)	Number of completely new customers obtained in a given period	22%	26%	16%	18%	8%	3.1
(vi)	Ratio of orders to calls	11%	20%	38%	20%	8%	2.6
(vii)	Other ratios similar to (vi)	9%	10%	19%	30%	32%	2.0
(viii)	Average profit per unit of sales	12%	18%	32%	24%	14%	2.5
(ix)	Management's assessment of a salesperson's personal qualities such as diligence, effort, co-operation, initiative and reliability	32%	30%	29%	9%	0%	4.2
(x)	Management's assessment of a salesperson's knowledge of the enterprise's products, customers, markets and competitors	40%	32%	22%	6%	0%	4.2

Key: 5 = Very important factor; 4 = Important factor; 3 = Moderately important; 2 = Relatively important; 1 = Factor not considered; M = Mean value.

Section 2: Evaluation of Salespeople

Please indicate the extent to which you agree or disagree with each of the following statements.

1. When recruiting salespeople we take the view that:

		5	4	3	2	1	M
(i)	an individual's vigour and enthusiasm are just as important as his or her educational background	18%	21%	26%	19%	16%	2.5
(ii)	it is more important for a salesperson to be assertive and individualistic than to be good at working in teams	16%	16%	31%	15%	22%	2.3

2. As far as the Chinese operations of this enterprise are concerned, we believe that:

		5	4	3	2	1	M
(i)	a salesperson who possesses extensive contacts with people who influence decisions in other organizations is more valuable than one who is currently achieving high level sales	18%	18%	30%	20%	14%	2.7
(ii)	it is more valuable to the firm for a salesperson to spend time cultivating relationships with important people outside the enterprise than to spend time gathering information about customers and competing firms	16%	20%	30%	18%	16%	2.6
(iii)	our salespeople must always repay favours, even if this involves a cost to the firm	13%	19%	32%	22%	14%	2.5
(iv)	knowledge of key people in other organizations is at least as important as knowledge of customers' reactions to the enterprise's products, prices, aftersales service, etc.	16%	24%	30%	20%	10%	2.8
(v)	it is not possible to succeed in the Chinese market without becoming dependent on close long term relationships with people in other organizations	22%	28%	28%	14%	8%	3.6

Key: 5 = Strongly agree; 1 = Strongly disagree.

Section 3: the Enterprise and its Local Environment

Please indicate the extent to which you agree or disagree with each of the following statements.

		5	4	3	2	1	M
1.	Local demand for the enterprise's goods is volatile and uncertain	16%	26%	30%	16%	12%	2.8
2.	The behaviour of competing enterprises is unpredictable	18%	24%	32%	14%	12%	2.9
3.	It is easy for us to recruit fresh salespeople	22%	18%	22%	22%	16%	2.4
4.	We supply a complicated item that requires our salespeople to have much product knowledge	16%	20%	24%	22%	18%	2.1
5.	The activities and performances of our salespeople are easy to measure	20%	24%	30%	18%	8%	2.9

6.	Our salespeople are highly motivated within themselves and can be trusted to work hard without our having to force them	26%	32%	24%	14%	4%	3.5

Finally

7. Relative to your competitors, how would you describe the rate of growth of your sales within China during the last five years (or since you commenced operations if this period is less than five years)? (Mean = 3.2)

Excellent	18%
Good	30%
Moderate	28%
Disappointing	12%
Very disappointing	12%

8. How long has your company been operating in China? (Mean = 8.3 years)

9. As the person filling in this questionnaire, what is your own personal country of origin? (*Please tick*)

Hong Kong	35%
Singapore	4%
Taiwan	3%
USA	24%
Canada	3%
European country (please specify)	22%
Japan	3%
Other (please specify)	6%

REFERENCES

Alston, J.P. (1989), 'Wa, *Guanxi* and *Inhawa:* Managerial Principles in Japan, China and Korea', *Business Horizons*, March–April, pp. 26–31.

Ambler, T. (1994), '*Guanxi*: Marketing's Third Paradigm', *Business Strategy Review*, Winter, pp.69–80.

Anderson, E. and Oliver, R.L. (1987), 'Perspectives on Behaviour-Based versus Outcome-Based Salesforce Control Systems', *Journal of Marketing*, Vol.51, No.4, pp.76–88.

Arias, J.T. (1998), 'A Relationship Marketing Approach to *Guanxi*', *European Journal of Marketing*, Vol. 32, Nos 1/2, pp.145–56.

Barker, A.T. (1995), 'Differences between Salesforces Using Behaviour-Based and Outcome-Based Control Systems', in *Making Marketing Work*, Proceedings of the 29th MEG Conference, University of Bradford, July 1995, Vol.1, pp.11–19.

Bjorkman, I. (1995), 'Organization Theory and Management Practices in Chinese/Western Joint Ventures', in H.C. de Bettignies (ed.), *Changing Markets in Asia*, Proceedings of the LVMH Conference, 3–4 Feb. 1995. Fontainebleau, INSEAD and Stanford University, pp.92–127.

Bjorkman, I. and Koch, S. (1995), 'Social Relationships and Business Networks: The Case of Western Companies in China', *International Business Review*, Vol.4, No.4, pp.519–35.

Boisot, M. and Xing, G. (1992), 'The Nature of Managerial Work in the Chinese Enterprise Reforms', *Organizational Studies*, Vol.13, No.2, pp.161–84.

Buttery, E.A. and Leung, T.K. (1998), 'The Difference between Chinese and Western Negotiations', *European Journal of Marketing*, Vol.32, Nos.3/4, pp.374–89.

Campbell, N. (1987), 'Experiences of Western Companies in China', *Euro-Asia Business Review*, July, pp.35–8.

Chan, A. and Leng, J.T. (1995), 'Changing Trends of Fashion Retailing in Urban China', in H.C. de Bettignies (ed.), *Changing Markets in Asia*, Proceedings of the LVMH Conference, 3–4 Feb. 1995. Fontainebleau, INSEAD and Stanford University, pp.128–48.

Chen, M. (1994), '*Guanxi* and the Chinese Art of Network Building', *New Asia Review*, Summer, pp.40–3.

Child, J. and Maroczy, L. (1993), 'Host Country Managerial Behaviour and Learning in Chinese and Hungarian Joint Ventures', *Journal of Management Studies*, Vol.30, No.4, pp.611–31.

Churchill, G.A., Ford, N.M. and Walker, O.C. (1993), *Salesforce Management*. Homewood, IL: Irwin.

Davies, H. (1995), *China Business: Context and Issues*. Hong Kong: Longman Asia.

de Bruijn, E.J. and Jai, X. (1993), 'Transferring Technology to China by Means of Joint Ventures', *Research Technology Management*, Vol.36, No.1, pp.17–22.

Forestier, K. and Abdoolcarim, Z. (1994), 'China Investors Play a New Game', *Asian Business*, Vol.30, No.9, pp.20–4.

Hu, M.Y. and Chen, H. (1996), 'An Empirical Analysis of Factors Explaining Foreign Joint Venture Performance in China', *Journal of Business Research*, Vol.35, No.2, pp.165–73.

Hwang, E.R. (1987), 'Face and Favour: The Chinese Power Game', *American Journal of Sociology*, Vol.92, No.4, pp.35–41.

Kao, J. (1993), 'The Worldwide Web of Chinese Business', *Harvard Business Review*, March–April, pp.24–36.

Luo, Y. (1997), 'Guanxi and Performance of Foreign-Invested Enterprises in China: An Empirical Enquiry', *Management International Review*, Vol.37, No.1, pp. 51–70.

Martinsons, M.G. and Tseng, C. (1995), 'Successful Joint Ventures in the Heart of the Dragon', *Long Range Planning*, Vol.28, No.5, pp.45–58.

Menard, S. (1995), *Applied Logistic Regression*. Thousand Oaks, CA: Sage.

Pearce, J.A., Robbins, D.K. and Robinson, R.B. (1987), 'The Impact of Grand Strategy and Planning Formality on Financial Performance', *Strategic Management Journal*, Vol.8, No.1, pp.125–34.

Piercy, N.F., Cravens, D.W. and Morgan, N.A. (1998), 'Salesforce Performance and Behaviour-Based Management Processes in Business-to-Business Sales Organizations', *European Journal of Marketing*, Vol.32, Nos.1–2, pp.79–100.

Punnett, B.J. and Yu, P. (1990), 'Attitudes towards Doing Business with the People's Republic of China', *International Studies of Management and Organization*, Vol.20, No.1, pp.149–60.

Reuvid, J. (1997), *Doing Business with China*. London: Kogan Page.

Roehrig, M.F. (1994), *Foreign Joint Ventures in Contemporary China*. New York: St Martin's Press.

Shao, A.T. and Herbig, P. (1995), 'Marketing inside the Dragon, Despite China's Bureaucracy', *International Marketing Review*, Vol.12, No.1, pp.65–76.

Shenkar, O. (1990), 'International Joint Ventures' Problems in China: Risks and Remedies', *Long Range Planning*, Vol.23, No.3, pp.82–90.

Tai, L.S.T. (1988), 'Doing Business in the People's Republic of China', *Management International Review*, Vol.28, No.1, pp.5–9.

US Department of Commerce (1990), *Special Report on US Investment in China*. Washington, DC: National Council for US–China Trade.

Wong, Y.H. and Chan, A. (1997), 'Relationship Marketing in China: Guanxi and Relationship Quality Performance', in *Marketing without Borders*, Proceedings of the 31st MEG (Academy of Marketing) Conference, Manchester Metropolitan University, July 1997, Vol.2, pp.1105–18.

Yau, O. (1988), 'Chinese Cultural Values: Their Dimensions and Marketing Implications', *European Journal of Marketing*, Vol.22, No.5, pp.44–57.

6

Management in the Chinese Construction Industry

PING LAN

When traditional systems of collectivized agriculture, planned industry and commerce, and the pursuit of self-reliance failed to produce satisfactory results, the Chinese government embarked upon a major programme of economic reforms in the late 1970s. As a builder of physical facilities and a provider of work for surplus rural labourers, the Chinese construction industry plays an important role in the dual transformation of the country – that is, from an agricultural society to an industrial society, and from a planned economy to a market economy. Since 1980 the total output of industry has been growing at double-digit rate and reached RMB Yuan 1,246 billion (US$150 billion) in real terms in 1997. This level is thirty six times that of 1980. At the same time, the share of the construction industry in China's gross domestic production (GDP) rose from 3.6 per cent in 1979 to 6.7 per cent in 1997.

The Chinese construction industry has been a beneficiary of the reform era policies. Chinese construction enterprises first adopted a 'contracting responsibility system' in the urban industrial sector, which originated from rural households in the early 1980s. They have been operating in a rapidly growing market during the last two decades. However, while the industry as a whole experienced high growth, the relationships of main stakeholders in the industry changed dramatically. Many problems have resulted, such as corruption and stagnation of reform in construction enterprises (Lan and Jackson, 1998a).

Much has been written on China's economic reform, particularly on state-owned enterprise management (Granick, 1990; Child, 1994; Broadman, 1996). However, few studies address the restructuring of the Chinese construction industry under new competitive driving forces, though selected aspects of the reforms in the industry have been tackled. For example, He (1996) outlines the changes of the cost estimation system in China. Research undertaken by the Australian Government (EAAU, 1997) examined how China's infrastructure shortcomings constrain growth, and how the Chinese government is addressing these impediments.

There are multiple reasons for a lack of relevant studies. The most important of these is that studies inside China are fragmented and incomplete. Due to the limitations of funds, unclear ideas regarding the scope of the construction industry, and without a fully developed building economics discipline, most Chinese researchers focus on technical issues or definitions of the scope and role of the industry (Lu and Zhang, 1997). In general terms, the overall research is theoretically underdeveloped, heavily repetitive and disorganized. This is compounded by the fact that Chinese construction practices are different from those in the free-market world and make it difficult for Western researchers to conduct comparative studies.

In attempting to fill the gap in the literature this contribution combines two models into one analytical framework so as to thoroughly investigate the major changes in the Chinese construction industry brought about by economic reforms. One model, developed by Porter (1980), deals with industry competition. The other focuses on monitoring economic transformation, as used by the International Monetary Fund (IMF) in 1993. Based on the framework, the following issues are scrutinized: the emergence of competition among construction enterprises, the shift away from strong government intervention, the increase in the bargaining power of clients, the changes in the relationship between contractors and suppliers, and market entry by newcomers both locally and internationally.

This analysis is organized thus: following this introduction, the second section attempts to analyse the driving forces that determine an industry's competition, and discusses important indicators which explain the nature of an economic system. Based on the synthesis of these discussions, the subsequent five sections analyse forces which are currently reshaping the Chinese construction industry. the third investigates the current characteristics of

Chinese construction enterprises; the fourth describes the changes in the roles played by the Chinese government; the fifth investigates the reasons why clients have gained their bargaining power; the sixth examines why building material suppliers lost their bargaining power in relation to consultants; and the seventh describes two kinds of new entrants: rural construction teams at the low end of the market and foreign contractors at the premium end of the market. The final section of this contribution draws conclusions from the research.

The information used here was collected from two sources. One was through various documents, both published and unpublished, and the other was through a survey conducted by the author in China and Australia between 1996 and 1997. As part of the survey, various Chinese construction enterprises and government agencies in Beijing, Shanghai, Guangzhou and Zhengzhou were visited. At the same time, 22 Australian companies with current operations in China were contacted. The information gathered in China forms the bulk of the discussion and is supplemented by the Australian data. The use of Australian data aims to place the Chinese construction industry in an international perspective.

COMPETITIVE DRIVING FORCES AND ECONOMIC TRANSFORMATION INDICATORS

The aim of economic reform in China, or more generally speaking in all planned economies, is to let state-owned enterprises compete in an environment in which market forces become dominant and government intervention is reduced. In order to trace this transformation it is necessary to understand the nature of industry competition in a free market and the factors involved in creating a market economy from a planned economy.

Porter's work (1980, 1985, 1990) offers useful insights into industry competition. According to Porter, the basic unit of analysis for understanding competition is industry. Firms' competitive strategy must grow out of a sophisticated understanding of the structure of the industry and how it is changing. In any industry, whether it is domestic or international, the nature of competition is embodied in five competitive forces. These forces determine industry profitability as they shape the prices firms can charge, the costs they have to bear, and the investment required to compete in the industry. The strength of each competitive force, as shown below, is a function of industry structure, or the underlying economic and technical characteristics of an industry:

- *The bargaining power of buyers*: a function of such things as the number of buyers, and the degree to which a firm's sales are dependent upon any one buyer.
- *The threat of new entrants*: these can limit the overall profit potential in the industry.
- The threat of substitute products or services: the presence of close substitute products limits the price that competitors can charge without inducing substitution and eroding industry volume.
- *The bargaining power of suppliers*: powerful suppliers are able to increase their profits by bargaining.
- *The rivalry among the existing competitors*: the higher costs required by competition or by the need to pass on profits to customers in the form of low prices.

It is apparent that Porter's 'driving forces' model well describes the market side of industry structure analysis (Watson, 1992). However, the threat of substitute products or services in the model is not as relevant in the construction industry as it is in the manufacturing industry. This is due to the non-substitutional nature of most products or services provided by construction enterprises.

IMF research (1993) into the changes in China's economic system highlights several factors which indicate transition in the economy. According to the IMF, the transformation of an economic system from a centrally planned economy to an economy in which resources are allocated primarily through market mechanisms can be examined with regard to the following elements:

- *If the price mechanisms operate freely*; that is, prices are set by the independent interaction of producers and consumers in most or all sectors of the economy.
- *If all sectors of the economy are open to international trade*; that is, minimal tariffs and non-tariff barriers or other forms of government trade control apply.
- *If competition is strong in all industry sectors of the domestic*

market, referring to a lack of regulatory or legal barriers to the entry or exit of firms.

- *If the state plays a minimal role in the domestic economy*, whereby the role of government is mainly limited to providing public goods and collecting taxes necessary to finance these activities.
- *If an institutional framework supporting market activities is well developed*, a framework which includes an effective rule of law and an independent judiciary, well developed regulatory standards and a responsive and transparent bureaucracy.

These criteria reflect both the relative importance of market forces and government intervention in an economy. However, applying the criteria to the construction industry is problematic in that the international trade issue is not nearly as relevant. Construction is a special industry. The products of the industry are immobile and are usually tied to the final market. International trade control affects little of the industry.

By dropping the irrelevant elements and combining the two models, a framework is set up to guide this research (Figure 1). There are several considerations. Firstly, all indicators of economic transformation, except those of government intervention, are discussed with the key players in the industry as they are interwoven with the four driving forces. For example, increasing competition can be observed among contractors, suppliers and new entrants. Institutional frameworks also affect the behaviour of contractors and clients.

Secondly, as government intervention is a special part of an economic system it is discussed separately. The analysis covers several roles governments can play, both directly and indirectly, in affecting the operations of the driving forces, such as client, financier and regulator.

Thirdly, rural construction teams are treated as entrants not suppliers. Although many rural construction teams serve as labour suppliers for construction enterprises, many of these also act as independent contractors in construction projects, particularly in small scale projects. Foreign construction companies are also treated as new entrants, though their entry into the construction market subjects them to government intervention.

Finally, building material manufacturers and consultants are

FIGURE 1
FRAMEWORK FOR ANALYZING THE TRANSFORMATION OF THE CHINESE CONSTRUCTION INDUSTRY

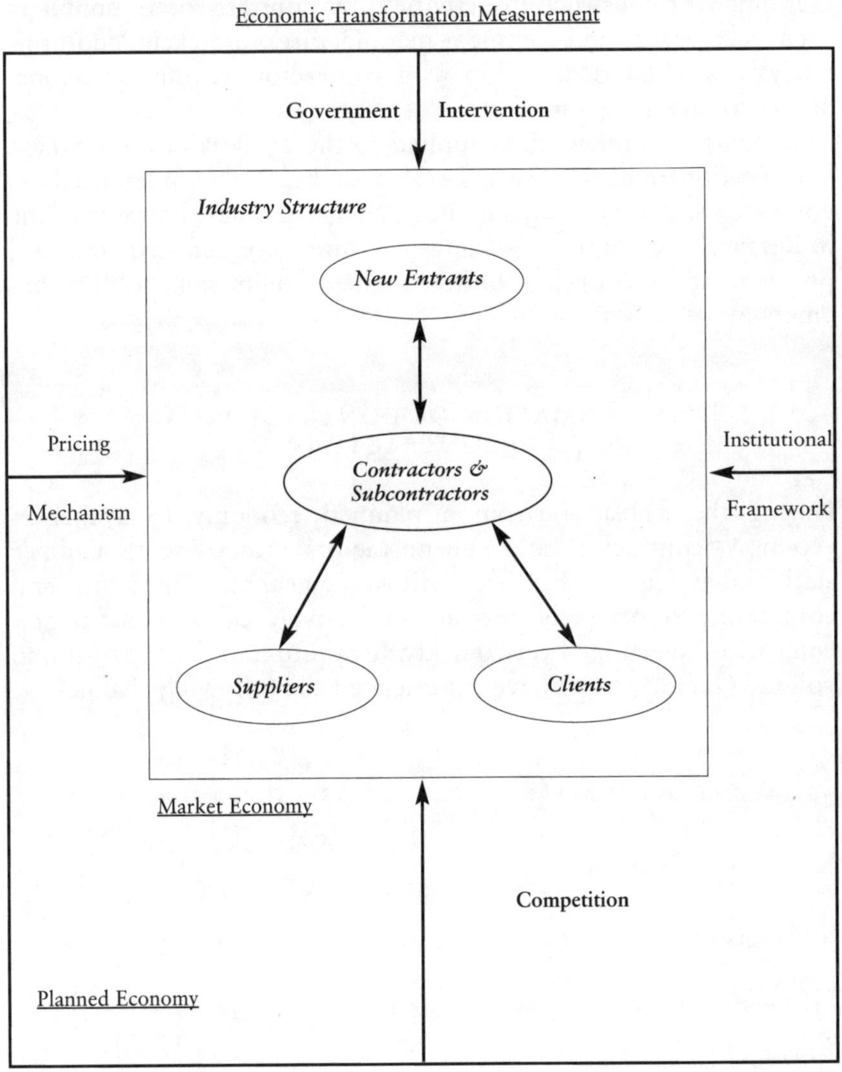

Source: Developed by the author based on Porter (1985) and IMF (1993).

placed into the category of suppliers. The reason that only building material suppliers and various consultants are chosen as suppliers is that they provide materials and services, which are continuously consumed in construction activities. By contrast, other suppliers such as construction equipment manufacturers are excluded in this analysis, as their relationship with contractors is only occasional and is comparatively weak.

When this framework is applied to the analysis of the Chinese construction industry, the behaviour of key stakeholders such as contractors, government, suppliers, clients and new entrants in the industry shows dramatic change. A more complicated and still problematic relationship between these main stakeholders has emerged.

TRANSFORMATION OF CONTRACTORS AND SUBCONTRACTORS

During the transition from a planned economy to a market economy, contractors and subcontractors (according to China's statistical practices, they are defined as general contractors and contractors respectively and are collectively called construction enterprises) developed very quickly. In addition to the expansion in volume (Table 1), they have experienced the following changes.

TABLE 1
MAIN INDICATORS FOR CHINESE CONSTRUCTION ENTERPRISES, 1980–1995

Items	*1980*	*1985*	*1990*	*1995*	*1997*
Number of enterprises	6,604	10,351	12,275	24,133	39,522
Employment (1,000 persons)	6,480	8,491	9,265	14,979	19,768
Total output (US$ million)	3,457	7,549	14,734	69,804	84,523

Note: Calculation is based on US$1 = Yuan 8.3.

Source: China Statistical Yearbook 1998.

Firstly, state-owned contractors have to search for work through market competition. Prior to the reform, Chinese contractors were assigned construction work by the government with no formal relationship between contractor and client. Projects were constructed by the contractors based on a design budget that was determined by the government or a government design institute.

Since the early 1980s, Chinese contractors have adopted a 'contracting responsibility system' which separates ownership and management and is now applied to all industries. The deregulation and withdrawal of government as a client encouraged and even forced the contractors to ensure their projects reached the marketplace. For example, in the late 1980s, only about 2 per cent of total construction in China was contracted by tendering, but by 1995 this figure had increased to one-third (Jin, 1996).

Secondly, the prices for construction services are no longer fixed by the government and are subject to market fluctuations. Traditionally, the cost of construction materials, construction machinery, labour, and profit margins for contractors were set by the central government. Inputs required by construction were distributed by a national distribution system. Furthermore, the Construction Bank, a body responsible for financing all government projects in China, controlled all transactions related to a project. Given this background, prices for construction activities were standardized.

As the government neither assigns construction work nor distributes construction materials to construction enterprises, construction costs as well as prices for construction are flexible. Although it is still the practice of a design institute to estimate construction costs according to the national 'budgetary estimate norms', there is much more scope for Chinese contractors to deal with construction costs and to determine their profit margins. Project funding is available from many different sources. The cost of construction materials, machinery and labour are subject to market fluctuations. There are many channels to deal with transactions. Based on these changes, prices for construction services are currently set by the interaction of contractors and clients within an ever-widening circle.

Thirdly, a two-tier subcontracting system was set up to accommodate construction enterprises. During the decades of centralized control, the main contractor in China was responsible for all the work involved in a project. In recent years, due to the fast rate of development and the huge demand for construction labour, adopting a subcontracting system has become unavoidable. At present, a two-tier hierarchy covers all construction enterprises in China.

According to the framework, all contractors are divided into two types. The first includes general contractors. In general, they have the capacity to design, build, deliver a project and undertake related research and development (R&D). General contractors are divided into two classes, according to their work history, licences obtained, numbers of qualified staff and capitalization.

Further down the contractual chain are construction contractors. Their role is to build the projects. These contractors are divided into 33 categories according to the nature of projects – electronic contractor, foundation contractor, tunnel contractor, etc. In each category, there are between two and four classes. The criteria are similar to those for general contractors, but with the emphasis on certain specified technical requirements. According to this division, most Chinese construction enterprises fall into this category.

Along with these changes two problems have emerged, which hinder the further development of Chinese construction enterprises. Firstly, there is the relative stagnation of reform among the contractors and, secondly, contractors are prevented from attaining further specialization due to incomplete contractual chains.

Although Chinese contractors were pioneers in adopting the 'contracting responsibility system' in the 1980s, their reforms in the last decade have not gone beyond that domain (cf. Forrester and Porter contribution). Ownership reform, for example, is behind other industries. By 1996, shareholding companies accounted for less than 2 per cent of total construction firms, in terms of the output, while the average in manufacturing was over 5 per cent.

Confined by the institutional tradition of a planned economy, it is more difficult for Chinese contractors to deal with market competition. This can be observed from their inability to deal with mergers and takeovers. For example, in the recent national campaign for promoting the 'modern enterprises institution', which aims to group firms into large conglomerates through mergers and takeovers, little has been achieved in the industry.

Most of about 500 Chinese construction enterprise groups are formed based on the traditional division of local-owned and ministry-owned structures (CCIA, 1996).

The incomplete contractual chain in China is mainly reflected in the unclear relationship between contractors and subcontractors, and insufficient links between the various contractors on a project. In most free market economies, regardless of whether contractors are service-orientated or production-orientated, their relationship with subcontractors is reasonably clear, though it varies significantly from long term strategic alliances to 'one-off' project-based cooperation. For example, a subcontracting system is well developed in Australia, where contractors are service-orientated and subcontractors deliver between 75 and 85 per cent of the value of the industry's production (DPWS, 1996).

In China, however, a system for governing subcontracting has not been set up. It is unclear what percentage of construction jobs the subcontractors undertake. Also unclear is the pattern of relationship between contractors and subcontractors. The Chinese government is now concerned about over-subcontracting, with many contractors and designers seeking profits by illegally leasing their licences or by subcontracting their jobs to unqualified firms. Therefore, Clause 3.29 of the new Construction Law requires contractors to undertake 'main structure' construction of the project alone, and forbids subcontractors to further subcontract out any work.

Lack of a clear contractor–subcontractor relationship and the impracticability of limiting the contractual chain to only two links hinder the further development of specialization amongst construction firms. First, subcontractors have to be comprehensive instead of specialized. This does not allow them to concentrate on developing their core competence. Second, competition among contractors and subcontractors is over a wider range, which can have a detrimental effect on the performance of most construction enterprises. According to official statistics, the average profit margin (rate of profit / gross output value) in all Chinese construction enterprises between 1995 and 1997 was only about 1.2 per cent. In order to obtain new orders, many enterprises had to work at even lower margins. By the middle of 1996, over half of state-owned construction enterprises were losing money or just breaking even (Li, 1996).

Given this situation, the difference in rates of efficiency in China and Australia is obvious, as shown in Table 2. The Australian construction industry, according to Mitchell (1996), demonstrates world class efficiency in terms of productivity.

TABLE 2
CONSTRUCTION COSTS RATIOS BETWEEN CHINA AND AUSTRALIA IN THE MID 1990s

Items	*Construction Costs Ratios*
Building materials	1: 8
Wages	1:24
Unit rates	1: 7
Building costs	1: 2

Note: Calculation is based on 1AU$=Yuan 6.3. Costs are averaged across a range of 12 building materials, 13 occupation groups, 14 categories of work and 6 building types.

Source: Author's compilation of various sources.

The first two indicators in Table 2 can be seen as pure input measurements. The last two indicators can be seen as measurements of output efficiency from the standpoint of construction. They represent total machinery, materials and labour committed to particular construction jobs. It is apparent that the differences between the two countries in input indicators are much bigger than those in efficiency indicators.

SHIFTING OF GOVERNMENT INTERVENTION

Since the adoption of the 'reform and openness' policy in the late 1970s, the role of government has been changing dramatically. The most distinguishable change is that governments at different levels no longer assign construction work to construction enterprises. They have withdrawn from the operations of these firms. In addition, the intervention of government in the construction market has shifted from direct ownership of projects to indirect control through financial leverage. Furthermore, the national government has conditionally opened its construction market to foreign investment and foreign contractors. However, unlike Western countries, Chinese government intervention in the construction market and in the construction industry is still pervasive and influential, as the discussion below will demonstrate.

Government acts as a client. With the deregulation of the Chinese command economy, this role of government as client is decreasing. For example, the share of the state budget in total investment in fixed assets (Table 3) dropped from 28 per cent in 1981 to less than 3 per cent in 1997. It is worth noting, though, that different governments still influence the construction market through various instruments. Firstly, the national government continues to directly run large public projects such as the Three Gorges Dam. Secondly, it still, to a certain extent, directly controls state-owned enterprises, which remain a main market for construction projects. Thirdly, the more entrepreneurial local authorities remain deeply involved in local economic development. Every local authority sets up its own 'priority projects' annually to intervene in the operation of the construction industry.

TABLE 3
TOTAL INVESTMENT IN FIXED ASSETS BY SOURCES (%)

Sources of Funds	*1981*	*1985*	*1990*	*1997*
State budget	28.1	16.0	8.7	2.8
Domestic loans	12.7	20.1	19.6	18.9
Foreign investment	3.8	3.6	6.3	10.3
Fundraising and other	55.4	60.3	65.4	67.7
Total	100.0	100.0	100.0	100.0

Source: China Statistical Yearbook 1998.

Government acts as a financier. Differing from Western countries, the Chinese government is directly involved in the operations of 'commercial banks'. Therefore, about 20 per cent of construction projects, which rely on domestic loans, are directly controlled by different levels of governments. The intervention of government, through the operations of 'commercial banks', spreads to many other construction projects, though their investment is not as tightly controlled.

Government acts as a regulator. While the role of government as a client is decreasing, the role of government as a regulator is increasing. Many more regulations were made in the 1990s than in the 1980s. The scope of regulation is also enlarged. At the national level, the following issues have been the priorities of regulation making: introducing a licensing system, regulating the chaotic construction market, improving project quality, estimating construction costs and reforming construction enterprises (Table 4).

TABLE 4
PROMULGATED NATIONAL REGULATIONS RELATED TO CONSTRUCTION INDUSTRY

Main Concern of Regulations	*Numbers by Promulgated Year*						
	1980s	*1990*	*1991*	*1992*	*1993*	*1994*	*1995*
Licence system	0	0	1	3	1	2	2
Construction market	1	0	2	3	1	2	1
Quality and safety	4	2	3	1	2	2	0
Technology progress	1	0	1	0	1	1	1
Construction cost	0	0	1	3	1	1	0
Enterprise reform	1	0	2	4	4	2	5
Total	7	2	10	14	10	10	9

Source: Compiled by author based on MOC (1996) A Collection of Documents for Project Construction and the Construction Industry. Beijing. Metallurgical Industry Press.

In addition to promulgating various rules to regulate or change the operational environment of construction enterprises, the Chinese government has conditionally opened its market, though there is still strong protectionism. At the national level, the Ministry of Construction in China, by a licensing system, limits overseas contractors' local operations to the following four cases:

- Projects funded solely by overseas investment or grant funds.
- Projects with loans from multinational institutions and open to international bidding.
- Projects jointly invested in by Chinese and overseas companies where Chinese enterprises have difficulties in contracting alone due to technical difficulties.
- Projects with total Chinese investment, which cannot be constructed by Chinese contractors alone. Overseas companies are allowed to jointly contract these projects with their Chinese counterparts upon the approval of the relevant construction administrative departments at provincial level.

It is apparent that the national Chinese government sets technology and capital as two preconditions for foreign contractors into China. This can also be observed from China's control over the inflow of foreign investment into its construction industry. In order to gain more advanced technology, China does not allow foreign contractors to set up wholly owned subsidiaries in its territory and limits foreign contractors' local operations to the same scope as their local partners. In order to generate more capital input, the Chinese government requires that the registered capital for foreign-funded construction enterprises be over US$16 million (MOC, 1996).

At the local level, local authorities have concerns with employment. Governments at all levels are keen for the construction companies within their region to win contracts. When competition is intense, interference from local government is strong. By the end of 1995, over one-third of municipalities and provinces in China were formulating special regulations to protect 'their' construction market. It is understandable that foreign contractors are subject to more government intervention than other foreign investors in China. For example, among 22 Australian companies operating in China, contractors (which account for half of the surveyed firms) report that two-thirds of them face strong government intervention both at central and local level. By comparison, only one-third of the Australian investors in other sectors report the same case.

THE INCREASE OF CLIENTS' BARGAINING POWER

Clients create demand and have the power to directly influence industry performance. Their influence can be positive or negative, depending on circumstances. In China, as in other countries, clients are a heterogeneous group. Their interests and the approaches they take to project initiation and delivery tend to be diverse. Nevertheless, Chinese clients have several distinguishing features at the present stage in the country's development.

Firstly, the state-owned sector still plays an important role in China's economy, particularly in absorbing investment, though its share in production has dropped dramatically. For example, state-owned industrial enterprises accounted for 77.6 per cent of gross industrial output value in 1978. The figure dropped to 40 per cent in 1995 and further to 25.5 per cent in 1997. However, over half of current construction and installation work in China still comes from the state-owned sector (Table 5). This disparity on the one hand shows the difficulty for reforming Chinese state-owned enterprises (Qin, 1996); and on the other hand it indicates that allocation of resources in China is not fully governed by the market force.

TABLE 5
STRUCTURE OF CHINA'S CONSTRUCTION AND INSTALLATION MARKET

Type of Client	*Market Share (%)*	
	1995	*1997*
State-owned units	50.1	51.5
Collectively owned units	19.1	13.8
Individuals	17.6	19.9
Jointly owned units	0.5	0.5
Share holding units	3.5	4.4
Overseas funded units	8.7	9.3
Others	0.4	0.7
Total	100.0	100.0

Sources: China Statistical Yearbook 1996, 1998.

Due to incomplete reform, many clients in China take short term views on their projects, or only have a short term planning for their projects. Market-embracing reform effectively changed state-owned firms from pure production units to increasingly independent market players. Now they are partly responsible for their own profits and losses. However, the transformation is far from complete. Most state-owned enterprises are currently at a stage akin to 'semiconductors'; that is, they are sensitive to some market signals. They rush to produce certain products when market signals are flashing. However, they are not aware of the consequences of oversupply or simply do not take the full responsibility for the oversupply they have created as their losses can be labelled 'tuition fees' and be written off from their bank loans, either totally or partially. For example, in 1996, there was a 2.2 million tonne cement surplus from 70 surveyed cement producers and an oversupply of 5 million cases of glass from 23 surveyed flat glass manufacturers (Lan and Jackson, 1998b). In such circumstances, long term concerns give way to short term concerns such as the immediate costs of construction.

Undercapitalization is another characteristic of Chinese clients. It is common in China that a client develops a project without the necessary capital. The following factors contribute to the problem:

- During the rapid expansion of the economy, enterprises in China were perpetually short of capital.
- It is a tradition for Chinese enterprises and/or local authorities to have a 'hidden capital gap' when they submit their project proposals to relevant authorities or the central government for approval. A recent official survey on various projects with total investment US$ 800 million reveals that this gap is 80 per cent of the total budget on average (Chai, 1998).
- 'Debt triangles', in which firms delay or refuse due payments to each other, are common.

Thus in many cases a client's capital as it appears in their balance sheets is not available in practice. When China tightened its capital supply in the early 1990s to fight double-digit inflation, the shortage of capital among clients became more obvious. Therefore, more and more clients are asking contractors to undertake projects with their own capital. According to a survey, the total due payment for construction and installation projects is over Yuan 50 billion in 1996 (DOCI, 1996).

The third feature of Chinese clients is that they tend to use improper, sometimes illegal practices in the management of their projects. By the end of 1995, only about one-third of all projects in China involved open tender. Many of the deals were made 'under the table'. Since the open tender system is not yet widely applied, corruption is pervasive in the Chinese construction industry. It is common for clients to ask for 'kick-backs', to insist on using certain poor quality building materials, or to seek to minimize the cost of construction by selecting the lowest bid. Their behaviour has not yet been regulated effectively due to problems in the enforcement of various regulations (Li, 1996). The promulgation of the first Chinese Construction Law, which came into effect on 1 March 1998, aims to tackle these issues.

The fourth feature of clients in China is the increase in their overseas numbers. The market share of foreign clients increased from nil in early 1980s to about 10 per cent in 1997. Inflow foreign direct investment (FDI) is concentrated in several sectors, such as manufacturing, real estate and transportation. These investments are closely connected with the construction industry. The inflows of FDI, generally speaking, increase construction standards and offer more learning opportunities for local contractors, whether they serve as contractors or subcontractors.

The combination of the above changes has dramatically transformed the relationship between clients and construction enterprises in China. More complicated relationships are being forged as various independent investors have replaced the government as the main clients of construction enterprises, so diversifying links between a construction enterprise and its clients. However, clients are more adept at playing the market than contractors, partly because of the stagnation of contractors in ownership reform (Table 6). As a consequence, the bargaining power of clients shows an increasing trend, which can be seen from the increasing number of contractors willing to undertake projects with their own capital.

TABLE 6
COMPARISON OF OWNERSHIP STRUCTURE BY TOTAL OUTPUT (%)

Type of Ownership	*Contractors*	*Manufacturers*
State-owned	49.6	41.0
Collectively owned	43.0	29.3
Individuals	0.5	–
Jointly owned	0.3	–
Share holding	4.8	7.0
Overseas funded	1.5	20.4
Others	0.3	2.3
Total	100.0	100.0

Note: Manufacturers are at and above township level.

Sources: China Statistical Yearbook 1998.

CHANGES OF RELATIONSHIP BETWEEN CONTRACTORS AND SUPPLIERS

Building material manufacturers' bargaining power, generally speaking, has been eroded during the last decade, though building materials account for a large portion of total building costs. Reasons for this relate back to the oversupply of conventional building materials caused by deregulation, the low concentration of production among the manufacturers, and the inroads made by contractors in the production of building materials.

Before the economic reforms, the manufacture of building materials in China was controlled by the State Administration of Building Materials Industry (SABMI), and all construction materials were distributed by the government. Following deregulation in the 1980s there was a fever of investing in building material production by different industries in different regions. It is known as 'investing into building materials by all the sectors' in China. As a result of the investment fever, SABMI's monopoly on building material manufacturing was broken, and the boundary between the building materials industry and other industries became unclear. Currently, only a minority of the total output of building materials is controlled by SABMI. For example, in Shanghai, only 20 per cent of cement production and 25 per cent of ready-mixed concrete supply are under the control of the local branch of SABMI.

As a consequence of this investment fever, concentration of building material manufacturing in China is very low. For example, there are over 7,000 cement producers. The top 67 firms account for only 10 per cent of total cement production. Of the 140 glass producers the top 23 firms account for 43 per cent of production (SABMI, 1996). The very low concentration of building material production may be attributed to two reasons. One is the domination of rural firms in this sector. There were over 200,000 building material suppliers throughout China in the mid-1990s. Among them, rural manufacturing firms account for 70 per cent of enterprises and 40 per cent of total output. The other reason is that there are no ministry-owned firms in this sector, unlike in other industries. Ministry-owned firms are usually regarded as key players. As a result of their national importance they usually receive privileged treatment such as early possession of advanced new technology. A lack of such key players would make it difficult for small suppliers to gain economies of scale, to influence the market, and to promote technological progress nationwide.

Since the replacement of a centrally controlled construction materials distribution system by a market procurement system, many Chinese contractors, particularly large construction companies, have become both manufacturers and final users of building materials as part of their diversification strategies. In Shanghai, 20 per cent of ready-mixed concrete and 25 per cent of plasterboard is manufactured by the Shanghai Construction Group (SCG), the largest construction enterprise in Shanghai. Setting up joint ventures with foreign investors has become a shortcut for contractors to make inroads into building material manufacturing, because of a lack of technology and capital. For example, SCG set up a joint venture with CSR, an Australian building material manufacturer, to manufacture plasterboard with a production capacity of 25,000,000 square metres per year. This is equal to half the market size of Shanghai. This backward integration of contractors further diminishes the bargaining power of building materials suppliers.

In contrast to building materials suppliers, consultants' impact on construction enterprises in China has become more influential. The most outstanding feature of consultant services in China is its dual structure: that is, state-owned institutes tackle technical issues, and private consultants deal with personal contacts (Lan and Jackson, 1998b).

Highly specialized technical jobs such as architectural and design works in China, as in other countries, occur at the 'front end' of projects and so are well placed to set the framework for improving short and long-term project outcomes. Currently, there are about 800,000 surveyors and designers working in this sector. Architectural and design works are mainly undertaken by the design institutes set up by the Chinese authorities. Typically, these design institutes depend on government works, with private projects being of only secondary importance. They are run by experienced professionals at the top level, but a gap exists in the middle layer of professionals and the lower end includes many poor-quality designers. Although private consultants are increasing in number, the monopoly of state-owned institutes in this sector remains. One reason for such institutes having strong influence on contractors is that they still enjoy Chinese government protection. A foreign firm, particularly an architectural firm, is required to have a local partner to ensure that their submissions for doing business in China are approved. The local partner usually needs to be located in the appropriate city, since registration recognized in one city does not necessarily mean recognition in another, despite the national character of registration.

Regarding non-technical issues, particularly those related to personal contacts which are crucial for winning contracts, consultant services are mainly operated by private individuals. This kind of service focuses on forging various personal relationships. It is not confined to the 'front end' of projects and permeates the whole life cycle of a construction project. Those who provide such services usually possess highly personalized networks. The key to the network is to have good relationships with various authorities. Many advantages, therefore, can be generated from having good personal relationships.

The general recognition of the importance of personal contacts sets the market for such services. People who hold positions in the relevant authorities, who have relatives or are close to officers in these authorities, who have good relationships with banks and clients, are well placed to be the providers of the services. Unlike design and other technically specialized consultants, 'personal contact' consultants are dominated by private concerns. They may be run in various forms, legal or illegal. Compared with other consultants, 'personal contact' consultants are more market driven and more flexible.

Although there is not a clear picture about the bargaining power of these *guanxi* or 'personal contact' consultants nationwide, the survey found that many contractors in China are willing to pay generously for their services, believing this will lead to winning a contract. A new slogan among the Chinese construction companies, 'Personal contacts are a productive force', is evidence that contractors regard these consultants as important suppliers for their business.

TWO TYPES OF NEW ENTRANTS

Chinese contractors currently face two kinds of threats generated by new entrants into the industry. One is the penetration of foreign contractors with capital and superior technology at the top end of the market, and the other is low cost, rural construction teams flooding into the lower end of the market.

China's rural economic reform increased the productivity of agriculture. At the same time, it freed up surplus labour in rural areas. From 1980 to 1995, it was estimated that over 20 million of the 300 million surplus labourers in rural areas entered the construction market (Jin, 1996). According to official statistics, the number of rural construction teams reached 71,017 in China in 1995, which is about three times the number of construction enterprises. The total output of these construction teams was US$ 44 billion. This is sixty-one times that of 1980, and doubles the average growth rate of the industry.

Although growing rapidly, these construction teams are poorly equipped and poorly managed. When they first entered the market, they mainly undertook unskilled labouring work. As they gained certain technical and management skills, some of them began to compete with construction enterprises. Due to their very low overheads, low labour costs, low profit margins and usually lawless management, they not only took construction work in rural areas, small towns and the periphery of cities, but also penetrated into urban areas. Some of them have developed into independent subcontractors and even contractors. Rural construction teams from Jiangshu, Zhejiang and Shandong province are more active. The emerging closer relationship between unregulated clients and lawless rural construction teams has become an immense concern for construction enterprises and the government. Many problems, such as project quality, illegal practices and corruption, are tied to this relationship (CCIA, 1996).

Although there are some limitations to the entry of foreign contractors and foreign investors into the Chinese construction industry, many gain access in China as a result of their strength in technology and capital.

Generally speaking, there are two ways an overseas construction company can operate in China. One is to undertake construction projects without having Chinese 'legal person status'. Under a decree of the Ministry of Construction, an overseas contractor applies for a licence from a particular provincial government if it operates only in that province, while it must apply for a licence from the Ministry of Construction if it operates in more than one province. By the end 1996, there were thirty foreign contractors operating in China in this way and holding licences from the Ministry of Construction in China (Yao, 1996).

When analysing information about the contractors, several facts are worth noting. Firstly, most of the foreign contractors in the list show a certain technological superiority. For example, Spaceframe, a small Australian contractor that specializes in pre-engineered buildings for warehouses, factories, cold stores, etc., has two pre-engineered portal frame building systems. Both systems are totally computerized, so that the firm can price a building within ten minutes and prepare detailed engineering, architectural and shop drawing within 30 minutes. Because of their advanced design techniques and superior building technology, the firm developed rapidly in China. Secondly, Hong Kong and Japanese construction companies are dominant. Hong Kong contractors entered the Chinese market earlier and on a large scale. Japanese construction companies, such as Kumagai Gumi, Shimizu and Taizei, target large projects. Korean constructors, although they came later, are also very active in the market. Thirdly, European and American contractors are mainly engaged in equipment installation, factory construction and engineering construction. For example, in the construction of Xiaolangde Hydraulic Power Station on the Yellow River, 13 of the 14 foreign contractors are from Europe.

The other way for an overseas construction company to operate in China is to have a local subsidiary, usually a joint venture. Since opening its doors, China has accommodated about 1,600 foreign-funded enterprises related to the construction industry. Among them, there are over 100 comparatively large ones with investments of over US$10 million. Several changes have occurred over time among these foreign-funded construction enterprises. First, fewer foreign contractors now operate in areas without much technological value, such as earthworks. Secondly, infrastructure construction, particularly in the transportation and energy sectors, has been the main target for foreign-funded construction companies. However, the pattern is shifting away from purely highway construction towards a combination of power station and highway construction and management. Thirdly, the operating scope of foreign-funded construction companies is getting wider over time. Other infrastructure projects, such as water supply projects, are receiving more consideration from overseas contractors.

CONCLUSIONS

Against the framework set up at the beginning of this contribution, the above analyses of the main stakeholders in the Chinese construction industry show several characteristics in the changes of contractual relationship and transformation of the industrial structure. Firstly, the industry currently is becoming more market driven. Government no longer assigns construction work to construction enterprises. Its intervention has shifted from directly providing construction jobs to project financial control. Contractors and subcontractors have to search for contracts through market competition. The conditional opening of the construction market caused an influx of foreign direct investment and foreign contractors. The loosening of control over the movement of surplus rural labour has generated a flood of rural construction teams. All these factors have increased competition in the industry.

Second, the Chinese construction industry has become more fragmented and poorly regulated. Due to the low entry barriers, the importance of local personal contacts and the variety of local regulations, there is a large number of small and medium sized companies in the industry, some with potential to grow rapidly. But the lack of an effective framework for setting up a full construction industry hierarchy among contractors and subcontractors continues to hinder the development of construction firms' specialization. Indeed, various wrongdoings or illegal practices, fermented by the relationships between lawless rural construction teams and unregulated clients, erode the reinforcement of laws and regulations. Therefore, the potential profits of construction enterprises are easily bargained away by clients and certain suppliers. More generally, the potential for the orderly development of the industry is reduced.

Third, although economic reform has brought Chinese construction practices more in line with international conventions, they are still quite different from those in the free-market world. For example, government intervention is still very strong, though the intervention instruments are now more diversified; whereas the relationship between contractors and clients is more complicated, the behaviour of contractors and subcontractors remains more or less confined to a planned economy; the tendering system is still not widely applied and many deals are made 'under the table'; asking private consultants to deal with personal relationships has become an inseparable part of doing business in the Chinese construction market; some regulations on many construction activities are unclear and often confused; and there is also a lack of correspondence between standards for building design and construction in China and the free-market world. Therefore, more openness and further reform are required to accelerate the transformation of the industry. At the present stage, establishing a complete contractual chain among contractors and subcontractors, and promoting open tendering systems, should be the priorities.

REFERENCES

Broadman, H.G. (ed.) (1996), *Policy Options for Reform of Chinese State-Owned Enterprises*. World Bank Discussion Paper, No.335.

CCIA (China Construction Industry Association) (1996), 'On the Strategies for Advancing the Development of the Construction Enterprises Group', *Construction Economy*, No.1, pp.8–13.

Chai, M. (1998), 'Why the Efficiency of Yuan 6.8 Billion Investment Is So Low', *Economic Information*, 19 March.

Child, J. (1994), *Management in China during the Age of Reform*. Cambridge: Cambridge University Press.

DCI (Division of Construction Industry) (1996), *Research References for Developing the Construction Industry*, Vol. 2. Beijing: Ministry of Construction.

DPWS (Department of Public Works and Services) (1996), *The Construction Industry in New South Wales: Opportunities and Challenges*. NSW Government Green Paper.

EAAU (East Asia Analysis Unit) (1997), *China Embraces the Market: Achievements, Constraints and Opportunities*. Department of Foreign Affairs and Trade, Australia.

Granick, D. (1990), *Chinese State Enterprises: A Regional Property Rights Analysis*. Chicago: The University of Chicago Press.

He, Z. (1996), 'Understanding the Chinese Construction Costing System', *Cost Engineering*, Vol.38, No.1, pp.19–21.

IMF (International Monetary Fund) (1993), *China at the Threshold of a Market Economy*. Washington, DC: IMF.

Jin, M.Q. (1996), 'The Only Way Out to Develop Vigorously the Construction Industry', *Construction Economy*, No.1, pp.3–7.

Lan, P. (1996), *Technology Transfer to China through Foreign Direct Investment*. Aldershot, England: Avebury.

Lan, P. and Jackson, J.T. (1997), 'Problems Faced by Australian Contractors in China', *The Building Economist*, No.4, pp.4–9.

Lan, P. and Jackson, J.T. (1998a), 'Catching the New Opportunities in China's Construction Market', *The Building Economist*, No.2, pp.24–9.

Lan, P. and Jackson J.T. (1998b), *Current Characteristics of the Main Stakeholders in the Chinese Construction Industry*. Marketing and International Business Working Paper Series, No. 7. Queensland University of Technology.

Li, D.Q. (1996), *Research into the Improvement of State-owned Construction Enterprises*. Report for the Ministry of Construction, China.

Lu, Y. and Zhang, Q. (1997), 'Building Economics Research in the People's Republic of China: A Review', *Construction Management and Economics*, Vol.15, No.5, pp.421–8.

Mitchell, A. (1996), 'Tariffs Are No Boon to Battlers', *The Australian Financial Review*, 20 November.

MOC (Ministry of Construction) (1996), *A Collection of Documents for Project Construction and the Construction Industry*. Beijing: Metallurgical Industry Press.

Porter, M.E. (1980), *Competitive Strategy: Techniques for Analysing Industries and Competitors*. New York: The Free Press.

Porter, M.E. (1985), *Competitive Advantage: Creating and Sustaining Superior Performance*. New York: The Free Press.

Porter, M.E. (1990), *The Competitive Advantage of Nations*. London: Macmillan.

Qin, X. (1996), 'Restructuring Large State-Owned Enterprises: Internal Mechanisms for Allocating Resources as a Substitute for the Market', in H.G. Broadman (ed.), *Policy Options for Reform of Chinese State-Owned Enterprises*. World Bank Discussion Paper, No.335, pp.157–84.

SABMI (State Administration of Building Materials Industry) (1996), *Information for the Building Materials Market*. Beijing.

Watson, G.H. (1992), *The Benchmarking Workbook: Adapting Best Practices for Performance Improvement*. Portland, OR: Productive Press.

Yao, Bing (1996), *The General Introduction of Overseas Enterprises Contracting Projects in China*. Beijing: Ministry of Construction.

7

Transferring Ownership-specific Advantages to a Joint Venture in China

SIMONETTA ILARI and ADRIENNE LA GRANGE

The major advantage of foreign direct investment (FDI) for transnational companies is that it provides an opportunity to exercise a controlling interest in the use to which foreign investment is put and to be directly and actively involved in the management of a foreign affiliate, rather than merely provide capital. Firms seeking to expand internationally often choose to retain ownership control of their operations, even when there are significant costs in doing so (Hymer, 1976; Vernon, 1966; 1971; Aliber, 1970; Buckley and Casson, 1976). Following John Dunning's eclectic approach, ownership advantages might include intangible assets of the firm (such as its management and marketing systems, and human resources), derived from a firm's intention to organize its operations on a cross-national scale (including the greater availability of production materials, established relations with a network of suppliers, production flexibility and better knowledge of international markets), the capacity of the firm to organize interfirm relationships and transactions in a competitive way, and the managerial know-how that enables it to operate efficiently (Dunning 1977, 1992, 1995).

Until the mid-1970s there was relatively little foreign direct investment in China. The country was not perceived to be a very attractive investment proposition by transnational companies, and FDI was actively discouraged by the Chinese government, particularly during the Cultural Revolution (1966–76) (Riskin, 1987; Howell, 1993; Wang, 1993). The Open Door policy (1976 to present) initiated a new era of FDI in China, as the Chinese government actively fostered foreign investment by providing greater incentives and opportunities. Indeed, reliance on foreign capital was a fundamental component of China's broader reform blueprint (Redding, 1990; Pearson, 1991; Ma, 1995). Its expectations of FDI specifically were threefold: that it would accelerate the process of industrial construction and restructuring by providing much needed funds; that it would promote technical knowledge and production equipment renovation through the inflow of equipment and information from overseas; and that it would improve the balance of payments through increases in exports and import substitution. It was also anticipated that FDI would generate new job opportunities, increase the range of products and services available on the Chinese market, and stimulate the development of local economies (China Investment Guide, 1995).

A number of transnational automotive firms (such as Volkswagen, Peugeot, Citroen, Fiat and Honda) had examined the potential in investing directly in China's automotive industry, and the manufacture and distribution of cars and two-wheelers has been an important component of FDI (Mann, 1989; Hoon-Halbauer, 1994; Peng, 1994). The motorcycle industry in particular is well placed to take advantage of greater market opportunities in China, not only because of its rapid development since the 1980s, but also through the scope for further growth. During the first decade of the reforms, motorcycle output increased from 12,000 in 1979 to 1.17 million in 1988, while the number of brands increased from three to eleven. In the first half of the 1990s, China's motorcycle output increased on average by 54 per cent annually (Ilari, 1997). By 1993, China had become the world's second largest motorcycle producer (Peng, 1994). Yet although China's motorcycle industry has the highest growth rate in Asia, rates of ownership of two-wheelers lag behind those of the rest of Asia. In 1991, there were only five two-wheelers in China for every 1,000 people, compared to 35 in Vietnam, 96 in Thailand, 168 in Malaysia and 481 in Taiwan. Thus China's motorcycle sector may be regarded as in its infancy, with explosive growth feasible if not likely before the turn of century (Ilari, 1997).

In late 1993, a major European automotive manufacturer signed a joint venture agreement to produce and sell its scooters in China. In essence the firm's strategy was virtually to 'replicate' its successful European operation in China, thereby harnessing important ownership-specific advantages that it enjoyed. These included but were not limited to its production process, its marketing and distribution system, and its organizational structure and work concept. The purpose of this contribution is to explore the extent to which the company was able to harness ownership-specific advantages of FDI during an important part of the establishment period, 1994–95.

THE X-MOTOR CASE-STUDY

Euro-Motor is an Italian motorcycle manufacturer with an international presence in about 130 countries and a product range that enjoys worldwide recognition. When the company began negotiations for a joint venture in 1993 there were already clear signs that the Chinese government intended to promote the creation of a local automotive industry and that the imminent reform of China's turnover tax system would impose further barriers on the import of these products (Industrial Policy of the Motor Industry, 1994; Wei, 1994). Under the new tax regime, effective since 1994, imported motorcycles would be subject to a value added tax of 17 per cent and a consumption tax of 10 per cent of total sales value (Asia Law and Practice, 1994). Custom duties on imported two-wheelers would be levied at 120 to 150 per cent of the retail price. Moreover, duties on imported parts would range from 25 to 100 per cent of the retail price. It was apparent that China's fiscal and import policies were likely to have a negative impact on the competitiveness of imported products (Peng, 1994), which influenced Euro-Motor's choice of a direct investment strategy rather than a 'shallow penetration' strategy based on trade. Soaring retail prices of imported vehicles would have considerably reduced the appeal of a brand that did not yet enjoy widespread public recognition, particularly at a time of increased competition from local manufacturers.

In 1994, Euro-Motor established a joint venture to produce scooters for the Chinese market in Foshan, a prosperous industrial city in the Pearl River Delta, Guangdong Province. Its affiliate, X-Motor, is a joint venture between three companies. The local partner (Pearl Motor) is a Chinese state-owned motorcycle manufacturer, and a former licensee of Euro-Motor. The third partner is a large overseas-Chinese, family owned firm (SIAL

Group), which would contribute cash resources and act as an interface between Euro-Motor and Pearl Motor.

Euro-Motor had high hopes for its Chinese affiliate. By establishing the joint venture Euro-Motor hoped to enjoy greater flexibility and uniformity in internal clearing and purchasing procedures, integrate China into a centralized and globalized system of components supplies, and to some extent reduce the legal costs and risks incurred in the draft of separate technology agreements with local firms. In particular, China does not recognize foreign manufacturers' rights to impose restrictive conditions on the transfer of technology, a factor that greatly contributes to the risk of licensing and leasing agreements rather than direct investment.

Moreover, Euro-motor's management came to perceive China as a focal point for its global expansion (EIU and Andersen Consulting, 1995). Sales in China could not only balance cyclical market downswings in Europe, but also had the potential to become the core of the corporation's business in due course. This was a major consideration in Euro-Motor's drive to expand overseas sales through direct investment in production facilities in South East Asia (the cornerstone projects being China and India).

Purpose and Methodology

The purpose of this analysis is to evaluate Euro-Motor's efforts to harness the ownership-specific advantages of FDI in China during the start-up phase of its affiliate. Its performance is important for a number of reasons. Firstly, the Chinese government is seeking to channel foreign investment to industries whose development would best meet China's long term growth. While early joint ventures in China were concentrated in low technology fields such as textiles and shoes, since the mid-1980s China has increasingly attracted medium technology enterprises. The success of these ventures is very important to China, because they are perceived not only as an opportunity to boost the country's technological level of development, but also because China hopes to attract high technology FDI in due course. More specifically, China is seeking to expand its domestic automotive industry and is reliant on technology transfers from overseas joint ventures to promote the development of this sector.

Transnational companies from industrialized economies have become increasingly eager to invest in the China market in the

1990s, particularly as urban household incomes have risen and restrictions on domestic sales have been slowly but progressively eased. China has become increasingly important to transnational firms as a customer, and is playing an expanding role in many firms' global business strategies. Thus this case-study has relevance not only because it is typical of the new wave of joint ventures seeking not only to sell their products to China's domestic market but also to control their distribution and marketing – rather than only manufacture in China to take advantage of its cheap labour and resources. The case-study also has relevance because, as is increasingly the case for transnational companies, success in China has wider implications for global operations.

Finally, while the case-study company is far from the first transnational automotive company to invest directly in China, it is the first to maintain a controlling interest in its affiliate. The joint venture's ownership structure permits the transnational firm to retain control not only of the production process but also of the distribution and marketing of its product. This compares to other automotive joint ventures where foreign firms have had either a minority or equal stake in the investment.

Findings presented here are based on fieldwork conducted by one of the authors (Simonetta Ilari) over a twelve-month period from late 1994 to late 1995. During this period she had a hybrid role in the joint venture affiliate as an observer and employee. It was agreed that she would be permitted to attend meetings and interact with the staff in order to assist her in her research. In particular, senior staff were aware of and supportive of her research, and were therefore helpful, though also cautious. There was also agreement about the data to which she would have access, and the areas she would be permitted to investigate. Because the joint venture was in its start-up phase, communications between the staff were relatively fluid and informal, and this greatly enhanced her observer status.

In 'exchange' for her observer status, it was agreed that she would work as Assistant to the General Manager. This position provided numerous opportunities to interact with both senior and more junior staff on an informal basis in all the major areas of X-Motor's operation. It also enabled her to become well acquainted with her colleagues quickly. Moreover, the position necessitated regular attendance at management team meetings, and involved participation in meetings and negotiations between the affiliate's management and senior political figures in Foshan, as well as with the parent company and its core suppliers. In addition, formal and informal meetings with personnel in other joint venture companies provided a comparative perspective.[1] Obviously, much of the information that the researcher came across was confidential, and care has been taken not to abuse the openness and cooperation of those involved. The real names of companies and individuals have also not been disclosed.

This account does not attempt to tell the whole story of the joint venture, but rather deals with events that took place from late 1994 to late 1995, the period of the researcher's direct and intimate involvement in the company. This period coincided with a critical phase in the establishment of the joint venture, and thus provides an opportunity to comment on the preliminary success of the parent company in harnessing the advantages of FDI over most of the establishment period.

OWNERSHIP-SPECIFIC ADVANTAGES OF EURO-MOTOR'S DIRECT INVESTMENT IN CHINA

Euro-Motor perceived several important ownership-specific advantages of investing directly in China. One advantage was that it could hope virtually to 'replicate' its European production process by importing state-of-the-art equipment to assume a comprehensive range of manufacturing and assembling activities (EIU and Andersen Consulting, 1995). The development of a large scale, high-tech production facility would enable the affiliate to produce elegant and reliable products that could be positioned at the upper end of China's scooter market and fill an important market niche. The intention to transfer modern technology and expertise would also strengthen Euro-Motor's negotiating position for the new investment project with Chinese authorities. Moreover, development of a state-of-the-art production facility in China would enable the affiliate to play an important role in Euro-Motor's global expansion plans and become part of its strategy to source components and supplies globally.

Central to Euro-Motor's vision of recreating its European production system in China was the localization of components and supplies. The target was to localize 80 per cent of content within three years. This was motivated in part by the high duties and shipping expenses of importing components, which would significantly increase the cost of producing scooters in the competitive Chinese market; a selected group of domestic suppliers would be given technical assistance and training to develop their capability to produce simpler components to Euro-Motor's quality standards. Localization of supplies was also seen as a way of ensuring the quality of components crucial for vehicle reliability and performance: Euro-Motor hoped to persuade its core suppliers, particularly of components that required complex and capital-intensive manufacturing processes, to set up production facilities in China. The relocation of existing suppliers, with whom Euro-Motor had extremely close relationships, appeared less risky and more advantageous than finding indigenous suppliers for the high tech components. The long-established work relationship between Euro-Motor and its suppliers was not only an implicit guarantee of component quality and the timely delivery of supplies, but also existing suppliers were familiar with Euro-Motor's work procedures and technical personnel. Euro-Motor would help core suppliers relocate to China by providing them with information and helping to identify and negotiate with prospective joint venture partners.

Another important ownership-specific advantage of FDI was perceived to be control over the marketing, distribution and after-sales service of Euro-Motor's products. In 1992, Euro-Motor had entered into a licensing agreement with a local motorcycle manufacturer (who later became their joint venture partner) but had no effective control over the marketing, distribution, pricing and after-sales service of the licensed product. Because Euro-Motor's products are positioned at the top end of the market, a substantial risk was perceived in creating a poor market image due to inadequate marketing and after-sales service. Furthermore, the brand was new on the Chinese market, and marketing mistakes would probably tarnish the company's reputation for a long time and negatively affect future sales. It was proposed to create a capillary distribution network of up-market but non-exclusive dealerships, very closely modelled on Euro-Motor's successful European network.

Finally, Euro-Motor perceived significant ownership advantages in transferring its organizational structure and dynamic work concept to its affiliate. Euro-Motor's intention was to create a flexible, matrix organizational structure with minimal hierarchical divisions, able to respond quickly and creatively to emerging situations. This would not only facilitate relations between the parent and affiliate, but would also enable X-Motor to achieve efficient internal coordination between different departments. The creation of good functional linkages with Euro-Motor would be pursued in a direct way by training Chinese staff in Italy, and in an indirect way by sending a number of permanent managers and frequent teams of technicians and specialists from the parent to Foshan to establish and supervise particular activities and to work together with the local staff on individual projects. Remuneration and promotion would be performance related to reinforce the emphasis on initiative and team work.

Persuading Core Suppliers to Establish Production Facilities in China

The construction of a state-of-the-art production facility was a cornerstone of Euro-Motor's investment strategy in China. It was also clearly perceived that preserving its relationships with its core suppliers was central to 'replicating' its European production facility. While it was envisaged that simpler components would be produced by local suppliers, there were serious doubts about the ability of local manufacturers to produce high-tech components to Euro-Motor's specifications. It was therefore imperative that the core suppliers should be persuaded of the wisdom of relocating part of their production to China, preferably to Foshan itself. To this end, when Euro-Motor negotiated for its factory site in Foshan it also arranged for an adjacent site to be reserved as the location of core suppliers' production facilities, and obtained agreement that the land price would be frozen for three years.

Between 1994 and 1995, the period during which the researcher was associated with X-Motor, a serious effort was made to find suitable local suppliers to manufacture the less complex components. Although this was not resolved by the time the researcher left the company, it appeared that by the time the new production facility was operational, local suppliers would be able to meet X-Motor's requirements in large measure. In addition, over the same period, six of Euro-Motor's suppliers (from Europe and Japan) signed joint-venture contracts with Chinese partners, one of which located near Foshan, and for this group X-Motor represented an important but complementary source of business.

The major effort made over this period was to woo Euro-Motor's small to medium sized high-tech core suppliers, mostly located close to its headquarters in Italy, to China. These firms produced components essential to the quality and performance of the finished vehicle, including brake systems, variable transmission, alloy wheels and die-cast aluminium components, shock absorbers, electronic components and plastic parts. For many of these core suppliers, Euro-Motor was their most important client.

A series of 'bilateral' visits between Italy and China was organized in 1995 to promote the idea of investing in China. A senior delegation from Foshan visited Euro-Motor's core suppliers in Italy, and senior managers from the core suppliers were brought to Foshan. Despite Euro-Motor's intense 'bridging' activity, the core suppliers could not readily be persuaded to commit to investing in China. In this regard, 'replicating' the European production facility was proving very difficult to realize.

Several cases highlight the suppliers' concerns about the proposed China venture. Bright Gear Company, for example, produces aluminum alloy wheels and brake system components for major motorcycle producers worldwide, though Euro-Motor is a very important client. In an informal discussion with the vice-mayor of Foshan, its Chief Executive Officer offered the following view.

> I am well aware that the future is in South East Asia . . . But in order to be competitive, you have to keep pace with technological development and even possibly anticipate it. To me the possibility of utilizing low cost labour is not a key advantage but rather a disadvantage, because manual intervention on the machinery we use is reduced to a minimum and the operator has rather a control function, for which he/she needs to be qualified. Instead, I have to think how much will it cost me (in time and resources) to build a new plant from scratch in Foshan and make it productive in terms of human resource development, training programmes and new equipment purchase . . . I should be prepared to deploy my best human resources to work there, take frequent

> trips myself and on top of that I am very uncertain about the outcome. I do not see a specific local government commitment to human resource training, nor can X-Motor guarantee me certain volumes, despite their ambitious expansion plans. Land and electricity costs are also not low for a developing country . . . Given these conditions, I think it is still more convenient for me to produce here and export all over the world, at least for the moment.

Flywell Company is a medium size manufacturer (200 employees) of electronic components for motorcycles (flywheels, ignition coils, permanent magnet starters, etc.). Its general manager perceived that the main problem of manufacturing in China was the huge strain that the venture's training requirements would place on the company's resources. His questions to Foshan's vice-mayor focused on two issues: the availability of local government programmes for human resource and technical personnel training, and the role of local government in helping to recruit skilled staff. He offered the following view about his recent visit to Foshan to the researcher.

> Flywell is not a large firm . . . The firms that I saw do not look like they have personnel of the right technological level. They need to be formed. But if I start redeploying people here, how can I manage things in the parent factory? On the other hand, particularly in the start-up phase, the training of local personnel has to be done carefully and thoroughly. You cannot just send anybody; it needs to be somebody who is an insider in the factory and knows about the process and the work method.

By comparison, Best Plastic Company, a highly automated firm specializing in moulding and painting plastic materials, seemed a more viable proposition to be persuaded of the benefits of investing in China at this time. X-Motor's general manager introduced the firm to a Chinese state-owned enterprise which was actively seeking foreign investment to enable it to obtain access to state-of-the-art equipment and boost exports. The enterprise had already established six joint-ventures, two of which specialized in the production of plastic objects (telephone sets and plastic precision objects, whose manufacturing process required significant expertise and accuracy). Thus for Best Plastic Company the risk that a China venture might excessively strain its human and physical resources was considerably mitigated by its prospective partner's existing technological capacity. When the researcher left the employ of X-Motor there appeared to be a realistic possibility for joint-venture formation.

As a consequence of Euro-Motor's efforts to persuade its core suppliers to invest in Foshan it was likely that one important core supplier would do so, and of course others may follow later. What became apparent over this period, however, was the difference in perceptions between Euro-Motor and its core suppliers about the logic, if not the actual necessity, of investing in China. Euro-Motor worked from the premise that the benefits of such an investment were self-evident and compelling, and that core suppliers would be aware of the dangers of losing global market share in the long run if they did not participate in the China venture. To some extent this was a consequence of Euro-Motor's perhaps somewhat patriarchal attitude to its core suppliers, who were not seen to be entirely independent of its 'wisdom and direction', rather than being based on a careful assessment of their needs and opportunities. Suppliers that already had an established base of international clients, including other Sino-foreign car manufacturers or X-Motor's Japanese competitors, were relatively willing to invest abroad. By comparison, Euro-Motor's core suppliers were concerned about the perceived high costs of skilled personnel, difficulties in recruiting skilled staff, and the lack of local government support for the project (Stewart, 1990; EIU, 1994). They were also concerned about Euro-Motor's unwillingness to provide any financial support or to guarantee stable purchase volumes. As a consequence, they would be fully exposed to the volatility of the motorcycle components local market. Indeed, some of the senior managers of these firms believed that the burden of setting up a new venture in China could jeopardize their productivity in Europe.

Their difficulties in persuading their core suppliers to relocate part of their production to Foshan was a blow to Euro-Motor, as they perceived their production capability as comprising their own production facility and their European core suppliers' facilities in an integrated way. In essence, they arguably perceived themselves and their core suppliers as a production facility 'package'. To some extent this was a result of their history and relationship with a number of the core suppliers. In some cases, Euro-Motor had invested in the development of their core suppliers and in a particular instance a core supplier was a sister company of Euro-Motor. Therefore, from Euro-Motor's perspective, its failure to persuade its core suppliers to relocate part of their production to China meant that it could not reap the full ownership advantage of establishing a production facility in China. This situation also diminished Euro-Motor's bargaining power with the Chinese Government (Yan and Gray, 1995), because the company had presented its joint venture proposal to the municipal authorities as comprising themselves and their core suppliers.

Replicating Euro-Motor's Marketing and Distribution Network

Euro-Motor's marketing and distribution network and its excellent after-sales service were regarded as decisive elements of its competitive advantage internationally, and replication of its European network was perceived to be central to its successful expansion into China. Reliance on a local commercial network was not favoured because X-Motor would have little or no control over marketing, distribution or after-sales service (World Bank, 1994). Instead it was proposed to authorize non-exclusive, up-market dealerships. This would enable Euro-Motor to establish direct affiliate control over marketing and distribution, which would help to establish the brand name, facilitate the creation of an image of quality, style and reliability of technical service, allow the company to position its products at the upper end of the market, and permit a unified and consistent pricing policy for its products.

Indeed, Euro-Motor's standard dealership contract was adopted without substantial modifications for China. Specific conditions apply to authorized dealers, including showroom layout, product display, sales personnel training, suggested retail prices, and terms of payment. The premises where products are displayed have to meet certain requirements in terms of area and location, and must be fitted in a standard way including the use of light boxes, which are provided by the company to facilitate brand name recognition and maintain the image of classy and reliable products promoted in the company's advertising campaigns. Dealers are also required to establish technical assistance units, provide personnel for mechanical training, and perform repairs according to company standards. In order to preserve dealers' sales margins and avoid excessive competition between them, the company tends to establish few or sole dealerships in an individual city.

As in Europe, the company's commitment to the establishment of dealerships in China would be limited to the provision of technical training to technical and sales staff of service stations and sale centres, and to the organization and financing of promotion activities and advertising campaigns to promote brand name recognition and launch new products. Dealers would thus be expected to invest a significant amount in shop decoration as well as in establishing service stations to provide the required after-sales service to their customers.

This distribution concept has served Euro-Motor well in Europe and elsewhere. Yet several factors reduced its efficacy in the China context. One factor was China's institutional framework. Two-wheelers need to be officially approved (Peng, 1994), a process that is cumbersome and lengthy. The Chinese Ministry of Automotive Industry (CMAI) publishes a catalogue of approved models annually, and only approved vehicles may obtain registration plates from traffic authorities. The price of plates varies considerably from one locality to another, but in general is high. For example, research by X-Motor suggested that in Fuzhou (Fujian Province), the 1995 price of a new plate cost between RMB 10,000 to RMB 40,000 (about US$1,100 to $4,900), depending on the two-wheeler model.

Yet the purchase of an approved vehicle does not guarantee that a plate will be available. New plates are restricted to an annual quota for all categories of vehicles (cars, vans, scooters, motorcycles) issued by the traffic department of the local police bureau. The composition of vehicles allowed to circulate in a given urban area is individually decided by local authorities. Therefore the issue of new plates can be limited or even suspended by local urban administrations, depending on their assessment of prevailing traffic and environmental conditions.

China's regulatory environment is not only complex and cumbersome by Western standards, but tends to be quite arbitrary and also to change quite quickly (Boisot and Child, 1990; Carver, 1996). For example in 1993, Euro-Motor imported a large number of mopeds to Shanghai, where they were extremely popular because of their lightness, ease of driving, slow speed and relatively low engine power and fuel consumption. At this time mopeds were excluded from the restricted category of motorcycles and scooters, but neither fitted the category of motor-assisted bicycles. Sales of mopeds expanded rapidly in large measure because they could circulate in Shanghai as bicycles – that is, without plates and without the need to undergo the listing procedure. It was soon clear that the moped's unregulated status was jeopardized by its very popularity, and its consequent impact on traffic, safety and the environment. Since 1994, mopeds have been required to comply with the standards for motor-assisted bicycles, and the regulatory framework has grown increasingly restrictive and unclear. This meant of course that what was initially perceived to be a profitable market niche soon disappeared. The business lessons to be learnt from these kinds of events were learnt well and quickly by motor vehicle dealers and others.

Another factor militating against the successful implementation of Euro-Motor's distribution network was the perennial danger of counterfeiting (Freeman, 1994; Zhang, 1996), of which potential dealers would also be well aware. In less than a year of Euro-Motor launching its high quality but costly mopeds in Shanghai, local manufacturers began producing their own, lower quality mopeds or copying Euro-Motor's models. These local brands were about 20–30 per cent cheaper than Euro-Motor's products, and although the quality of their engines and overall vehicle performance were generally significantly inferior, some of the copycat manufacturers could reproduce the exterior of Euro-Motor's vehicles with great accuracy and attention to detail.

As little could be done to stop the production of counterfeit products, Euro-Motor responded by launching a large scale advertising campaign to promote its products and brand image, and by pursuing the development of its after-sales service network to compete more effectively on the 'quality of service' front. While the advertising campaign was certainly successful in promoting brand name recognition, the copycat producers were also bold in harnessing the positive effects of the publicity, and false X-Motor logos were confidently displayed in their shops to attract customers. To compound their difficulties, Euro-Motor's authorized dealers found that mopeds distributed for sale in neighbouring provinces were returning mysteriously through indirect channels to the Shanghai area, where they entered into direct competition with their authorized products. This of course led to rivalries and accusations of unfair territory invasion.

In many ways, therefore, the situation in China was not comparable to other areas where Euro-Motor had successfully established its marketing and distribution network. From X-Motor's perspective the establishment of dealerships would also be time consuming, not only because quality retailers with the right characteristics and expertise were hard to find, but also because of eligible candidates' reluctance to invest in shop fit-out and the advance purchase of vehicles, given the extreme volatility of the regulatory framework and other factors that might negatively affect sales.

Recreating Euro-Motor's Work Style in Foshan

Euro-Motor regarded the principles of its organizational structure and work concept as important ownership-specific advantages in 'replicating' its European operation in China. It was envisaged that the transfer of technological equipment and processes would be supported and complemented by a parallel transfer of these principles. The intention was to create a flexible work structure with minimal hierarchical divisions, which would be reflected in the wage structure, based on a small number of categories. Salaries would be composed of a relatively small fixed component and a larger floating component. The floating component would be calculated on the basis of an individual's on-the-job performance and was aimed at improving work efficiency. Staff would receive a monthly bonus linked to performance. The bonus would be about 60–65 per cent of the basic salary in all categories. An annual bonus would also be provided and would depend on an employee's position in the company.

Euro-Motor also envisaged that it would replicate its work concept, which could be characterized as comprising fluid relationships between staff, low levels of formalization, and an emphasis on teamwork. Employees should also be encouraged to contribute ideas to improve the work process and take up new assignments as required. This approach of course necessitates the free flow of ideas and information as well as cooperation between staff and departments to resolve specific problems and to achieve specific targets and deadlines. The implementation of these work concepts at X-Motor would ensure good communications not only within the affiliate but also between Euro-Motor and X-Motor.

Euro-Motor was very keen to implement its vision of good work practice for several reasons. One was that it wished to implement 'best practice' in order to provide a competitive advantage for the company internationally. Furthermore, X-Motor was envisaged to play an important role in its globalization strategy, and it was therefore seen as imperative that its organizational structure and work practices be modelled after cutting edge practices in the industry.

X-Motor's long term recruitment need was to find indigenous middle management personnel in various departments to work in close association with foreign managers and to be trained in the process. Although China has a shortage of skilled labour (EIU, 1994), X-Motor was confident that it would be able to attract suitable staff by offering technical training, good chances of career advancement, and wider decision making scope than is usually available to comparable professional staff in Chinese state-owned enterprises. In-house training would not only improve employees' vocational skills but also foster Euro-Motor's particular work concept based on the free exchange of information and the delegation of responsibility (Osland, 1993).

From the beginning, X-Motor's employment philosophy was poorly received by local employees. Wage levels were considered low relative to the perceived risks of being employed in the private sector. This probably meant that Euro-Motor had overestimated salary differences between major cities and a smaller city like Foshan in the same province. Furthermore, there was a serious scarcity of the kind of skilled personnel they required, for whom they were also in competition with other joint venture companies.

A very controversial issue was the risk factor in the pay system, notably that salary reviews and the size of annual bonuses were linked to employee work performance and subject to evaluation (Ng, 1990). Local employees were also generally unwilling to enter into formal work contracts with X-Motor, which is not a practice in state-owned enterprises. Furthermore, senior technical staff felt downgraded by the simplicity of the wage structure, and believed strongly that a wider and more articulated variety of job titles and wage categories should be introduced to take into account the qualifications, degrees of technical specialization, and amount of work experience of staff members. A newly employed engineer offered the following view.

> I think the job title is very important. In your [X-Motor's] system there are only a few categories, so if I do not qualify for the highest position I end up one level lower than I am at present. How can I have face to direct the people below me? Even if the difference in salary is minimal compared to lower positions, the tangible demonstration of your prestige and importance within a company is the face you have.

While X-Motor's management was aware that newly recruited staff were disgruntled about the prevailing conditions of employment, it envisaged little scope for compromise on these issues. X-Motor was conceived as a high-tech firm requiring a flexible, non-hierarchical structure to capture maximum competitive advantage. Demands by staff to be employed more in line with conditions pertaining to state-owned enterprises were perceived to be economically inefficient. Instead, staff should be helped to develop a more market-orientated attitude and abandon the work mentality prevalent in state-owned production units. Indeed, in management's view candidates applying for managerial positions were implicitly required to adhere to the concept of pay-for-performance and accept the risks involved.

Another major difficulty was X-Motor's attempts to implement Euro-Motor's work concept, which implied that staff delegate authority, accept broader job responsibilities and cooperate extensively with other individuals and departments – unfamiliar practices in Chinese firms (Child, 1994; Hoon-Halbauer, 1994). The creation of such a work spirit was hampered not only by the resistance of X-Motor's Chinese staff but also by a significant divergence in management styles between the overseas-Chinese partner (SIAL Group) and X-Motor's Italian staff. X-Motor's management found that its Chinese employees tended to regard job responsibilities as 'task'- rather than 'function'-orientated – a more Euro-Motor concept. Consequently there was extensive fragmentation of job responsibilities and their distribution among a wider number of staff with lower skills. Each staff member increasingly became responsible for a small and well defined portion of work.

As a simple example, it had been proposed to create a general administrative unit to provide routine secretarial services such as translation, photocopying and fax distribution as well as to gather information on legal and commercial developments affecting the business. The general manager envisaged the general office employing several dynamic people undertaking various activities on a rotating basis. Instead, the general office was organized around single machines. Every machine (switchboard, photocopy machine, fax) had its own attendant, who was exclusively responsible for handling the machine and keeping accurate records of usage by individuals and departments. Cooperation between employees to complete an urgent task soon required a tortuous process of negotiation with supervisors, and in general the administrative staff were unwilling to do work that did not comprise their normal duties. By the time the researcher left the company, X-Motor's employment structure was becoming stubbornly hierarchical at its core (Lockett, 1988).

There were perceived to be advantages to placing the overseas-Chinese partner (the affiliate's deputy general manager from the SIAL Group) in charge of personnel matters, particularly to ease cultural understanding between the Chinese staff and the foreign affiliate. Deviating significantly from Euro-Motor's work style, the deputy general manager concentrated on establishing internal guidelines to manage personnel activities down to the smallest detail (including work attendance, leave application, annual holiday, telephone calls, use of the company van, petty cash applications, and business trip management). The draft of such policies was intended to provide personnel with a clearer idea of their rights and obligations in relation to the company and establish internal discipline. However, the consequence was that the personnel department exercised a strong, centralized control over many employee activities that were quite unrelated to personnel issues. Furthermore, many relatively routine activities required written approval from the deputy general manager, and operations were delayed while he considered all applications and requests with a considerable degree of care.

This all had a number of negative consequences for replicating Euro-Motor's home operation in Foshan. One was that local staff soon came to realize that their scope for autonomous routine decision making was substantially restricted by the continual need to submit and justify requests to the deputy general manager.

Another was that the control exercised by the personnel office was poorly received by X-Motor's Italian managers. They felt that the matrix principle of functional and administrative control was not being implemented in a balanced and efficient way, and that their professional decisions were in jeopardy of being overturned or modified at any time. It also had a negative impact on the company's ability to attract (and retain) suitable candidates. A senior engineer had looked forward to working in a modern, international environment, but offered this opinion soon after joining X-Motor.

> The engineering department should be one of the most dynamic departments inside the company and have the key function of designing the products in relation to the demand from the Chinese market and provide the necessary link with the European headquarters to design models specific to the Chinese market . . . However, after a few days in X-Motor I immediately realized that the engineering department here is not conceived as in modern Western enterprises, but rather resembles the same department in a Chinese state enterprise.

The organizational structures and work concepts of modern, capitalist enterprises are generally regarded to be significantly more efficient than those of enterprises in socialist or command economies. It is also widely accepted by leaders of transitional socialist economies that there are major efficiency benefits of adopting the organizational structures and work concepts prevalent in market economies. Euro-Motor's preliminary efforts to transfer these structures and concepts to China highlights the major difficulties in accomplishing this.

IMPLICATIONS OF THE DIFFICULTIES IN REPLICATING EURO-MOTOR'S OPERATION IN FOSHAN

The section above suggests that there were serious obstacles in harnessing the ownership-specific advantages of Euro-Motor's foreign direct investment in China. These related to important aspects of replicating their manufacturing facility, their marketing and distribution system, and their work concept.

Production

There were two major components to replicating Euro-Motor's Italian production facility in Foshan: the construction of a state-of-the-art production facility itself, and the relocation of its core suppliers to Foshan. Construction of the production facility was not sufficiently advanced when the fieldwork for this analysis was conducted to comment on the outcome of this aspect of the joint venture. However, although Euro-Motor tried hard to persuade its core suppliers to establish joint ventures to manufacture their products in China, it met with significantly more resistance than it had anticipated. Perhaps this reflected the fact that while Euro-Motor was implementing its long term globalization strategy, smaller high-tech firms were watching the difficulties that larger firms, not only Euro-Motor, were experiencing in realizing their investment strategies in China. In particular, core suppliers were concerned about the shortage of skilled personnel as well as the high costs and uncertainties associated with operating in China. Thus while a major competitive advantage for Euro-Motor was its close (indeed almost paternal) relationship with core suppliers, it did not appear that the advantage of these relationships would be very easily transferable to China.

A failure to persuade core suppliers to relocate part of their operation to China would have important consequences for Euro-Motor. Firstly, X-Motor would be reliant on Chinese suppliers to manufacture components that were arguably beyond their technical capabilities. These would probably be of a lower standard that those produced by Euro-Motor's core suppliers, or would require considerable investment by Euro-Motor to upgrade their production facilities and/or train their staff. This would not only have an impact on the quality of two wheelers sold in the domestic Chinese market, but also had potentially serious implications for Euro-Motor's global strategy, as it excluded *tout court* the possibility that excess capacity could be exported from the China plant to other (even more developed) markets. While one of the advantages of globalization for firms such as Euro-Motor was the flexibility to respond to changing market conditions by redistributing their global production and distribution, this flexibility would be seriously jeopardized if a poorer quality product were to be produced in China. Instead, X-Motor would produce in China for China, which was far from the original vision for the enterprise.

Further, Euro-Motor would be required to undertake the painful process of building long term relationships with new key suppliers, a task made more difficult by cultural differences between Euro-Motor and Chinese firms (Davies, 1995). These difficulties would probably be exacerbated by Euro-Motor's greater exposure to Chinese law, institutions and business customs (Freeman, 1994). Euro-Motor's difficulty in persuading core suppliers to relocate part of the production to Foshan would also reduce their bargaining power with the local authority, because they were not attracting the high-tech component firms that the authority particularly wished to promote in Foshan.

The alternative to relying on existing core suppliers was to shift emphasis and resources to the development of domestic suppliers. In 1994, large purchasing teams were sent from Italy by the parent to help identify suitable local suppliers of components and materials. The Euro-Motor team estimated that a significantly lower rate of localization could be achieved by using domestic suppliers than was assumed by X-Motor's purchasing department. Differences existed between the parent's purchasing team and the affiliate's purchasing department in the method of evaluating and selecting suppliers, even though the process was primarily factual and based on a standardized data collecting system. For example, the Euro-Motor team focused on the poor management of the local suppliers, while the affiliate's purchasing department was less concerned with finding suppliers with optimal management structures than with meeting the need to source materials locally as quickly as possible and to achieve substantial cost savings.

Another example of the visiting team's 'conservative attitude' related to the analysis and weighting of data from various suppliers. Local suppliers were evaluated according to formalized criteria that included their technical profile, delivery performance, quality, reliability and price, as well as their financial solvency and ability to meet long term obligations. However, this information is often patchy and not readily accessible or available in China. As a result, the team sent by the parent adopted a very cautious approach in evaluating local suppliers' potential. By insisting that local suppliers' performance weighting should be compared with Euro-Motor's existing suppliers, the visiting team often emphasized its position that there was but one way to achieve localization: that of relocating existing suppliers to China.

Major issues associated with the sourcing of high-tech components internationally and less complex components locally still awaited resolution when the researcher left the company. While these issues would probably be resolved one way or another in due course, they pointed to grave difficulties in implementing Euro-Motor's vision for its production facility in Foshan – the simultaneous globalization of its high-tech core suppliers complemented by sourcing less complex materials and components locally. This suggests, perhaps, that relationships that worked so well in the circumstances of Italy were not necessarily transferable to Foshan – a serious divergence of interests between Euro-Motor and its core suppliers was quite apparent. It also pointed to Euro-Motor's difficulties in adapting to the realities of working in the less advanced and less sophisticated milieu of Foshan. This raises the question of the appropriateness of transferring what is a very complex and sophisticated production model to the significantly economically less developed environment of China.

Marketing and Distribution

Euro-Motor was concerned essentially to reproduce its European marketing, distribution and after-sales network in China, based on non-exclusive but tightly managed authorized dealerships. Difficulties encountered in the establishment phase of the joint venture suggest that this would not be easy to accomplish.

One option to resolve the difficulties associated with up-market, non-exclusive dealerships would be to reduce the quality of their Chinese two-wheelers and lower the price. However, this would be problematical for several reasons. In the first instance this would affect X-Motor's profit margins. Further, if X-Motor compromised its exclusive and high-end market image, it would be difficult to differentiate its products from the many similar products already well established in the Chinese market. A new entrant with a product not readily distinguishable from well established and popular brands would have difficulty competing in the market.

Another alternative to relying on up-market but non-exclusive dealerships to distribute their scooters would be to use the Chinese distribution network for two-wheelers, which comprises a system of state wholesalers and state and private retailers. Manufacturers sell to wholesalers covering given geographic areas, who sell to dealers, who in turn sell to sub-dealers. X-Motor's management firmly believed that this was not a sensible marketing and distribution strategy. Firstly, in this system manufacturers have no control over the retailers, and cannot select dealers in specific locations, or shops with high standard fit-outs. There is also no guarantee that their products will be appropriately marketed, nor can manufacturers evaluate dealers' performance with the intention of rewarding successful dealers and reducing their reliance on unsuccessful ones (Davies, 1995). Clearly, such a distribution system, based on a large number of sales outlets (many of dubious quality) is best suited to brands that are well established and popular (such as certain Japanese two-wheelers) or to those that are extremely competitive pricewise, even though they are of lower quality (such as certain domestic two-wheelers), rather than to X-Motor's scooters.

Investing directly in dealerships was also not a realistic option. Although Euro-Motor had a presence in over 130 countries, they never invested directly in dealerships, in large part because of the inherent risk of this type of activity. Yet even if they were willing to invest in shops in China, Chinese law would not easily permit this. At best, X-Motor would be a minority owner of each shop, which would still preclude their control over marketing and distribution in spite of their investment. It would also be difficult to justify establishing shops selling X-Motor or Euro-Motor products exclusively, because the anticipated turnover would not merit such a large investment; yet if the dealerships were not exclusive, effort and investment by X-Motor in the non-exclusive dealerships would potentially be subsidizing their competition. Although Euro-Motor's products are sold in many developing countries, it had relatively limited experience in establishing marketing and distribution networks outside Europe, and perhaps significantly underestimated the difficulties in exercising effective control in the circumstances pertaining in China.

Work Structure

As discussed above, Euro-Motor experienced significant difficulties in recreating its organizational structure and work concept in China. Its flexible and non-hierarchical work structure was poorly received by local employees, as was the emphasis on performance-related remuneration. Although it was envisaged that X-Motor would introduce a flexible matrix organizational structure, which had served Euro-Motor well in Europe and elsewhere, by the time the fieldwork was completed X-Motor was becoming hierarchical at its core.

Arguably, these difficulties have quite serious implications for implementing Euro-Motor's vision for its Chinese affiliate. In the first instance, it might have a potentially serious impact on the efficiency of the operation if staff adopted a more passive attitude to their jobs, took less responsibility and accomplished less, as a consequence of relatively narrowly defined job structures. Although no hard evidence is at hand, this would probably have an impact on the quality of the product, X-Motor's capacity to respond to both domestic and global trends in the two-wheeler industry, and its ability to take advantage of advances in component production, or the start-up of new component firms serving the industry. Moreover, this has wider implications for China's development of its domestic automotive industry. China's stated intentions of moving to more market-orientated employment practices would be aided by joint ventures playing an exemplar role, and Chinese automotive enterprises would not be able to look to X-Motor to provide guidance in implementing a new, and arguably more appropriate, work style.

This raises the issue of the need for X-Motor to explore realistic and culturally sensitive ways of achieving its objectives. While the Chinese staff were refusing to adopt clearly superior ways of doing things, X-Motor's management was refusing to do things in any way other than the way familiar to them, and the way that served them well in the particular circumstances of Europe. The issue does remain, however, that a state-of-the-art facility in China would be hampered by cavalierly adopting the work practices and work ethos of a Chinese state-owned enterprise. This is indeed a seeming *impasse*.

CONCLUSIONS

Since the 1970s, transnational companies from developed economies have increasingly sought to harness the advantages of globalization. Firms seeking to expand internationally have often chosen to retain ownership control of their operations in order, *inter alia*, to harness ownership-specific advantages. In the 1990s, China has been an important recipient of FDI from developed countries, as a consequence of improved investment opportunities and access to local markets. A challenge for both foreign firms and China alike is to find ways to enable FDI enterprises to harness ownership-specific advantages on a larger scale.

In 1994, a Sino-Italian joint venture was established in Foshan (China) to manufacture and sell motorcycles. China was a rapidly expanding market for motorcycles, and its fiscal and regulatory framework was fast becoming non-conducive to indirect forms of investment such as licensing or franchise agreements compared to manufacturing and selling the company's products directly. The Italian parent company perceived major ownership-specific advantages of FDI. This included its freedom to largely reproduce in China its successful state-of-the-art European production facility as well as its successful relationships with core suppliers. This would enable its affiliate to produce classy and reliable products to be positioned at the upper end of China's motorcycle market. It also perceived a major competitive advantage in virtually reproducing its European marketing, distribution and after-sales service network, as well as its flexible organizational structure and dynamic work concept. Based on fieldwork conducted by one of the authors (Simonetta Ilari) over a twelve-month period from late 1994 to late 1995, this contribution explored Euro-Motor's progress in realizing the perceived ownership-specific advantages of FDI during the establishment phase of its Chinese affiliate, X-Motor.

This analysis has highlighted major difficulties experienced by Euro-Motor in replicating its European operation in China, with regard to production, distribution and marketing and its work concept. Yet any significant effort to resolve these difficulties would probably necessitate a shift to existing Chinese practice, which was not perceived to be economically efficient, or require a dilution of its controlling interest in its affiliate, in which case it would effectively sacrifice its ownership-specific advantages. In sum, the establishment of Euro-Motor's affiliate suggests that increasingly prevailing practice was being created in China and intended for China. International 'compatibility' and therefore 'economies of connectivity' of Chinese foreign invested projects still appear to be very limited.

It is likely, of course, that over time major difficulties in harnessing the ownership-specific advantages of FDI would be overcome, and that Euro-Motor would realize its vision for its Chinese affiliate. It is conventional wisdom that the establishment of sophisticated enterprises in developing countries is a difficult, time consuming and costly endeavour. With considerable justification, China is perceived as one of the most important long term prospects for transnational firms seeking to globalize their activities. However, this case-study highlights the complexity of harnessing ownership-specific advantages of FDI in the China context.

ACKNOWLEDGEMENTS

We would like to thank Professor Peter Hills of the University of Hong Kong, Ms Viviana Capomaccio of the Italian Trade Commission (Guangzhou), and all the executives, officials and employees who shared their valuable time and ideas with Simonetta Ilari. We are also grateful to Professor Paul Wilding and the anonymous referees for their helpful comments on an earlier version of this contribution.

NOTE

1. The research benefited greatly from the helpfulness and cooperation of many people involved in the joint venture, as well as the researcher's fluency in Chinese, Italian and English, the major languages of the joint venture operation.

REFERENCES

Aliber, R.Z. (1970), 'A Theory of Direct Foreign Investment', in C.P. Kindleberger (ed.), *The International Corporation*. Cambridge, MA: MIT Press.

Asia Law and Practice (1994), *China's New Tax Regime*. Hong Kong: Asia Law and Practice.

Boisot, M. and Child, J. (1990) 'Efficiency, Ideology and Tradition in the Choice of Transactions Governance Structures: The Case of China as a Modernizing Society', in S. R. Clegg and G. S. Redding (eds), *Capitalism in Contrasting Cultures*. Berlin: Walter de Gruyter.

Buckley, M. and Casson, P.J. (1976), *The Future of the Multinational Enterprise*. London: Macmillan Press.

Carver, A. (1996), 'Open and Secret Regulations in China and their Implications for Foreign Investment', in J. Child and Y. Lu (eds), *Management Issues in China*. London: Routledge.

Chen, E.K.Y. (1994), 'Transnational Corporations and Technology Transfer to Developing Countries', in E.K.Y. Chen (ed.), *Technology Transfer to Developing Countries*. London: Routledge.

Child, J. (1994), *Management in China During the Age of Reform*. Cambridge: Cambridge University Press.

China Investment Guide (1995), *China Investment Guide*, Department of Foreign Investment, MOFTEC. Hong Kong: Longman.

Davies, H. (1995), 'Interpreting *Guanxi*: Tthe Role of Personal Connections in a High Context Transitional Economy', in H. Davies (ed.), *China Business: Context and Issues*. Hong Kong: Longman.

Dicken, P. (1992), *Global Shift. The Internationalization of Economic Activity*, 2nd edn. London: Paul Chapman.

Dunning, J.H. (1977), 'Trade, Location of Economic Activity and the MNE: A Search for an Eclectic Approach', in B. Ohlin *et al.* (eds), *The International Allocation of Economic Activity*. London: Holmes and Meier, pp.395–418.

Dunning, J.H. (1992), *Multinational Enterprises and the Global Economy*. Wokingham, England: Addison-Wesley.

Duning, J.H. (1995), 'Reappraising the Eclectic Paradigm in an Age of Alliance Capitalism', *Journal of International Business Studies*, Vol.26, No.3, pp.461–91.

EIU (Economist Intelligence Unit) (1994), *China Hand: The Complete Guide to Doing Business in China*. Hong Kong: EIU.

EIU and Andersen Consulting (1995), *Moving China Ventures out of the Red into the Black: Insights from Best and Worst Performers*. Hong Kong: EIU.

Freeman, D. (ed.) (1994), *Life and Death of a Joint Venture in China*. Hong Kong: Asia Law and Practice.

Fry, M.J. (1993), *Foreign Direct Investment in Southeast Asia: Differential Impacts*. Singapore: Institute of Southeast Asian Studies.

Hoon-Halbauer, Sing K. (1994), *Management of Sino-Foreign Joint Ventures*. Lund: Lund University Press.

Howell, J. (1993), *China Opens its Doors*. Hemel Hempstead: Harvester Wheatsheaf.

Hymer, S.H. (1976), *The International Operations of National Firms: A Study of Direct Foreign Investment*. Cambridge, MA: MIT Press.

Ilari, S. (1997), Transnational Investment in China – A Long March towards Integrated Global Production: A Case Study of a Manufacturing Firm in Guangdong Province'. Unpublished Ph.D. Dissertation, The University of Hong Kong.

Industrial Policy of the Motor Industry (1994), Policy adopted by the State Planning Commission on 19 February 1994, *China Auto*, Vol.4, No.4, July/August, pp.31–42.

Kanter, R.M. (1995), *World Class*. New York: Simon & Schuster.

Lall, S. (1985), *Multinationals, Technology and Exports*. London: Macmillan.

Lockett, M. (1988), 'Chinese Culture and the Problems of Chinese Management', *Organization Studies*, Vol.9, No.4, pp.475–96.

Ma, C.S. (1995), 'Issues in Fine-Tuning Foreign Investment Policies', *JETRO China Newsletter*, No.116, May–June, pp.2–9.

Mann, J. (1989), *Beijing Jeep: The Short, Unhappy Romance of American Business in China*. New York: Simon & Schuster.

Negroponte, N. (1995), *Being Digital*. London: Coronet Books.

Ng, S.H. (1990), 'The Ethos of Chinese at Work: Collectivism or Individualism?', in J. Child and M. Lockett (eds), *Advances in Chinese Industrial Studies*, Vol.1, Part A, pp.315–28.

Osland, G.E. (1993), 'A Bilateral Analysis of the Performance of US–China Equity Joint-Ventures'. Unpublished Ph.D. Dissertation, Dept of Marketing and Logistics, Michigan State University.

Pearson, M.M. (1991), *Joint Ventures in the People's Republic of China*. Princeton: Princeton University Press.

Peng, J.Z. (1994), *All About the Chinese Automobile Industry*. Redondo Beach, CA: Interlingua, on behalf of the Central Japan Industries Association.

Redding, G.S. (1990), *The Spirit of Chinese Capitalism*. Berlin: Walter de Gruyter.

Riskin, C. (1987), *China's Political Economy*. New York: Oxford University Press.

Stewart, S. (1990), 'Where the Power Lies: A Look at China's Bureaucracy', in N. Campbell, and J.S. Henley (eds), *Advances in Chinese Industrial Studies*, Vol.1, Part B, pp.51–8.

Swyngedouw, E.A. (1992), 'The Mammon Quest. "Globalization", Interspatial Competition and the Monetary Order: The Construction of New Scales', in M. Dunford and G. Kafkalas (eds), *Cities and Regions in the New Europe*. London: Belhaven Press.

Vernon, R. (1996), 'International Investment and International Trade in the Product Life Cycle', *Quarterly Journal of Economics*, Vol.80, May, pp.190–207.

Vernon, R. (1971), *Sovereignty at Bay: The Multinational Spread of US Enterprises*. New York: Basic Books.

Wang, Y.F. (1993), *China's Science and Technology Policy: 1949–1989*. Aldershot, England: Avebury.

Wei, J. (1994), *Chinese Foreign Investment Laws and Policies: Evolution and Transformation*. Westport, CT: Quorum Books.

World Bank (1994), *China: Integrated Market Development and Regulation*. Washington, DC: World Bank.

World Investment Report (1993), *Transnational Corporations and Integrated International Production*, UNCTAD. New York: United Nations.

World Investment Report (1994). *Transnational Corporations, Employment and the Work Place*, UNCTAD. New York: United Nations.

Yan, A.M. and Gray, B. (1995), 'Bargaining Power, Management Control and Performance in US–China Joint-Ventures: A Comparative Case Study', in K. Chatterjee and B. Gray (eds), *International Joint Ventures: Economic and Organizational Perspectives*. Dordrecht: Kluwer Academic Publishers.

Zhang, S.Q. (1996), 'Strategic Intention of Parent Companies and Property Rights in Joint-Ventures'. Paper presented at the conference 'Managing Joint Ventures in China', Hong Kong, 9–11 April.

8

Managing Corporate Networks from America to China

JOHN CHILD and SALLY HEAVENS

Over 200 of the world's top 500 corporations have now invested in China. They have been responsible for many of the larger foreign investment projects, and are regarded as the most important sources for the transfer of foreign technology and management expertise into China. Research indicates that multinational corporations (MNCs) have a strong and consistent impact on management practice in Sino-foreign joint ventures (Child and Yan, 1998). Some of them have established their own management and technical schools in China, as well as offering training to state-owned enterprises and providing funds to support education in deprived regions (Beijing Review, 1998). They are therefore making a significant contribution to the country's development. Most foreign operations in China have been joint ventures in which one or more local partners are involved with ownership rights, though since 1997 the number of new wholly owned subsidiaries has outpaced that of joint ventures.

Operating in a singular environment like China, however, adds to the management challenge already faced by MNCs (Strange *et al.*, 1998). These corporations have to manage a high level of complexity which, as Doz and Prahalad (1993) have argued, stems from a combination of heterogeneity and multi-dimensionality. Heterogeneity results primarily from the particular trade-offs between businesses, countries, functions and tasks that best suit the economic and political circumstances of different countries. Multi-dimensionality reflects the range of products or services, geographical regions and supporting functions that diversified MNCs encompass. The need to articulate forms of organization that can cope with growing MNC complexity has been increasingly recognized in recent years (cf. Bartlett *et al.*, 1990; Ghoshal and Westney, 1993). Less hierarchical, network structures are being adopted (Marschan, 1997), and there is increasing interest in the processes whereby fundamental requirements such as control, flexibility and learning can be achieved within this form.

China is a highly complex business environment that is undergoing quite radical changes concomitant with economic reform, rapid industrialization and evolving government policies (Child, 1999). In view of this complexity, MNCs face the question of whether to treat China as just another country or to give it greater than usual prominence within their organization, thereby adding to their heterogeneity. There are several considerations favouring the latter. China's size and high rate of growth make it a particularly important market. At the same time, as it is a developing country, operations in China require special assistance. They will often be dependent upon substantial technology transfer, as well as help in supplier and distributor development. Chinese partners typically supply the bulk of the ventures' managers and staff, who are normally not used to, and will not necessarily identify with, the norms and procedures of the MNC without foreign managerial guidance. Joint ventures in China may therefore require an unusually heavy managerial investment by foreign partners, at least in their early years, drawing heavily on the different dimensions of MNC organizational expertise. The management of external relations is also particularly important, because central and local government authorities exercise considerable influence on the operations of foreign affiliates. This influence takes a direct form through the power of officials to interpret legal provisions, tax obligations, and approval of expansion plans. In the case of joint ventures it also takes an indirect form in that most of their Chinese partners report to higher governmental authorities. As Nolan (1995: 9) comments with reference to one of Coca-Cola's joint ventures in China, the state is 'an important shadow figure' on the board of directors.

The particular characteristics of China as a business environment also impinge on the product, regional and functional aspects of MNC multi-dimensionality in three ways. First, there is a need to assist and monitor technology transfer, for which the relevant expertise is likely to be located within an MNC's product groups or businesses. Second, an MNC has to view China as consisting of several internal markets because of its scale, infrastructural limitations, and regional differences in economic development. This requires a regional organization with the sensitivity to manage the differentiation and heterogeneity of its markets. Because of the country's size and regional diversity, many MNCs now have multiple joint ventures in China. They may have to coordinate the relations between these joint ventures and the central authorities, as well as exploit marketing and supply economies among them. Third, there is a need to provide functional support, which is not always available from local partners, in areas such as finance and accounting, HRM and legal affairs.

China is therefore a unusual business environment that creates a particular challenge for MNCs endeavouring to integrate local joint venture operations into their global management systems. This article examines how eight prominent American MNCs are handling the process of linking the management of their China joint ventures into their global structures. It begins by describing the scope and method of the study, and the analytical perspective employed. Findings are then presented in five sections. The first looks at how China joint ventures are located within the MNCs' global management structures. The second section discusses key levels and actors in the China–corporate management networks. The third section considers the relation between structure and process. The fourth addresses the reconciliation of control with flexibility. The last section looks at the processes of learning and adaptation within the networks. A conclusion draws together key points.

SCOPE AND METHOD OF THE STUDY

The study is of eight MNCs with head offices in the USA and joint ventures in China. The eight corporations are located in the non-consumer electronics and fast-moving goods (FMCG) sectors – four in each sector. In the following text and tables, the electronics companies are identified by the prefix E and FMCG companies by the prefix F.

Primarily qualitative information was gathered on the processes involved in managing the corporate networks between these two locations, and on the structural frameworks within which these processes took place. A joint venture established in China by each of the MNCs was visited to collect information on its links with the parent company.[1] Expatriate general managers, and in one case the American head of operations, were the informants within the joint ventures for the material discussed in this article. Interviews were subsequently conducted in the USA with twelve senior corporate executives who had responsibility for China or who were otherwise closely involved with their corporation's policy towards its China ventures. A further six persons in the Hong Kong regional offices of five of the companies, who had responsibility for their China ventures, were also interviewed. The procedure adopted for each interview was to ask open-ended questions based on standardized check-lists. These check-lists only served to provide a common baseline, and in virtually all of the interviews it was possible to explore issues with the managers concerned at length by means of a relatively free-form discussion. All the corporate and regional level interviews were tape recorded, as were some in the joint ventures depending on the acceptability of this procedure to the interviewee.

A NETWORK PROCESS PERSPECTIVE

A 'network process perspective' will be applied to the results of the investigation, and this requires some explanation. It is broadly comparable to viewing 'transnational corporations' as 'integrated networks' (Bartlett and Ghoshal, 1989: Chapter 5). It should be noted that the concept of network adopted here is 'corporate' or *intra*-organizational in scope, and not the *inter*-organizational network on which much of the literature has focused (such as Nohria and Eccles, 1992; Cravens *et al.*, 1996). Relations between MNCs and their China joint ventures are for present purposes regarded as proceeding through an internal organizational network linking the joint ventures to MNC corporate head offices.

Van de Ven (1992: 170) provides a definition of 'process' that is apposite for understanding the management of international corporate networks:

[The] most frequently used meaning of process is as a

> category of concepts of individual and organizational actions, such as communication frequency, work flows, decision making techniques ... In this usage, process refers to a category of concepts that is distinguished from other categories of concepts, such as organizational environment, structure and performance.

The term 'network' is widely used in discussions on the organization of contemporary business but, because its characteristics still constitute a subject for debate and inquiry, a commonly accepted definition has not emerged. It carries connotations of a web of relationships that are built and used to advantage by people – or, in our present case, by the members of an organization. Nohria (1992: 5) expresses the nature of networks within organizations, and how the concept adds to our understanding of a company's organization *per se*, in the following passage:

> formal or prescribed relations (such as those that show up on organization charts or on input–output tables) do not entirely capture the network of relationships that shape an organization. Informal or 'emergent' relationships ... are just as important in understanding networks in organizations. These relations can be of many different types. Among other things, they may be based on friendship, advice, or conversational relationships within and across an organization's formal boundaries.

Nohria (1992: 7) also takes the view that

> networks constrain actions, and are in turn shaped by them ... While network analysts would maintain that the patterns of relationships in any organization are to a large extent fairly stable and recurring, they recognize that new network ties are being constantly formed and that over time these new ties can change old network patterns in quite dramatic ways.

This is akin to saying that a full understanding of how MNCs are managed requires that we examine the structural and processual aspects of management networks in relation to each other. As the theory of 'structuration' suggests (Giddens, 1984), action and structure have a symbiotic relationship in organizations such that, while action can modify structure, it is also shaped and constrained by it. Therefore networks can both be *prescribed* by the patterns they have formed and the ways in which they have become routinized (that is, by structural features), and they can be *emergent* though the initiatives of organizational members (Tichy, 1981). Emergent networks may in time become routinized and hence prescribed. In short, network processes constitute the operational realization of structures, while at the same time they contribute to the evolution of those structures.

In setting out the analytical framework for their research project on 'Managing International Networks', Forsgren and Pahlberg (1992) recognize that networks within international firms are to some extent framed by the 'focused levels' within such firms. These are assumed to be the most important vertical strata for understanding the processes within the corporate network, such as communication and decision making. Forsgren and Pahlberg distinguish three focused levels: the corporate ('corporate executive committee'), the division, and the subsidiary. A similar structure of focused levels is likely to apply to many large MNCs with joint ventures in China, where division will sometimes become 'region' and subsidiary will be 'joint venture'.

Forsgren and Pahlberg also assume that there will be 'focused actors' within an organizational network. These people are the key participants and drivers of a network – for example, those between whom important communications flow, those who consolidate information and act as its main point of transmission to other nodes and levels in the network, and so forth. Focused actors may play this role by virtue of their formal hierarchical positions (they may, for example, link the focused levels), and also by virtue of the way other attributes, such as specialized competence and knowledge, allow them to offer significant contributions within the network.

The following analysis of findings from American companies with China joint ventures is couched within the network process perspective. As just noted, this attends to vertical and horizontal linkages within MNC corporate networks, and to the role of focused levels and actors in facilitating the processes of management within such networks.

THE LOCATION OF CHINA JOINT VENTURES IN GLOBAL MANAGEMENT STRUCTURES

It is useful to distinguish between the *transactional* (input–output) and *managerial* links of the China joint ventures into their foreign parents' multinational networks. They were, in fact, considerably less integrated into global transactional networks than they were into the foreign parents' international management systems.

Only one of the joint ventures was selling any outputs to its MNC parent. The exception was Corporation E4, which had allocated the worldwide production of an older electronic process control system to its China joint venture. This corporation was therefore selling 25 per cent of its output value to other parts of its MNC parent's network. Rather more joint ventures were integrated with their MNC parents on the supply side. Three of the four electronics joint ventures purchased components from their MNCs. E3 took 80 per cent by value, E4 took 45 per cent, while E2 took 30 per cent. Among the fast-moving consumer goods joint ventures, only F2 received an appreciable amount of its process inputs from its MNC parent, at 40 per cent by value. The other FMCG joint ventures received under 5 per cent of their inputs from the American parents.

This low level of transactional integration is explained largely by the fact that all the MNCs had as their overriding priorities for establishing joint ventures in China the establishment of a strategic position *vis-à-vis* competitors and access to the market. They were not primarily motivated by supply side factors such as the availability of low-cost materials or labour. Their intention, at least initially, was to produce for the Chinese market rather than to integrate China into their international production networks.

The relatively limited transactional integration of these China joint ventures justifies focusing on managerial integration. The points at which China joint ventures are linked into the wider corporate structure of MNCs depends on how the issue of multi-dimensionality is resolved. This is clearly easier in the case of a single joint venture producing one product than that of several joint ventures producing different products, possibly destined for different segments of the Chinese market. In the former case, a straightforward product divisional line linkage down to the China joint venture, through one or more regional levels and supported by functional services, will be appropriate (Stopford and Wells, 1972). In the latter case, with diversified product categories, the regional and/or China level office has coordinating and representative roles to play, and probably responsibility for new business development in China as well.

Meier *et al.* (1995) note that many MNCs have established 'China corporate centers' to assist business development and corporate positioning in China by coordinating and supporting business units in negotiating and establishing new ventures. They distinguish two main ways in which these centres can achieve effective coordination between product businesses or divisions active in China. One is the 'team approach' where 'the China center comprises senior representatives or heads of the local business units, plus a senior country representative' (p. 25). It can, however, be difficult to achieve collaboration in this way between the business managers and the country manager. An alternative approach is therefore to have line responsibility ('focused leadership') with the China centre 'led by a China CEO with country P&L responsibility to whom the China business units report' (ibid.).

A further consideration which bears upon the role performed by the regional or country office is the operational status given to the China joint venture(s). There are several options relating to the level of local initiative that is favoured. Joint ventures can, for example, be defined as business units, with their own technological and functional resources and the autonomy to undertake their own commercial initiatives. Another option is to locate the formation of their strategy and most of their support at a China country or Asia-Pacific regional level, and to run the joint ventures primarily as manufacturing and sales branch units with perhaps the additional responsibility for relations with local governmental authorities. The issue of how much decentralization is accorded to the joint ventures is thus bound up with the role that is given to the country or regional office. It is part of the wider issue of how decision making autonomy for China is distributed through the MNC structure and how responsibilities are allocated to different levels and groups within that structure.

The eight corporations investigated attached great importance to the design of their global structures. These corporations found the question of how such design should map onto their joint ventures in China a significant challenge. Two important design decisions concerned the main lines of control and coordination relating to the joint ventures, and the autonomy they were accorded within the MNC framework. Five of the companies were actively experimenting with their structures for China. All were continuing to explore issues of balance and coordination between vertically and horizontally differentiated units within the overall matrix. As one corporate FMCG senior director commented on proposals to reorganize within China into business units:

> This calls the China structure into question again. We've argued the functional structure versus the autonomous business unit structure ad infinitum. ... It has been the most difficult challenge that we have had [in the corporation globally] and it has been ugly, it really has been ugly. (Corporation F3)

The corporate strategy director of an electronics corporation indicated that his company faced similar uncertainties over appropriate reporting lines for its China joint ventures:

> That's switched back and forth a few times: whether it's a solid line into the product divisions, which figure out the products the market needs during engineering, design and delivery, and dotted line into the geographic structure – or solid into the geographic and dotted into the divisions. (Corporation E2)

Table 1 summarizes how the eight MNCs were structured globally, the roles of their regional and China offices, the number of joint ventures they had in China, and how these formally linked into their structures. Four of the eight corporations were organized on the basis of global product businesses; three in electronics and one in FMCG. These businesses normally had worldwide responsibility for R&D, manufacturing and in some cases marketing. They carried profit responsibility and were the main investment arms of their corporations. Their regional offices had responsibilities primarily for business development, market coordination and functional support. One electronics corporation (E3) operated a balanced matrix of product and geographical units. The remaining three FMCG corporations were organized primarily on a geographical basis. As expected, the product dimension tended

TABLE 1
THE LOCATION OF CHINA JOINT VENTURES IN MNC STRUCTURES

Company	*Global structure*	*Role of regional office*	*Role of China company*	*Number of JVs, reporting to*
E1	Product based	Primary role is as regional offices for product divisions. Also new territory development; functional support inc. IT & legal; government relations.	*Limited team approach.* Primarily consolidation and co-ordination, government relations; profit consolidation; securing potential inter-JV synergies; functional support inc. quality	6 JVs, reporting to region-based product division managers.
E2	Product based	China market strategy; sales & service; functional support.	*Team approach*. Consolidating and coordinating JVs and field operations; functional support. In process of taking on China strategy	3 JVs, reporting primarily to China company JV manager
E3	Matrix	Business development; marketing; functional support.	*Line responsibility. Reports directly to corporate CEO*. Govt relations; coordinating business units in China for market advantage; functional support, inc. operations & legal	9 JVs, reporting to CEO of China company
E4	Product based	Assist business units (JVs, subsidiaries) in market development, coordination of marketing and technology transfer	*No China company*	1 JV, reporting to regional manager

Continued

TABLE 1 (Continued)

Company	*Global structure*	*Role of regional office*	*Role of China company*	*Number of JVs, reporting to*
F1	Product based	Policy and consolidation for regional group of countries within product business; functional support	*China office for each product business. Line responsibility for JVs.* Central government relations; functional support (inc. marketing & operations)	13 JVs in main product sector, reporting to VP Sales Operations in China Office
F2	Geographical	Responsibility for Asia-Pacific regional performance; functional support. Also product category officers to disseminate and oversee product strategy	*Line responsibility for JVs.* Central Asia office with Country Manager overseeing China businesses; functional support (inc. marketing, government relations, China information)	4 JVs, reporting to Country Manager, China
F3	Geographical	Overseeing country units; functional support	*Line responsibility for China businesses* especially marketing; functional support (inc. R&D)	3 JVs, reporting to Managing Director for China
F4	Geographical	General overseeing of geographical divisions within regional groups; functional support	*Line responsibility for JVs*; functional support (inc. legal, marketing, IS, PR)	17 JVs, reporting to Executive VP in China company

Note: Unless otherwise mentioned, functional support in all cases includes finance, HR/personnel, and technical.

to be more prominent in the electronics sector and the geographical dimension in the FMCG sector.

Multiple-product business MNCs faced a greater challenge in how to organize for China than those that had all their products falling within the same category, especially when, at the same time, there were potential synergies in China between the product groups. The status and role of the unit dealing with China varied between the five MNCs (E1, E2, E3, F1 and F2) with diversified products. The organization of their China centres varied from few links between product personnel at the China level (F1), through a limited team approach to a highly focused line responsibility.

In short, senior executives in each of the MNCs were exploring how best to locate China joint ventures within their global structures. This was a significant issue within the wider problem of how best to organize the management of worldwide activities. When their structures reflected the primacy of one dimension, such as differentiated product businesses, they endeavoured to incorporate other complementary dimensions. China's huge size, and the unusual significance of governmental authorities in its business environment, obliged MNCs to pay particular attention to the coordination of their China policies. Focused levels and focused actors play a key role in this coordination.

FOCUSED LEVELS AND FOCUSED ACTORS

All but one of the eight corporations recognized four discrete levels within its structure: worldwide corporate, divisional (regional and/or product), China company/office and joint venture. The exceptional case (company E4) had only one joint venture in China and did not therefore have a China company or office as a separate organizational level responsible for the coordination and support of several units within the country.

The extent to which these levels were *focused* ones, in the sense of having particular centrality in communication and decision making, varied to a greater extent than is depicted by the formal structure alone. For example, the role of the regional office ranged from being a key location for the consolidation of upward information and the active determination of joint venture policy (such as in companies E2 and F2), to serving as little more than a functional support unit (as in E1 and F3). Likewise, in some of the MNCs the China level unit took a wide range of decisions on behalf of the joint ventures, whereas in others its activities were confined to government relations and the provision of some functional support.

In most of the MNCs, the regional office was a particularly key unit in the organizational structure, with respect to the management of China joint ventures. The economy of concentrating support activities at the regional level, plus the fact that they had good air transport links with the main Chinese cities, preserved an important role for the regional offices even when the joint ventures reported in the first instance to a China company or office. However, the CEO of F2 noted that 'the regional people have to be close enough to reality, that they can properly apprise you of what is doable, realistically doable, as opposed to wishful thinking. They really have to be well grounded in what's going on'. This perspective was elucidated by the president of the same corporation's regional office in Hong Kong, who was in close touch with the manager of its China office located two rooms away:

> nothing in Asia Pacific is staid, it's fluid. In setting up the organization here, we established a mission, and that was to grow our business in (our) core categories ... To do that we act as, not a holding company, but we essentially act as a regional star where we support, monitor, encourage, plan and are held responsible for the results of the businesses which we control.

When a region is responsible for the achievement of targets, this also makes it into a focal level that has to manage the tension between empowerment and control of an MNC's China operations. The regional president of F2 noted that 'we tend to log onto people's judgement as to where decisions should be made. We're trying to push it down, to empower people.' However, at the same time he acknowledges that 'Hong Kong ... would be involved in almost all the decisions in China ... because lots of general managers are relatively new, and because we run a global company, we like to keep very much up to speed with issues ... Very few decisions are taken without us being aware of them.' Corporate and regional executives generally stressed the significance of the control process. The vice-president of strategic planning within the Asia-

Pacific regional division of F1, for example, noted that: 'F1's culture is very strong in making sure that the general managers, and the country managers, and the division presidents, make the numbers. If you make the number, you are a hero; if you don't, you're done. It is not a very forgiving company.' Generally, it is the regional office which assumes the major responsibility for China within this process – for consolidating information, monitoring against targets and assuming prime responsibility for joint venture results. In some cases, most notably E3, a China company has assumed this focal role and, as MNCs increase the number of their ventures and subsidiaries in China, the China level company or office is increasingly likely to take over this role from the region (cf. Meier *et al.*, 1995). E2 was making this transition from a regional to a China company focus at the time of the study.

Correspondingly, a focused actor occupying a 'boundary-spanning' role in the organization was often found at the regional level or, less often, as with E3 and F4, heading the China company/office. Focused actors can be seen as a mediating element in the 'hierarchy–heterarchy dichotomy' (Birkinshaw and Morrison, 1995: 737). Their role may be defined in both processual and structural terms: 'Communication systems may rely on specialized actors to transfer information ... The firm's absorptive capacity depends on the individuals who stand at the interface of either the firm and the external environment or at the interface between subunits within the firm' (Cohen and Levinthal, 1990: 132).

This point is borne out by our case studies. For example, the CEO of F2 described the role played by his Asia-Pacific regional president in the following terms: 'this person is doing a lot of government relations, negotiation, political work, in the PRC ... it is almost as if he is chairman of the PRC, and head of the joint ventures as a sort of a chief operating officer, PRC.' An organizational actor such as this is key both in terms of hierarchical process (that is, consolidating information from lower down the organizational structure) and also in terms of lateral process (that is, in horizontal communications and linkages). This can be seen to introduce the political perspective of 'gatekeeping' (Pettigrew, 1973), highlighting the strategically sensitive points in the organizational communications structure at which information is conveyed, but may also be reinterpreted or suppressed. We see this in the comments of the Chairman and CEO of E2's China company, and archetypal focused actor and gatekeeper:

> Before I came here I was a Corporate Controller, so I … dealt with the total company and was quite familiar with the proper management, and that is the reason that this office was established, to try and get a strategy for China … I deal directly with my boss (Corporate Vice President, International Operations) and I don't need an interface, and I try to eliminate as many of the coordinating functions or interface functions – you don't need those … . I am supposed to send regularly – I haven't done it so far – a once a month report to my boss, to keep him informed about major things that have happened or are likely to happen … so do all the other people. So I get reports on what is happening in their business, so you stay informed on the business aspects of the total corporation … and when I get them, I send them to the people that report to me. Occasionally, there are things in there that you don't want spread around too much, and you take that out.

Two further insights emerge from this manager's summary description of the part he plays as a focused actor within the corporate network. First, he is acting as a vertical coordinator across a key focused level within the MNC. As with all coordinators, the effective performance of this role depends on his personal credibility within the organization. He had previously served as the MNC's corporate controller. This gives him a set of personal connections at the corporate level and a personal standing at that level which allows him to operate with considerable discretion. Second, his self-admitted behaviour as a gatekeeper, controlling and editing information, points to the high dependence on focused actors which can emerge within an organization. If focused actors become bottlenecks for the distribution of information, this could have significant implications for the corporation's capacity to learn from its unfolding experience in a new and complex environment such as China.

STRUCTURE AND PROCESS

A significant feature of the management of corporate networks within MNCs lies in the ways that communication systems, both formal and informal, mediate and traverse both vertical and horizontal organizational units. This fluidity is today actively encouraged in many MNCs and it has been greatly facilitated by the use of information technology, especially electronic mail. At the same time, it appears to provide a good example of how process on the one hand transcends structure, particularly the traditional hierarchical form, and yet at the same time is facilitated by it.

There were many examples of how managers within the MNCs were endeavouring to ensure that process transcends structure. In company F4, corporate personnel were frequently stationed in the regional and China offices (which shared the same building), and also visited sites in China regularly. The purpose, according to a vice-president in its China company, is one of

> trying to cut down the response time ... in putting someone here, he or she can feel the pulse. When they go back, when we put a proposal, they will know rather than asking 1,005 questions, they will know.

To take another example, the director of corporate strategic planning at F1 noted that the process (in this case, of approval for extra-budgetary expenditure) is

> not nearly as hierarchical as I made it sound, with China, Hong Kong, to New York, to corporate [organizational levels]. It doesn't necessarily work that way. I mean, I will deal with a planning director in Hong Kong directly, on a project for instance... . at the end of the day, the most relevant information for me, and the job I have to do, is going to come from the people who are closest to the project ... So the lines of communication are open at all levels.

A regional vice-president in the same company echoed these sentiments, which are clearly part of its managerial culture: 'If I read something in a consolidated report that sounds interesting, in Hungary, or it sounds like something I would like to do in China, I phone Hungary... . I don't really care about the rank of this person; whoever knows most about this project – if I want to know about the deal – I will call him at his location.' The ability to adopt this flexible use of the corporate network, however, depends on the presence of certain basic structural provisions – in this case, a system to produce and distribute reports and a corporation-wide contact list identifying everyone with managerial responsibilities.

It is, of course, often the case that in order to achieve a situation where structure is the handmaiden to process rather than its jailer, formal organizational designations have to be devalued. An instance of this was provided by a senior executive in E3 commenting on the CEO of that corporation's China company. He noted that the CEO, who has overall responsibility for the matrix of regional units and business units in China,

> has been the greatest opponent to developing any kind of organization chart. He just doesn't like to see them. He's forcing fluidness on the organization.

A senior corporate vice-president of E1 claimed that his company's 'open style', lack of physical or organizational compartmentalization and 'tremendous verbal communications overhead' has led to an 'organic' management system in which access according to functional needs overrides hierarchy. He added:

> We basically tell people, to get your job done, if you need to talk to the President and you happen to be a production operator, if that's really the way to solve the problem, go talk to him.

Although immediacy, and fluidity, of communication are positive features of MNC networks, these networks do nevertheless have to be managed. It is clear from our investigation that, while organizational boundaries might be traversed, and informal communication processes such as electronic mail encouraged, such networks are powered by the hierarchy. Senior management can to an important degree determine the channels and form of fluid communication, their intention being that this will serve to promote a flexible response to changing situations and at the same time control performance. Such fluidity enables speed to be achieved in securing and responding to information, 'guaranteeing quick action' according to the president of company E4. The 'discipline' (as one respondent put it) of a hierarchical structure and its systems may, paradoxically, facilitate a flexible networking process. The models of hierarchy and heterarchy, which the literature tends to set in opposition (for example, Birkinshaw and Morrison, 1995) are thereby to some degree reconciled in terms of practice.

CONTROL AND FLEXIBILITY

A concern to reconcile control with flexibility within their corporate networks was manifest from all the interviews. This touches on the challenge addressed, *inter alia*, by Peters and Waterman (1982) in terms of attaining 'simultaneous tight-loose coupling'. Simons (1995: 80) phrases it in the following way:

> A fundamental problem facing managers in the 1990s is how to exercise adequate control in organizations that demand flexibility, innovation and creativity ... How do senior managers protect their companies from control failures when empowered employees are encouraged to redefine how they go about doing their jobs.

We were able to adopt two perspectives on the ways that the MNCs address this challenge. The first is through an examination of how decision making authority is distributed within their corporate networks. The second is through an insight into their control and communication processes.

Decision-making Authority

The distribution of decision making authority was in each of the MNCs investigated in terms of seven issues relevant to its China joint ventures. These are:

- capital expenditure for the joint venture
- policy on allocation of joint venture profit
- product modification
- choice of joint venture suppliers
- choice of the joint venture's markets
- appointment of a joint venture general manager
- remuneration policy for joint venture managers of PRC nationality

TABLE 2
DISTRIBUTION OF DECISION AUTONOMY WITHIN MNC CORPORATE NETWORKS

Decision	*Organizational Level*			
	US/Corporate	*Sub-Corporate: Region or Product Division*	*China*	*Joint Venture*
Approval for capital expenditure			E3 F2 F3 F4	E1 E2 E4 F1
Policy on allocation of JV profit	E1 E4 F3	F1 F2	E2 E3 F4	
Product modification	E4 F1 F3 F4	E1 F2	E2 E3	
Choice of suppliers				E1 E2[a] E3[a] E4 F1 F2[b] F3 F4
Choice of markets		E1	E2[c] E3	E4 F1 F2 F3 F4
Appointing JV GM	E1 E4 F3	F1 F2	E2[d] E3 F4	
JV remuneration policy (Chinese managers)	E4	E1 F2 F3	E3 F1 F4	E2

[a] For locally built and distributed products.
[b] For non-globally-sourced supplies.
[c] At regional level if choice affects a global customer.
[d] Decision goes to corporate level if appointee is an expatriate.

Table 2 outlines the extent to which authority for these decisions was decentralized down the MNC global structure at four levels: corporate, subcorporate (that is, product division or region), China company or office, and joint venture.

The distribution of decision autonomy within the MNC's corporate networks differs according to the type of decision and is also variable between the companies themselves. In the main, their China joint ventures can choose which suppliers to use, though this is often subject to certain restrictions. For instance, the supplier typically has to meet technical specifications for a global product or international brand, and in the case of the four FMCG companies the corporate level places pressure on the joint ventures to secure some supply from within the MNC or from its preferred global sources. The choice of markets to serve is also largely left to the joint venture in five of the companies, though in the FMCG sector the issue is of less significance either because the joint ventures cannot meet existing demand in China or because their overall territories are already defined. Company E1 is an exception to the localization of market choice. It has a strongly defined corporate policy on the areas of business in which its subsidiary units can compete. It does not, for example, offer system solutions to some sectors.

Approval to spend against capital expenditure budgets tends to be distributed across the levels of MNC structure according to the amount of expenditure involved and depending on whether the capital project has strategic implications. Four MNCs, three of them in electronics, decentralize capital expenditure approvals to their China joint ventures within approved financial limits. The other four, three of them in the FMCG sector, do not decentralize these decisions below their China company or office. This apparent difference between the two sectors may be due to the less integrated nature of production technology in electronics, where much capital expenditure can be made in smaller, discrete 'chunks'. It is also an important indicator of the extent to which the joint ventures are run as full-blown business units.

Policy on the remuneration packages offered to the local PRC managers of joint ventures is decided at various levels within the MNCs. (The equivalent for expatriate managers was in all cases determined in the USA as part of a corporate HRM policy.) This reflects a wide variation in the levels at which HRM policy is determined within the international operations of the MNCs. The difficulty of striking the right balance between maintaining corporation-wide norms and accommodating to local labour markets is particularly marked at present with respect to PRC managers' remuneration. The acute shortage of local Chinese managers with the levels of training and types of experience sought by MNCs has resulted in some companies bidding up levels of compensation. In China, local circumstances can threaten to dictate terms to international corporations that do not conform to the regional or global policies they seek to maintain.

Two other decisions cannot by definition be taken within the joint ventures. These are policy with regard to the allocation of surpluses which they generate, particularly whether to distribute or reinvest, and the appointment of a new joint venture general manager. Both decisions tend to be taken either by the China company or at the corporate level. Even when decisions on the allocation of joint venture surpluses are taken by the former, there is usually a general corporate policy framework that serves as a guide. The MNCs look upon China as a location for business development, and they prefer to reinvest surpluses within the country, whereas their local partners are generally looking for any profits to be distributed.

Product modification is, overall, the most centralized decision among those investigated. It is not an area for joint venture discretion. Indeed, decisions on modifications can be taken at the China company level in just two of the MNCs, and only then if they do not involve the introduction of a new product or do not have any wider global implications. The centralization of product modification reflects the vital necessity for MNCs to safeguard the integrity of their corporate names or their brands, in the world marketplace.

The distribution of decision making autonomy within the MNC managerial structures indicates that some areas are more tightly coupled to the corporate level, and hence within the MNC network as a whole, than are others. Capital expenditure is tightly coupled. In all the MNCs, capital budgets for China have to receive corporate approval, and this is accompanied by personal presentations which inform corporate officers of the relevant background. Expenditure within approved capital expenditure budgets is decentralized, but only within the limits and specifications approved at a higher level. Another tightly coupled area concerns product technology. Each corporation holds strictly to centrally determined technical standards for the global products allocated to the China joint ventures, though discretion to modify purely local Chinese products is in some cases decentralized.

Decisions on human resource issues are rather less consistently located within MNC structures. The terms and conditions of expatriate managerial appointments, and in several cases the specific appointments themselves, are generally approved at corporate level. This ensures the consistency of treatment that underpins the identity of such managers with the MNC's culture, which in turn provides an important integrating force within the MNC as a whole. On the other hand, decisions on remuneration policy for local PRC managers are in most cases made at regional or China company level, reflecting the desire of corporate policymakers to combine, in this instance, general principles and standards with the flexibility to respond to local circumstances. Decisions concerning joint venture transactions are generally localized. They are left to the discretion of the joint venture more than the other areas investigated, and are loosely coupled both with the centre and with other MNC affiliates. This is consistent with the generally low intensity of transactional networking between the China joint ventures and other parts of the MNCs.

While decision making autonomy varies among the MNCs according to the areas of decision concerned, there are also considerable differences between the MNCs themselves in the overall level of decentralization they display, as judged by the seven types of decision investigated.[2] Two electronics companies (E2 and E3) are, on this basis, the most decentralized, followed by the two beverage companies (F1 and F4) within the FMCG sector. Companies E1 and E4 are the most centralized, though for different reasons. E1 is noted for its strongly developed corporate culture and accompanying policies which consequently place constraints on initiative lower down its managerial networks. It is, in fact, an indicative case of how a highly organic, network-type company can be tightly controlled through strong corporate norms. In similar vein, Hedlund (1986: 24) pointed out that in heterarchies, 'integration is achieved primarily through normative control' and that 'paradoxically so, a heterarchy may contain more of hierarchy, in its etymological sense, than does bureaucratic hierarchy itself'.

E4 is a rather different case, since it operates with a regional office of quite limited scope and does not have a separate China office. As a result, decisions tend to pass up to the corporate level. Although it runs its joint ventures as business units, they are in fact tightly monitored by the corporate president, who claims to spend three weeks out of four travelling to different geographical areas of his corporation's operations, primarily to review their performance.

Control and Communication

Table 3 summarizes the main categories of information that were transmitted within corporate networks on a regular and formalized, predefined basis. Emphasis in upward communication is clearly placed on structured 'bottom-line' information for control purposes. This information was submitted by the China joint ventures, normally to the regional or China office, and then passed up to the corporate level in a consolidated form. Company E3 was the only exception to this process, where the financial and activity reporting systems were lodged within product divisions transmitting information to the corporate level before it was seen by the China holding company. This process was seen by one of its vice-presidents as fragmenting China-related information detrimentally. Information on quality and technical matters is passed upwards, as and when a problem arises or there is a request to modify a corporate standard. Such communication often passes directly from a joint venture to the appropriate corporate department and it can be relatively informal in nature. Surprisingly, only three of the MNCs required regular updates on the business situation in China. This is a self-imposed limitation on their corporate capacity to learn about the particular nature of the fast-changing China context.

Financial (such as budget) and technical parameters are centrally decided and defined at the corporate level. As a regional vice-president of company F4 graphically observed:

> We are given a circle, and within that circle we can dance, walk, whatever. But once you step outside, you must be very careful.

Some of the MNCs (E3, E4 and F3) conducted formal reviews of their China business more frequently than on an annual cycle. In fact, E4 has monthly regional business review meetings attended by the corporate president, the regional CEO and the managers of all the business units in the region:

> Each month [the China joint venture] will submit its financial performance, and a substantial number of charts that cover every aspect [of the business] ... So there is hands on management of the business units. We don't wait until three months go by and something happens.

TABLE 3
COMMUNICATION OF FORMALIZED INFORMATION WITHIN MNC CORPORATE NETWORKS

Company	*Communication upwards*	*Communication downwards**
E1	sales (weekly); financial (monthly)	technical specifications; instructions re. confidentiality
E2	sales (weekly); financial (monthly); business reports (monthly)	technical specifications;
E3	financial (monthly)	technical specifications; corporate planning targets (twice yearly)
E4	financial, sales & quality (monthly); 'strategic' business reports (monthly)	technical specifications; business reviews (monthly)
F1	financial (monthly)	product specifications
F2	operational highlights (weekly); financial & sales (monthly)	product and process specfications; product portfolios; marketing plans
F3	financial & sales (monthly); business development ('monthly management letters')	product and process specifications; business reviews (three times per year)
F4	financial & sales (every two weeks)	product specifications; packaging specifications; financial & legal directives

Note: *all the MNCs specify that business plans are reviewed at least annually, and all lay down formal procedures for capital expenditure requests.

Finance and technology are the areas in which the corporate network is tightly coupled through what Simons calls 'diagnostic control systems' (1995: 81), reflecting the centralization of decision making authority noted in the previous section. Other areas, such as HRM and marketing, tend to be more loosely coupled, with considerably more local initiative possible in most cases.

Parallel to the difference in degree of network coupling as seen in control and information systems are contrasts in the typical modes of communication. Regularized communication conveying precise information in standardized form is transmitted and recorded on paper, often by fax across organizational levels and geographical distances. 'Looser' and more spontaneous communication is typically conveyed by less formal systems – electronic mail, telephone, or informal meetings (either actual, or 'virtual' – that is, video-conferencing). Whereas the formal communication tends to follow vertical organizational channels, the less formal transcends these. However, as is noted later in the discussion of learning, some of the MNCs have come to adopt the practice of a wide distribution of regular formal reports across their geographically scattered units and they are increasingly using the convenience of e-mail for this purpose.

The need to maintain a balance between tight and loosely coupled systems, control versus autonomy, and centralization versus decentralization, is recognized as ongoing in the management of MNC networks. The president of E4, for example, is well aware of the issue and sees his own company's response to be the semi-autonomous profit centre. He acknowledges that the corporation's philosophy has been to promote self-sufficiency within its business units (including its China joint venture). 'The philosophy we have is the business unit ... is a profit centre and also has its own complete staff to run the business ... the business units are locally managed, with local staff, and self-sufficient.' He also states that 'we are coordinating their activities, not directing'. Elsewhere, however, he refers to the monthly reviews of business unit performance and the 'help' that is given to those that are not performing as they ought: 'those that don't achieve ... get more help than they would prefer. And if they're chronic problems, then we have to change the management.'

The maintenance of control is felt to be especially necessary for operations in China where local national staff are generally not familiar with international standards and where close attention may be required to ensure the proper use of funds. For these reasons, many MNCs operating in China insist on appointing their own general managers and financial managers to joint ventures with Chinese partners. The regional president of F2 states that:

> We try to run a decentralized, loose-tight coupling, simultaneously ... with our expat[riate managers] ... The general manager is ... charged with, having been trained

> in F2's way, to lead that company to the F2 standards from a reporting point of view, from a marketing point of view, from an operations point of view, from a quality point of view, and his task is to recognize the sort of standards and culture that we have, and try and put that into the organization. Knowing the Chinese joint venture, one has to tread lightly sometimes and strongly sometimes. So, the general manager really decides on lots of those issues.

This example and others indicate a quite widely held view that corporate 'standards and culture' are a *prerequisite for autonomy* further down the organization. Too much autonomy can indeed cause problems, as witnessed by the experience of company F1. According to one of its corporate vice-presidents,

> F1 is a very decentralized organization and there is a very strong belief at the corporate senior management level that one of the reasons we have been so successful is because we hire very good operating managers and ... let them run their businesses, without a lot of interference ... It is a constant balancing act, between the benefits we feel we get from decentralization and the real focus on the brand and the business you are in, and the obvious synergies you might get ... by centralizing certain functions. So far, we have tended to keep more to the decentralized side and try to push functions together and try to get some of those apparent synergies. But frankly, when we've tried in the past, those synergies have not always come through, and there's been more head-butting among the people that actually is counter-productive ... almost deleverage, as opposed to leverage effect. And that may partly be because of F1's culture, and the tradition of having these very autonomous units. People are reluctant to make the shift, so they make it very difficult, they make it counter-productive.

Of particular significance in the above observation is the reference to synergy, which takes the management of paradoxes within MNC networks beyond a simple balancing act to the potential for realizing a constructive dynamism, to drive success. A major catalyst in this process is the ongoing need for an organization to acquire information – and to *learn* – not least about changes in a volatile environment like China.

THE PROCESS OF LEARNING IN MNC NETWORKS

Huber (1991) makes the point that an organization frequently knows less than its constituent parts. It is vital, therefore, that network processes be managed so as to realize and capture potential intra-organizational knowledge synergies. This becomes even more critical in the case of diversified MNCs.

The need for information drives this supra-hierarchical process. Stata (1989: 64, 65) notes that:

> organizational learning occurs through shared insights, knowledge, and mental models. Thus, organizations can learn only as fast as the slowest link learns ... organizations are like giant networks of interconnected nodes. Changes intended to improve performance in one part of the organization can affect other parts of the organization with surprising, often negative consequences.

From our study, we see that this need for shared information can be just as true of learning at the corporate level. The director of business development at F3, referring to China, observes that 'if you don't understand the business, and you're learning, then you have to talk about it all the time'. A vice-president of F1 notes that 'the CFO of a division in New York is not going to tell me as much as talking to an analyst working on the project in Beijing'. Put another way, that vice-president learns more from this approach. He, and the analyst, are links in an organizational communication network which, through *not* observing a rigid hierarchical structure, facilitates the creation and re-creation of efficient linkages which communicate knowledge that is timely, and direct. Knowledge is delivered at the point at which it is most useful. This points to what might be termed *focused learning*, in which managers focus their attention on the source of the knowledge they require, regardless of the level of that source in the organizational hierarchy.

The issue of speed is central to the efficacy of such learning. Indeed, the process of learning, and the rate at which it can be achieved, fundamentally inform the creation and recreation of MNC networks. The need to acquire and implement knowledge which is both timely and effective – knowledge which perhaps may only be effective at a certain moment in time, and therefore demands immediacy of communication – underpins the heterarchical structure that some of the MNCs adopted. The source of knowledge rather than of authority has become the prime criterion directing communication flows outside of the formalized reporting systems. Electronic mail is of increasing significance in this regard. At the time of our visit, company E1, a computer company, already had two-thirds of all its worldwide employees on its e-mail system. A regional manager in F1 commented:

> The thing about e-mail is that, first of all, it gets you over the time difference... . when you come to the office in the morning, you find a reply to the e-mail you sent the night before because, while you are sleeping, they are working in the US! And it gives you the ability to try out the thoughts behind decisions, you can read it in sequence. Secondly, it is one way you can communicate with several people at the same time, by sending copies. And it's fast.

Both Stata and Hedlund have drawn attention to the significance of speed in the response of organizations to radical environmental changes. Stata (1989: 64) comments that 'the rate at which individuals and organizations learn may become the only sustainable competitive advantage'. Hedlund (1986) argues that global competition demands the rapid, rather than incremental, development of international strategy, and that:

> The heterarchical MNC could be seen as a *meta-institution*, which continuously creates new institutional arrangements, in the light of expertise concerning what works best for each specific purpose. This speeds up the process of institutional evolution in comparison with a 'Darwinian' process of selection ... the types of relationship between units in the company, as well as in relation to outside actors, will increase. (1986: 24)

Organizational learning is integral to this symbiotic relationship between 'institutional arrangements' (structure) and process. For it is realized via interactive processes that are contained – but not constrained – by a flexible organizational structure. Moreover, through informing 'new institutional arrangements' in the drive to locate and implement relevant expertise, learning contributes to the evolution of the 'meta-institutional' form; in other words, organizational learning as process impacts on the organization as structure.

It was not the structural positioning of an employee, group or unit in an organization, but rather the expertise they possessed, which was significant in the driving of corporate communications networks within the MNCs studied. What is known and where to find it within the network is the key issue. This is especially true in the heterarchical MNC, with its many and disparate centres, and 'a geographically diffused pattern of expertise ... corresponding to unique abilities in each node of the network' (Hedlund 1986: 21). Key to the successful management of learning within MNC networks is the awareness of such expertise – and the realization that, although *local* in origin, knowledge might be constructively applied elsewhere in the organization.

We see this in the example of company F1, and the relevance that experience within their Hungarian operations had for their China joint ventures. A regional executive was the medium for the transfer of this knowledge, having gone to Hungary *on his own initiative* specifically 'to learn how you start a greenfield project and run a (viable) operation in 18 months, in a previously Communist society, where people worked in a supply economy for 40 years and did not understand incentives (and where) there is a great discrepancy between their wages and the value of the product'.

One of the consequences of the discrepancy between the value of wages and the product was the need to control theft:

> I watched the procedure of checking the trucks out, of making sure everything is secure, and you load only the product that will be dropped off. It is not only for preventing theft, it is also an inventory to ensure that you do not waste the truck, to deliver something that you bring back in the afternoon... . And everything I learned

> during those two weeks, I learned from the people who do it ... warehouse supervisors, labour workers.

He spent two weeks in Hungary, going every morning to the plant at 5.00 a.m. to watch the trucks being loaded. Although he met with the CFO for Hungary (his closest functional counterpart) 'I spent no more than 15 minutes with (him) because ... he is not going to be able to tell me how his people prevent theft.' In such a learning situation, it is first hand experience, the *immediacy of contact* with those in possession of desired skills and expertise, which is of paramount importance. It is also worth emphasizing that, in this example, it is the manager who is doing the learning, gauging its worth before taking the decision to introduce the system (via the Hungarian expert) into the China joint ventures. The hierarchical concept of subordinate/superordinate has no relevance in this transfer of knowledge. As the F1 executive comments, 'The question is, ... who can benefit from that kind of experience. Do I check the inventory? No. But after seeing that in Hungary ... next time, if I hear about some of the same issues in Asia, I can tell my guys, give Hungary a call.'

The above example also points up the significance of *context of operation* for the learning process. Hedlund (1986: 21) comments that a prominent feature of the hypermodern MNC as heterarchy is that 'new ideas and products may come up in many different countries and later be exploited on a global scale'. The relevance of F1's Hungarian experience for its China operations partially illustrates this, but there is considerable scope for developing the contextual perspective in a discussion of heterarchy – and, in so doing, to elucidate the multifaceted nature of innovation and learning in MNCs. For it is not simply a case of 'new ideas' being generated locally for potential global benefit; the corollary to this is that the local context necessitates learning on the part of the established organization, with implications for corporate culture. In other words, there is a critical need for the MNC to learn about its various contexts of operation.

For example, the president of F2, who also adopts a 'hands-on' approach to learning, noticed on a visit to one of the company's China joint ventures that

> the [beverage] shipping carton is not strong enough for how product gets handled in China. The specifications

> were designed in the United States, but they are used to nice conveyors there, and here you have people throwing it up, and pallets up and under the truck, and off the truck, and here and there, and the stuff was all caved in and there is just, sort of, more get out and help, and make sure you're understanding from sales supervisors, their frustrations, things they'd like to do differently.

CONCLUSIONS

This analysis has applied a network process perspective to the management of MNC networks from America to China. The perspective has thrown light on ways in which the MNCs are addressing the tensions between maintaining control in relation to their worldwide financial and technical standards, while attempting simultaneously to adapt to the complex and dynamic economic environment of China.

The ways that MNCs linked their China joint ventures into their corporate structures reflected the balance between forces for global integration and those for local responsiveness. This tendency was weighed somewhat more towards global integration in the case of the electronics MNCs and towards local circumstances in the case of the FMCG corporations. Although the FMCG corporations had introduced their global brands into China, some of these were modified to suit the Chinese market and their promotion had to be sensitive to local culture and taste. Moreover, their production chains were more locally self-contained. The electronics corporations were required to be responsive to the local, often governmental, organizations who were their main customers in China, and also to government policy towards the high technology sector, but at the same time they exhibited a higher level of global transactional integration on the supply side. The power and role of worldwide product businesses were correspondingly greater in the electronics MNCs and they were the channels through which joint ventures reported into their multinational structures.

Despite these differences in emphasis, it was quite clearly the desire of MNC managers to reconcile the twin pressures for control and adaptation rather than satisfy one at the expense of the other.

This reconciliation, so far as China is concerned, is dependent on a relatively few focal actors. They are located at the interface between business units (the China joint ventures) and higher corporate levels, playing a mediating role somewhat akin to that of divisional managers in the resource allocation process of the multi-divisional firm (cf. Bower, 1970). Asia-Pacific regional heads, and increasingly the heads of China holding companies or offices, are the primary focal role-players. Their role combines priority-setting and functional support downwards for the general managers of China business units, with an upward reporting of consolidated results and interpretation of trends to the corporate level in the USA. The very focus they provide enables the MNC to operate a leaner network with a potentially faster and better-informed response to local environmental changes.

The concept of focal actor within corporate networks would seem to be a particularly fruitful one to explore in further research. One of the factors that seems to enhance the position of focal actors, and presumably their chances of success, is the trust vested in them by corporate level managers. This trust is founded on their previous track record and long service within the company, which is recognized within the hierarchy as having imbued them with the corporate culture. Responsibility for operations in an environment like China, which is viewed as significant for the future but especially challenging for the present, gives these focal actors a particularly critical role within the corporate network. It is recognized that they have to be afforded a high level of discretion and that corporate personnel, who are unfamiliar with the operating context, rely heavily upon their judgement and advice.

The focus in recent years on new organizational responses to radical environmental changes has tended to play down attention to control as an inherent process in any organized activity, as well as to the relation of structure to process. Investigation of the MNCs has indicated ways in which control is a necessary accompaniment to flexibility, and in which structure provides a framework for process. The points of reference provided by a structure and its systems may, paradoxically, facilitate a flexible networking process. Similarly, as Hedlund (1986) argued, what we are seeing within global diversified MNCs is not a dissolution of hierarchy, but rather its transformation into a more culture- and norm-based form, with the norms being heavily reinforced by personal contact and modern

IT-based quasi-personal communication. Focal actors are central to this development, as they realize the continuity of corporate culture while mediating the changes that are fundamental to successful operation in a highly competitive and complex environment like China. The corporate culture, supported by formalized corporate routines, contributes to 'pattern maintenance' – that is, consistent worldwide standards. Pressures for change, often presented in the form of business unit demands to the mediating focal actors, draw corporate attention to the need for 'adaptation'.

Although at first sight the internal management challenges faced by MNCs operating in China may appear to be largely their own problem, the significance of these leading corporations for China's economic development means that it is of paramount importance that they find ways to meet these challenges. Moreover, the organizational forms that MNCs are evolving may in turn become significant models for the leaders of China's state-owned enterprises to adopt as they internationalize and encounter similar needs to manage growing levels of complexity (Qin, 1999).

ACKNOWLEDGEMENTS

Grateful acknowledgement is made of funding provided by the Carnegie-Bosch Institute and the Leverhulme Trust to defray the cost of the research from which this study draws. The authors wish to thank Dr Yanni Yan for her assistance in conducting fieldwork.

NOTES

1. Although the research also examined relations with the Chinese parent companies, these lie beyond the scope of the present approach.
2. An indicator of overall autonomy was constructed by scoring each decision by its level of decentralization as follows, and then aggregating the scores for each MNC: Corporate = 1; Region/product division = 2; China company/office = 3; Joint venture = 4.

REFERENCES

Bartlett, C.A. and Ghoshal, S. (1989), *Managing across Borders: The Transnational Solution*. Boston, MA: Harvard Business School Press.

Bartlett, C.A., Doz, Y. and Hedlund, G. (eds) (1990), *Managing the Global Firm*. London: Routledge.

Beijing Review (1998), *Beijing Review* issues: 'Fast-food Management Training', 19 January, p.26; '5m Donation to Project Hope', 11 May, p.28; 'Motorola Trains Staff of State Enterprises', 20 July, p.25; 'Motorola Donates More to Project Hope', 17 August, p.29; 'P&G Donates Fund to Project Hope', 7 September, p.28.

Birkinshaw, J.M. and Morrison, A.J. (1995), 'Configurations of Strategy and Structure in Subsidiaries of Multinational Corporations', *Journal of International Business Studies*, Vol.26, pp.729–53.

Bower, J.L. (1970), *Managing the Resource Allocation Process*. Boston, MA: Division of Research, Harvard Business School.

Child, J. (1999), 'Management and Organizations in China', in A. Tsui, J.T. Li and K. Xin (eds), *Management and Organizations in China*. London: Macmillan (forthcoming).

Child, J. and Yan, Y. (1998), 'National and Transnational Effects in International Business: Indications from Sino-Foreign Joint Ventures'. Paper presented at the Inaugural Conference of the Asia Academy of Management, Hong Kong, December.

Cohen, W.M. and Levinthal, D.A. (1990), 'Absorptive Capacity: A New Perspective on Learning and Innovation', *Administrative Science Quarterly*, Vol. 35, pp.128–52.

Cravens, D.W., Piercy, N.F. and Shipp, S.H. (1996), 'New Organizational Forms for Competing in Highly Dynamic Environments: The Network Paradigm', *British Journal of Management*, Vol.7, pp.203–18.

Doz, Y. and Prahalad, C.K. (1993), 'Managing DMNCs: A Search for a New Paradigm', in S. Ghoshal and E.D. Westney (eds), *Organization Theory and the Multinational Corporation*. New York: St Martin's Press, pp.24–50.

Forsgren, M. and Pahlberg, C. (1992), *Managing International Networks*. Department of Business Studies, Uppsala University, Working Paper 1992/5.

Ghoshal, S. and Westney, E.D. (eds) (1993), *Organization Theory and the Multinational Corporation*. New York: St Martin's Press.

Giddens, A. (1984), *The Constitution of Society*. Cambridge: Polity Press.

Hedlund, G. (1986), 'The Hypermodern MNC – a Heterarchy?', *Human Resource Management*, Vol.25, pp.9–25.

Huber, G.P. (1991), 'Organizational Learning: The Contributing Processes and the Literatures', *Organization Science*, Vol.2, pp.88–115.

Marschan, R. (1997), 'Dimensions of Less-Hierarchical Structures in Multinationals', in I. Björkman and M. Forsgren (eds), *The Nature of the International Firm*. Copenhagen: Copenhagen Business School Press, pp.433–50.

Meier, J., Perez, J. and Woetzel, J.R. (1995), 'Solving the Puzzle: MNCs in China', *The McKinsey Quarterly*, 1995/2, pp.20–33.

Nohria, N. (1992), 'Is a Network Perspective a Useful Way of Studying Organizations?', in N. Nohria and R.G. Eccles (eds), *Networks and Organizations*. Boston, MA: Harvard Business School Press, pp.1–22.

Nohria, N. and Eccles, R.G. (eds) (1992), *Networks and Organizations*. Boston, MA: Harvard Business School Press.

Nolan, P.H. (1995), *Joint Ventures and Economic Reform in China: A Case Study of the Coca-Cola Business System, with Particular Reference to the Tianjin Coca-Cola Plant*. ESRC Centre for Business Research Working Paper Series, WP 24, University of Cambridge, December.

Peters, T.J. and Waterman, R.H., Jr (1982), *In Search of Excellence*. New York: Warner Books.

Pettigrew, A.M. (1973), *The Politics of Organizational Decision Making*. London: Tavistock.

Qin X. (1999), *A Conceptual Framework for the Strategic Restructuring of State-Owned Enterprises in China*. University of Hong Kong, Chinese Management Centre Working Paper, CMC1999-001-01, January.

Simons, R. (1995), 'Control in an Age of Empowerment', *Harvard Business Review*, Vol.73/2, pp.80–88.

Stata, R. (1989), 'Organizational Learning: The Key to Management Innovation', *Sloan Management Review*, Spring, pp.63–74.

Stopford, J.M. and Wells, L.T., Jr (1972), *Managing the Multinational Enterprise: Organization of the Firm and Ownership of Subsidiaries*. New York: Basic Books.

Strange, R., Kamall, S. and Tan, H. (1998), 'Operating as a Foreign Company in China', in R. Strange (ed.), *Management in China: The Experience of Foreign Businesses*. London: Frank Cass, pp.1–19.

Tichy, N.M. (1981), 'Networks in Organizations', in P.C. Nystrom and W.H. Starbuck (eds), *Handbook of Organizational Design*. New York: Oxford University Press, pp.225–49.

Van de Ven, A.H. (1992), 'Suggestions for Studying Strategy Process: A Research Note', *Strategic Management Journal*, Vol.13, pp.169–88.

9

Managerial and Organizational Learning in Chinese Firms

YANNI YAN

Control and learning are deeply embedded in the specific cultural and institutional ethos of an organization. The distinction between them tends to blur because of the nature of the interactions that take place. The nature of an International Joint Venture (IJV) shapes its complexity in terms of learning and control perspectives in comparison with a unitary organization, given that its parent companies have very different systems of governance and political, economic, social and cultural characteristics (Faulkner 1995a). The recognition of learning and control identity across organizational boundaries is a particular challenge, as there is a need to demonstrate an inherent coherence between the IJV's partners on the learning, as educed from the pressures of operating in a global competitive market, which require the partners to have an ability to adapt to a changing environment (Hamel, 1991) and control as derived from the exploration of partner's expertise and competence (Barnard, 1968; Machin and Lowe, 1983). Giddens (1984) takes an institutional view to organizations, which implies that learning can be reconstructed via interaction with different reference groups within an organization. Control requires the ability to change organization behaviour, and this depends upon an ability to induce the possible need for learning through defining the rules and formulating regulation structures. Child and Faulkner (1998) suggest that the balance of control between the partners of an IJV may be affected by the fact that the tacit knowledge held by one partner can be superseded by new knowledge brought in by another partner. The potential change in control may generate considerable resistance to transference of the new knowledge by the partner whose knowledge is being substituted.

The number of IJVs formed by partners from developed and developing countries have increased dramatically over the last 15 years (Inkpen, 1995; Faulkner, 1995b; Child *et al.*, 1997). China is one of the most important cases, as it has attracted more foreign direct investment than any other developing countries (United Nations, 1997). The IJV is the Chinese government's preferred mode of investment as it is specifically incorporated into national foreign direct investment (FDI) policy. The learning of management expertise and acquisition of advanced technology are ranked as the top two leading objectives for Sino-foreign joint ventures (Yan, 1997). The evidence from recent surveys suggests that some foreign firms are disappointed with the performance achieved by their Chinese investments due to such factors as the quality of learning achieved by the host managers and the cost of training those managers (Warner, 1995; Vanhonacker, 1997).

With these considerations in mind, this contribution is structured as follows: first, the organizational learning and control are both described in the context of IJVs. Secondly, the nature of the respective learning and control processes in an IJV are examined. These are assessed in terms of (1) learning inputs; (2) partners' mutual perceptions; (3) control based upon possession of superior competence; (4) the relation between a partner's achieved learning and its resource invested. Thirdly, the article describes the sample of 67 Sino-foreign joint ventures investigated, together with the methods employed for testing the hypotheses. Finally, hypotheses on performance outcomes are examined.

ORGANIZATIONAL LEARNING

The Learning Types

Learning is perceived as an organizational attribute, referring to the enhancement of the knowledge available to an organization (Child and Heavens, 1997). Knowledge enhancement, as applied to the case of an IJV, is both an outcome which shows enhanced capacity for organizational change and a process which demonstrates continuous improvement (Senge and Sterman, 1992; Dodgson, 1993). Fiol and Lyles (1985) show that lower 'types' of learning is geared towards ensuring control through repetitive routine improvements within the boundary of existing organizational knowledge. Organizational learning requires a context, as it generally leads to behavioural outcomes such as the following of rules, procedures and regulations. The higher 'types' of learning are characterized by insights gained that are non-routine. The development of regulation structures is based on proactive and generative learning approaches. This is because their outcomes tend to be cognitive in nature.

Argyris and Schön (1978) draw distinctions in the learning types through classification into single-loop, double-loop and deutero-loop learning. Single-loop learning refers to the lower-level response that optimizes performance within the limits of existing organizational frameworks. Learning takes place to correct the mismatch between intention and what actually happened. The nature of single-loop learning is suitable for routine or repetitive issues. Double-loop learning requires the ability to question existing systems and is orientated towards survival in a changing environment. Deutero-loop learning is learning-orientated and targets the organizational learning process itself (Schön, 1975).

The above classifications offer a rich and relatively unexplored domain in evaluating the validity of types of learning source transferred between partners in an IJV (Lyles and Salk, 1996). The technology and knowledge resource input transferred from partners has an impact upon the underlying value changes implicit in managing an IJV, because strategic knowledge derived from one of the IJV's partners is likely to be sensitive (Moingeon and Edmondson, 1996). Technical and managerial knowledge are often expressed in widely accessible international standardized forms and have relatively few boundaries between IJV partners (Senge, 1991). However, in the adaptation of the knowledge to specific contextual changes, problems may arise in an IJV if new knowledge requires innovative types of collaboration between people from different specialities, cultural backgrounds or the partner's contractual or non-contractual inputs (Child and Heavens, 1997). These difficulties may increase the problems of integration between an IJV and its parent companies (Reynolds, 1997).

The Learning Process

Learning consists of cycles of relevant activities, and the process elements should reflect those cycles by incorporating knowledge input, knowledge transformation and knowledge utilization (Pucik, 1988). The implementation of the learning process in an IJV may require safeguards for the partners who make valuable information available, and a willingness to collaborate on a basis of shared strategic, social, economic identity (Parkhe, 1991). An IJV organization may need to build some control mechanisms to ensure that the appropriate conditions exist for information to flow (Mumby and Stohl, 1991) and to promote the flow of relevant information in the learning process. Therefore, the establishment of commonly accessible formats between partners could be important (Simon, 1947, 1991; Clegg, 1981).

Dodgson (1993) indicates that learning is by no means a uniform process and that it varies in speed and direction depending on the people and organizations involved. This will complicate the understanding of the learning process between partner(s) at the formation of an IJV (Gherardi, 1996). The complementary technological expertise, managerial practices, and cognitive structure could be influenced by the variations in learning speeds of the respective partners. It also has to be noted that learning processes may be interrupted at any point and if this happens there will be incomplete knowledge retrieval and inadequate information processing (Hedberg, 1981). The creation of new knowledge or experiences within the context of an IJV involves a process of mutual learning and adjustment between partner(s) through an integration of the resource inputs provided by their parent companies. This presents a challenge to level of qualitative learning that can be achieved by the partners through the process of managing a joint venture (Argyris and Schön, 1974).

ORGANIZATIONAL CONTROL

Control is required in due proportion to the share of equity in order to protect investments in an IJV and to secure an acceptable return from them (Blodgett, 1991). The factors in a 'trade-off' between the level of equity held by the partners and the consequential learning outcomes are rarely taken into account (Lyles, 1988). However, the equity in an IJV can be used as a proxy for certain legal rights of control and this may present options of seeking a high level of equity in order to facilitate a learning achievement by the partner, or of securing an equal equity in order to achieve synergistic learning outcomes between the partners by transferring knowledge (Lindholm, 1997). Over the last 20 years, IJVs' control has tended to be measured by consideration of the levels of equity provided by the partners (Mjoen and Tallman, 1997). Previous investigations into the implications of partner control for IJV performance have produced mixed results (Geringer and Hébert, 1989).

Majority Equity

Killing (1983) advanced the proposition that IJVs having dominant control by one partner will be more successful because they are easier to manage. Killing found that ventures with 'dominant' parents 'significantly outperformed' those with shared management. This finding was based on two quite limited measures of joint venture performance which, nevertheless, provided a similar interpretation. These were the manager's own perception of his/her venture's performance, and whether the venture had either failed through demise or undergone a major reorganization because of poor performance. Killing did, however, qualify his conclusions by arguing that a critical requirement for joint venture success is that partners who have the required skills and knowledge should be able to exercise an appropriate level of control in those areas of competence. This means that in situations where, for example, one parent company has a special knowledge of technology, and the other a knowledge of the market, a shared management venture is the appropriate solution despite the likelihood that it will be more difficult to manage.

Killing's thesis on the performance advantages of dominant parents has received some further support, largely from studies of multinationals having IJVs in developing countries. For example, a study was undertaken by A.T. Kearney International of 55 large American and European multinational corporations operating in East Asia. This indicated that wholly owned subsidiaries accounted for almost 50 per cent of the cases achieving a return on investment greater than their cost of capital, while 50–50 and minority joint ventures and agent/partner arrangements made up more than 60 per cent of the operations with a return below their cost of capital (Business Asia, 1992).

Hu and Chen (1994) found from a survey of 382 Hong Kong

subsidiaries and ventures operating in China by 1986, that wholly owned subsidiaries were more likely to be successful than equity joint ventures or those based on contractual agreements. This again suggests that sole management control has performance advantages. The results must, however, be treated with caution since there were only 27 wholly owned subsidiaries in the sample, and very indirect measures of performance were employed: duration of the alliance and total partner investment in it. Yan and Gray (1996), in their study of Sino-US joint ventures, assessed performance in terms of the extent to which joint venture general managers or deputy general managers perceived each parent company's strategic objectives to have been achieved. Path analysis suggested that the higher the level of operational control a parent company exercises in the joint venture relative to its partner, the greater the extent to which that parent was perceived to be achieving its objectives. This finding appears to lend support to Killing's thesis that dominant control by one joint venture partner is associated with higher performance, but one should bear in mind that Yan and Gray's assessment was based on an evaluation of goal achievement rather than a direct measure of joint venture performance.

Shared Equity

Lyles and Salk (1996) found that 50–50 IJVs had significantly higher levels of knowledge acquisition than majority-controlled IJVs. Beamish and Banks (1987) found that shared control was related to satisfactory performance of IJVs in developing countries. Geringer and Woodcock (1989) found that 50–50 IJVs were more likely to survive. Janger (1980) used a classification scheme similar to Killing's in a study of 168 international joint ventures in both developed and developing countries. He did not, however, find that one type of joint venture tended to be more successful than another. Awadzi *et al.* (1986) failed to find any relationship between the extent of parent control and the performance of joint ventures. Bleeke and Ernst (1993) found among a sample of 49 cross-border alliances – chiefly, it appears, between partners from developed countries – that those with 50–50 ownership turned in a superior performance. Bleeke and Ernst considered that an alliance was successful if it passed two tests: both partners achieved their ingoing strategic objectives and both recovered their financial costs of capital. The reasoning they advance to account for their finding is particularly interesting because it stresses the benefits of strong management *within* an alliance rather than Killing's argument in favour of strong management *over* an alliance.

Beamish (1988) reviewed studies, including his own, on the control–performance link in developed and developing country alliances. Several of these investigations conclude that when alliances are formed between developed and less-developed country partners, there tends to be an association between satisfactory performance and less-dominant control by the foreign partner. The argument is that a sharing of control with local partners will lead to a greater contribution from them, which can assist in coping with circumstances that are unfamiliar to the foreign partner and therefore result in a higher return on investment.

THE FRAMEWORK OF LEARNING AND CONTROL IN AN IJV

The increase in numbers of IJVs has created the opportunity for many new factors to be investigated in the field of learning (Billett, 1996). The inputs from IJV partner(s) involves the transference of existing technology, management and local practice into an organizational setting where they represent new learning contexts and new learning sources for the IJV. An IJV appears to show all of the basic features of corporate life (Ebers, 1997), and its organizational change is driven by critical resources provided and enhanced by partners, which have brought about a recurring need for continuous learning and control in its organization (Bartholomew, 1997). Examination of organizational effectiveness requires a context of learning and control to exist. The context in the case of an IJV is perceived as equity and the existing resource including capital and non-capital inputs provided by its partners (Yan, 1997). Constructive learning can be seen to have occurred when organizations perform in changed and better ways. Foreign investing companies operating in China often face a choice between maintaining their standard of technology and managerial expertise or sharing their knowledge and expertise base with local Chinese partners (Boisot and Child, 1997). The choice for the local Chinese companies may be deciding between the options of maintaining

Chinese norms of complexity in terms of its social system, organizational structure and domestic market integrity or adopting Western technology and management structure.

The trade-off in an IJV context is between the knowledge input that a partner is willing to transfer to the IJV and the level of knowledge input that must be learned by the IJV in order to optimize its performance (Ouchi and Wilkins, 1983). The decision that a parent company takes in using or sharing areas of competence such as special technological and managerial expertise is likely to be affected by how much it feels it can control the actions of the IJV following the knowledge transference (Lin *et al.*, 1997). It should be noted that a partner's strategic objectives, and its culturally based responses to the specific levels of equity provided, may generate additional effects on an IJV's performance. If the strategic objectives sought by the partners are to be achieved, the potential social, economic and technical problems may be resolved through inter-partner learning activities (Argyris, 1983). This implies that there are certain learning requirements to incorporate each partner's strategic objectives as well as its ownership profile at the formation of an IJV (Lyles, 1996). The above considerations give rise to a first hypothesis, namely:

Hypothesis 1: The IJV performance will be based upon the level of equity that a partner contributes to the joint venture relative to the learning objectives it provides.

The integration of knowledge and learning processes between IJV partners can be facilitated by an organizational structural underpinning. Child and Leverage (1990) suggest, from their studies of how organizations in European service responded to the availability of new information technologies, that learning can be contested as well as collaborative between intra-organizational groups involved, such as technical specialists, higher management, HRM specialists, and employee representatives. Lawrence and Lorsch (1967) identify managers as the key personnel mediating the integration process. The degree of the learning importance to the IJV partner will depend on the configuration of the objective priorities, the level of equity and the provision of resource inputs (Bleeke and Ernst, 1993). The influence and control over an IJV may be derived from such provided configuration, since each partner has its own set of management and technological competencies. Mutually attractive capital, brand names and technology profiles can be offered if the expertise and resource boundaries between partners are bridged (Nonaka, 1991). As each partner brings with it appropriate competencies and knowledge from its home base, the combined resource profile enables them to redefine the frames of meaning within which those contributions are allocated in the IJV context (Argyris, 1990). The above considerations give rise to a second hypothesis, namely:

Hypothesis 2: The emphasis of learning and its outcome in an IJV is based upon the expertise and competence that each partner possesses.

The experience of Sino-foreign IJVs points to congruence of objectives between partners as a further contingency in terms of coupling a partner's level of control and its degree of learning improvement. A partner's ability to operate in the local Chinese environment will be considerably constrained if it depends on that environment for a key resource, or if the resource is provisioned by the other partner. The control perspective draws attention to the potential influence over the actions of organization managers enjoyed by external bodies via the supply of critical resources (Pfeffer and Salancik, 1978). The learning achievement of an IJV may be linked to the acquiescence of partners in terms of their willingness to transfer critical resources and knowledge (Hamel, 1991). The IJV learning process can be jeopardized if the disposition of a critical resource is highly concentrated in the hands of a single institutional body (Huber, 1991). This postulates that a partner may increase its appetite to learn when there is a match between a partner's level of equity and a strong desire to reduce the dependency upon its alliance. The argument is that a majority equity position is required in order to protect the resource, as it will enable a partner to formalize the organizational structure and facilitate learning through a joint venture partnership.

Killing's qualifying argument is that a critical requirement for joint venture success lies in a partner's ability to exercise control in areas of IJV activity for which it has superior competence. In other words, a functionally allocated distribution of control over an IJV is conducive to superior performance. In the case of Sino-foreign

IJVs, it is reasonable to single out finance, marketing and technology as areas in which foreign partners would normally possess superior competence, and the traditional aspects of personnel management, such as rewards and incentives, as areas in which Chinese partners would have superior relevant local knowledge. The above considerations give rise to a third hypothesis, namely:

Hypothesis 3: The more control that a parent company exercises over an IJV's activities for which it possesses superior competence, the higher will be the IJV's level of performance.

Boisot (1998) draws a three-dimensional concept of an 'information-space' model, made up of a codification, a diffusion and an abstraction dimension. The model identifies how these dimensions impact on the learning types and explains that learning cycle has associated costs, but may not always necessarily add value. Lovell and Turner (1988) recognize that learning does not always lead to performance improvement. Cognitive psychology has made a vital contribution to describing the outcomes of learning (Vosniadou, 1996). Dodgson (1993) suggests that there are linkages between various levels of learning and their likely outcomes. In the case of an IJV, levels of learning through cooperation provide potential leverage for improving and enhancing organizational performance. Learning achievements may be counterbalanced by the level of critical resource provided by the partners. These considerations give rise to a fourth hypothesis, namely:

Hypothesis 4: A higher learning outcome is achieved when the majority of resources are provided to an IJV by one partner. A lower learning outcome is achieved when the resource to an IJV is provided by both of the partners.

METHODS

The sample consists of 67 Sino-foreign joint ventures formed between Chinese and foreign owning companies. The foreign share of IJV equity ranges between 25 and 95 per cent. The research was conducted in collaboration with staff from the University of Cambridge and the International Technology and Economy Institute of the State Council in China during the period May 1994 to May 1995. Within the total of 67 joint ventures, 212 senior foreign and Chinese respondents from IJVs, including general managers, deputy general managers and function heads, were interviewed. The samples were located in two sectors, namely non-consumer electronics and fast-moving consumer goods. The choice of these two sectors was informed by the following considerations. In electronics, technology transfer and its management are key factors, as product design is a major focus of competence. In fast-moving consumer goods, marketing is particularly important, especially brand management and product promotion. The foreign parent companies chosen for the investigation were headquartered in the USA, Western Europe, Japan and Overseas Chinese territories (primarily Hong Kong and Taiwan). The IJVs were located in three areas of China: Beijing-Tianjin, Shanghai and Hangzhou, and Guangdong Province. The IJV sample varied in size between 50 and 2000 employees. The following variables were used for testing the hypotheses:

- *Objectives priorities*: The most senior foreign and Chinese manager in the joint venture was asked to select the five most important objective benefits which their parent companies sought from the IJV from a set of 12 items for foreign partners and a set of 17 items for Chinese partners.
- *Objectives achievements*: If an objective was included in the top five priorities selected, it was scored in a binary manner (provided = 1; not provided = 0). Objective achievements for both foreign and Chinese parent companies are scaled (1 = not achieved; 5 = fully achieved).
- *Equity share*: The share of equity held by foreign and Chinese parent companies. The control potential offered by equity capital relies upon the 'right to control' that a majority equity share conveys in the Western corporate tradition. There is evidence to indicate that equity share conveys control leverage in developing countries as well. Lecraw (1984), for example, found a correlation between the equity share held by transnational corporations in 153 ASEAN subsidiaries and their

level of overall management control in those subsidiaries.

- *Cultural capital-building context*: The items on (1) the common culture and identity-building and (2) symbols, slogans, rituals or ceremonies are organized for the IJV by one or other of the parent companies. The items are scored in a binary manner (not provided = 0; provided = 1).
- *Performance*: Subjective assessments were made by the most senior joint venture manager available in terms of the market share, growth, profitability, technology development, and development of local staff achieved. These are scaled (1 = not satisfied; 5 = highly satisfied). Objective assessments were made by the most senior available joint venture manager in terms of the profitability and growth of sales within the last three years.
- *Parent company control*: The most senior IJV manager available gave an evaluation on five-point scales of the degree of influence exercised respectively by the Chinese and foreign parent companies, or their representatives, over control issues in IJV management. When there was more than one Chinese or foreign parent company, the questions on influence were put with reference to the Chinese or foreign parent most involved in the joint venture's management.
- *Learning improvement*: The perceived learning improvement on skill, resource, quality of cooperation, market share, development of local staff, and technology development was assessed through five-point scales (1= priority improvement; 5 = less priority improvement).
- *Non-capital resource*: the composition of contractual and non-contractual inputs distinguishing between contributions in the form of product design, production technology, management systems, management services, and training. Provision and non-provision are scored in a binary manner (provided = 1; not provided = 0).

RESULTS

Table 1 shows the inter-correlations between the subjective evaluation of IJV performance and the partner's learning objectives. Two sample groups are chosen, differentiated according to the level of foreign equity: a foreign majority equity share group

TABLE 1
INTER-CORRELATIONS BETWEEN IJV PERFORMANCE ACHIEVED AND A PARTNER's LEARNING OBJECTIVES ATTAINED FOR EQUAL SHARE OR MAJORITY EQUITY GROUPS IN IJVs (N = 67 IJVs)

Learning	*Correlation between the subjective evaluation of IJV' performance and the learning objectives*[4]	
Objective priorities	*Equal equity (N=12)*	*Majority equity (N=40)*
Foreign strategic objectives[1]		
Attraction of Chinese market	–.15	.27*
Learning how to do business in China	–.36	.13
Chinese strategic objectives[2]		
Acquiring technology transfer	–.08	–.02
Learning how to export	–.26	.27*
Learning management expertise	–.09	.42**
Upgrading Chinese suppliers' technology	.36	–.02
Opportunity to train Chinese staff	.53*	–.07
Cultural capital building by partners[3]		
Common culture and identity building	.35	.27*
Symbols, slogans, rituals or ceremonies	.51*	.22

1 The most senior foreign manager in the joint venture was asked to select the five most important strategic objectives sought by the foreign parent company from the JV from a set of 12 items. The objectives are scored in a binary manner (1 = provided; 0 = not provided).

2 The most senior Chinese manager in the joint venture was asked to select the five most important strategic objectives sought by the Chinese parent company from the JV from a set of 17 items. The objectives are scored in a binary manner (1 = provided; 0 = not provided).

3 The most senior manager available in the joint venture was asked whether the items such as (1) common culture and identity building, (2) symbols, slogans, rituals or ceremonies, are respectively provided by foreign or Chinese parent companies (1= provided; 0 = not provided).

4 The performance indicators are the aggregation of the subject evaluations made by the available IJV managers on market growth, profitability and market share. The assessments were scored on a five-point scale (1 = not satisfied; 5 = fully satisfied).

(N=40) and an equal equity share group (N=12). The results emerging from the majority equity share group show that a good performance is achieved if the foreign partners have as an objective the penetration of the Chinese domestic market, or the Chinese partners have the objectives of learning how to export and acquiring management expertise, as these objectives are marked as positive and statistically significant. In the majority equity group, the common cultural identity building provided by the parent companies is perceived to lend constructive learning supports for an IJV to achieve a better performance. In an equal equity share group, the only two statistically significant items are the Chinese objectives of acquiring the opportunity to train Chinese staff, and the use of symbols, slogans and ceremonies provided by parent companies. The results suggest that the perception change via the use of organizational rituals and metaphors can affect a manager's behaviour in terms of learning to cope with new governance systems, as they will control the interpretative process through ideological reinforcement and human resources management. Hypothesis 1 is only partially supported.

Table 2 summarizes the primary learning experience gained throughout an IJV partnership. The results shows the main differences between Chinese and foreign managers are in the areas of: managing the companies' operations; communicating within or between departments; dealing with information and understanding culture in terms of values and objectives. For the Chinese partners, achieving an understanding of foreign culture and gaining experience of business management are mentioned frequently. The learning outcomes most often mentioned by the foreign partner groups are areas such as the way to approach local government, and the establishment of personal relationships and trust. The findings suggest that the foreign partners seem to demonstrate their need to maintain autonomy, but this often leaves very limited space to learn necessary Chinese business practices. The contrast in the learning frequencies of the foreign and Chinese partners reflects very different ways of thinking about how the IJV should be managed. From the foreign partner's point of view, communicating within or between departments and dealing with information can be regarded as a means of learning, as communication implies knowledge transfer as a method of control or establishment of a new form of legitimacy. From the Chinese partner's point of view,

TABLE 2
FREQUENCY TEST FOR THE MAIN LEARNING EXPERIENCE GAINED VIA AN IJV PARTNERSHIP (N = 67 IJVs)

Learning from working with counterparts	*Foreign partner (N=19)*	*Chinese partner (N=38)*
Managing the company's operations[1]	8	43
• competence in understanding management	4	27
• competence in understanding marketing	2	9
• communication within or between department	2	31
• dealing with information	2	31
Understanding of strategic issues[2]	5	19
• way of approaching with government	11	4
• strategic decision making	3	17
Understanding culture (values and objectives)[3]	15	37
• personal relationships and trust established	17	9
• language barriers	14	13

1 The most senior foreign and Chinese managers in the joint venture were asked to answer the questions on managing the company's operations in terms of the lists shown from the table. The number of cases dropped due to some of the answers being irrelevant to the above categories.
2 The most senior foreign and Chinese managers in the joint venture were asked to answer the questions on understanding strategic issues in terms of in terms of the lists shown from the table. The number of cases dropped due to some of the answers being irrelevant to the above categories.
3 The most senior foreign and Chinese managers in the joint venture were asked to the questions on understanding culture in terms of the lists shown from the table. The number of cases dropped due to some of the answers being irrelevant to the above categories.

granting the right to manage the joint venture to the foreign partner without some method of learning the discipline will generate negative effects on IJV performance. Hypothesis 2 is supported.

The foreign majority equity share and equal equity share groups are chosen in this study to see how they are related to the learning achieved in IJVs. The results suggest that there are no consistent differences in the learning outcomes from a comparison of the two groups. The areas where there are statistically significant differences between the two groups are: development of local staff (r=.06); technology development (r=.02); upgrading Chinese supplier's technology (r=.01) and establishing a strong business presence in China (r=.06). The mean values achieved based upon the above differences (4 items) are higher in the foreign majority equity share group. The results can be further interpreted as: when equity is dominated by one partner, constructive learning may be

TABLE 3
T-TEST FOR THE LEARNING OUTCOMES ACHIEVED IN IJVs OVER EQUAL EQUITY AND MAJORITY EQUITY GROUPS (N = 67 IJVs)

Learning outcomes	*T-test for independent samples*[3]		
	Equal equity (N=12)	*Majority equity (N=40)*	*Significance of p-value*
Learning in objectives achievements[1]			
Attraction of Chinese market	16	15	.84
Learning how to do business in China	18	16	.70
Establishing strong business presence in China	16	19	.06
Acquiring technology transfer	15	17	.61
Learning how to export	20	14	.34
Learning management expertise	17	16	.48
Upgrading Chinese suppliers' technology	5	16	.01
Opportunity to train Chinese staff	17	14	.57
Learning improvement[2]			
Skill improvement	27	26	.72
Quality of collaboration improvement	31	24	.17
Resource improvement	25	26	.87
Market share improvement	29	26	.39
Development of local staff	19	28	.06
Technology development	17	28	.02

[1] The most senior foreign and Chinese managers in the joint venture were asked to answer the objective achievement. The assessments are scored on a five-point scale (1 = not achieved; 0 = fully achieved).
[2] The most senior foreign and Chinese managers in the joint venture were asked to answer the questions on learning transformation. The assessment on the list above are scored no a five-point scale (1 = not high priority; 5 = very high priority).
[3] Foreign equity shares was used as the indicator of 'equal equity' (= 50–50 equity) or 'majority equity (> 50–50 equity). T-test for independent mean samples the 67 IJVs.

achieved because equity may enhance control by reinforcing the legitimacy. This is particularly true in the Sino-foreign IJVs: when one of the partners becomes the dominant way of acting and enacting of managerial and technological expertise, learning appears to be a particular way to cope with changing environments without the risk of internal resistance. Partner control, to a large extent, is derived from provision of the technology and managerial expertise, as these can be used to define or condition the rules of interaction in other areas. The findings may reveal a general issue on the dilemma between the type of knowledge expertise committed and the degree of dominance by one parent company. This is because the technological expertise is associated with its own self-discipline, as the discipline can be seen as the ultimate way of obtaining control. The findings suggest that for the IJV partners

TABLE 4
CORRELATIONS BETWEEN THE LEARNING UTILIZATION AND THE PARTNERS RESOURCE INPUTS FOR THE USE OF EITHER A 'GOODNESS OF FIT' APPROACH OR A 'UNIVERSALISTIC' APPROACH IN IJVs (N = 67 IJVs)

Resource inputs	*Correlation between partner's resource inputs and learning achievements*[1]			
	Technology development		*Development of local staff*	
	Goodness of Fit Approach[2]	*Universalistic Approach*	*Goodness of Fit Approach*	*Universalistic Approach*
Equity inputs[3]	.06	.51*	–.03	.51*
Product design	.11	.45*	.07	.49*
Existing plant, facilities	.26*	.51*	.10	.26
Marketing support	.05	.36	.24*	.17
Contractual inputs[4]	.12	.06	.22	.10
Training	.05	.29*	.06	.13
Non-contractual inputs[5]	.04	.11	.21	.35*
Product design	.10	.23	.10	.34*
Professional service	.03	.38*	.02	.48*

[1] The most senior managers available were asked to give their subjective assessment on the learning achievement on technology development and development of local staff. The assessment was scored from (1= not satisfied, 5=fully satisfied).
[2] The 'goodness of fit' approach is used to examine the capital and non-capital resources provided by both foreign and Chinese partner to the joint venture
[3] The composition of equity distinguishing between contributions is provided by partners to the joint venture.
[4] The composition of contractual inputs distinguishing between contributions is provided by partners to the joint venture.
[5] The composition of non-contractual inputs distinguishing between contributions is provided by partners to the joint venture.

there is a trade-off between the expertise commitment and the control attached to the commitment. The resource provision to an IJV can be regarded as a means of gaining a fully accepted control through the resource discipline. Hypothesis 3 is not supported.

Table 4 shows the inter-correlations between the subjective evaluation of the learning achievements and the range of resource inputs supplied by the partners. The two learning outcomes, technology development and the development of local staff, are chosen to reflect the degree of learning achieved in the IJVs. The 'goodness of fit' or 'universalistic' approaches are used to show the ways resources are invested to IJVs. The correlations in the 'universalistic' group are shown to be slightly statistically more consistent and significant than the cases in 'goodness of fit'. The correlations in the universalistic group suggest the equity inputs (r=.51), the product design (r=.49), the non-contractual input (r=.35), the product design (r=.34 on non-contractual basis) and the professional service (r=.48) are statistically significant. The results indicate that when the parent companies commit more capital and technology to joint ventures, it becomes desirable in their eyes to have a greater control over their superior resource knowledge. Parent companies will not be satisfied with the IJV learning achievements in technology development and the general skill improvement achieved unless they have dominant control in those areas. Hypothesis 4 is only partially supported.

CONCLUSIONS

This contribution has utilized equity as a proxy for control to understand the relationship between control and learning in IJVs. There are several facets that deserve closer attention in the light of our findings.

First, the results show equity can be used as an appropriate indicator for examining both the process and the outcome of learning embedded in the organization. The distinctive contrast between equal or majority equity plays a central role in the establishment of the IJV's structure. Learning as both outcome and a process also impacts on the organizational structure, which can be actualized throughout an IJV's evolution. It seems to be the case in Sino-foreign joint ventures that the strategic learning objectives and cultural capital building provided by the partners shows positive effects on the performance. This may be due to the fact that learning is embedded in the procedures of control and is a powerful way of stabilizing or enhancing the legitimacy of decisions. This enables the parent companies to control the process and create appropriate learning conditions under which patterns of behaviour are learned and reinforced.

Second, learning achieved in an IJV may not necessarily relate to the control mechanisms exercised as it may link other aspects such as attitudes, cultural capital building, or even government policy. Foreign investing companies are often actively involved in an IJV's management activity by contributing their understanding of business practices. However, expatriate managers often tend to be overcritical of and impatient with their local counterparts, as they have no conception of the need to adapt to local practice. Joint ventures are intended by the Chinese authorities to play an important role in facilitating the learning of advanced management and technology expertise. When an IJV is established, the Chinese partners have a number of objectives in mind, prominent among which are the acquisition of technology and management knowledge. With reference to the primary learning experience gained from the joint venture, the local managers appear to be enthusiastic about learning, particularly in the context of management, marketing and strategic issues. The foreign partners only show an interest in learning about Chinese concepts of trust and relationship building. Such differences do not necessarily reflect any equity structural effect, but identify rather specific cultural and institutional roles that are present in most Sino-foreign joint ventures.

Third, there is evidence from this study that control and learning are closely interwoven where equity share is dominated by one of the partners. The results show the majority equity share can be used to safeguard its knowledge and competencies while simultaneously responding to the necessity to incorporate the knowledge and management practices of its partner. In most respects, the critical resources are usually associated with their self-discipline and legitimacy. The partner with the majority equity share is normally willing to share its knowledge with its partners, as this generally facilitates a process of learning that leads to a better performance. In addition, an imbalance of the equity could result in less conflict *per se* to take the action necessary for change and to increase management consistency within an IJV.

Fourth, this study highlights the relationship between the impact derived from the ways of committing the resources onto an IJV and its contribution to the learning achieved in an IJV. The specific factors can be elicited through the way in which partners adopt either a 'universalistic' approach or a 'goodness of fit' approach, since each context generates a different form of complexity. The way in which resource inputs are provided, either by applying universalistic or contingency approaches, generates different effects on the learning achieved in technology development and the development of local staff. The investigation of the 67 IJVs indicates that when the universalistic approach is used, it will normally be accompanied by a formalized learning process. The methodology of examining a partner's resource input profile would seem to be fruitful approach for further research into the IJV learning context.

The results of this investigation suggest a number of implications for foreign companies seeking to exercise direction over their China joint ventures. A larger equity share is found to support a parent's ability to influence its joint venture's strategic direction. Legal provisions designed to ensure joint ventures operate according to acceptable rules, regulations and policies that are still lacking in China. Therefore, it is important that foreign partners know where they stand in joint ventures, particularly where they may not have the equity share necessary to ensure control. The issue of equity rights in China can be analysed using a framework derived from Western management thinking.

The current structure of a joint venture imposed by foreign investing companies tends to concentrate upon how an individual joint venture's internal management system is vertically integrated into the foreign corporate structure. More attention needs to be paid to the horizontal links with the local institutional system. Long term interconnections between foreign partner executives based at regional and headquarters levels and the Chinese higher authorities will enable the foreign investing company's management to learn from the experience of operating in a relatively unfamiliar and difficult environment. Foreign investing companies that develop these horizontal links can take advantage of their international standing and prestige to secure influence with Chinese authorities.

ACKNOWLEDGEMENTS

Grateful acknowledgement is made of funding provided by the UK Economic and Social Research Council and the Hong Kong Research Grant Council to defray the cost of the research on which this study draws. The author would like to thank Professor Malcolm Warner and three anonymous reviewers for their valuable comments and also thank Professor John Child and Dr Yuan Lu for their assistance in fieldwork, which greatly contributed to this research.

REFERENCES

Argyris, C. (1983), *Reasoning, Learning and Action, Individual and Organizational*. San Francisco: Jossey-Bass.

Argyris, C. (1990), *Overcoming Organizational Defenses: Facilitating Organizational Learning*. Boston: Allyn and Bacon.

Argyris, C. and Schön, D. (1974), *Theory in Practice: Increasing Professional Effectiveness*. San Francisco: Jossey-Bass.

Argyris, C. and Schön, D. (1978), *Organizational Learning: A Theory of Action Perspective*. Reading, MA: Addison-Wesley.

Awadzi, W., Kedia, B.L. and Chinta, R. (1986), 'Performance Implications of Locus of Control and Complementary Resources in International Joint Ventures – An Empirical Study.' Paper presented at the Academy of International Business Conference, London.

Barnard, C.I. (1968), *The Functions of the Executive*. Cambridge, MA: Harvard University Press.

Bartholomew, S. (1997), 'National Systems of Biotechnology Innovation: Complex Interdependence in the Global System', *Journal of International Business Studies*, Vol. 28, No. 2, pp. 241–266.

Beamish, P.W. (1988), *Multinational Joint Ventures in Developing Countries*. London: Routledge.

Beamish, P.W. and Banks, J.C. (1987), 'Equity Joint Ventures and the Theory of the Multinational Enterprise', *Journal of International Business Studies*, Vol.18, No.2, pp.1–16.

Billett, S. (1996), 'Situated Learning: Bridging Sociocultural and Cognitive Theorising', *Learning and Instruction*, Vol.6, No.3, pp.263–80.

Bleeke, J. and Ernst, D. (1993), *Collaborating to Compete: Using Strategic Alliances and Acquisitions in the Global Marketplace*. New York: Wiley.

Blodgett, L.L. (1991), 'Partner Contributions as Predictors of Equality Share in International Joint Ventures', *Journal of International Business Studies*, Vol.22, pp.63–78.

Boisot, M. (1998) *Knowledge Assets: Securing Competitive Advantage in the Information Economy*. Oxford: Oxford University Press.

Boisot, M. and Child, J. (1996), 'From Fiefs to Clans and Network Capitalism: Explaining China's Emerging Economic Order', *Administrative Science Quarterly*, Vol.41, No.4, pp.600–28.

Business Asia (1992), 'Asia by Numbers. Corporate Structure: Stay Single, Stay Wealthy', *Business Asia*. London: Economist Intelligence Unit, December, pp.7–9.

Child, J. and Faulkner, D. (1998), *Strategies of Co-operation: Managing Alliances, Networks, and Joint Ventures*. Oxford University Press.

Child, J. and Heavens, S. (1997), *The Social Constitution of Organizations and Its Implications for Organizational Learning*. Research Paper in Management Studies, University of Cambridge. Working Paper No.3.

Child, J. and Loveridge, R. (1990) *Information Technology in European Services*. Oxford: Blackwell.

Child, J., Yan, Y. and Lu, Y. (1997), 'Ownership and Control in Sino-foreign Joint Ventures', in P.W. Beamish and J.P. Killing (ed.), *Cooperative Strategies: Asian Pacific Perspectives*. San Francisco: The New Lexington Press, pp.181–225.

Clegg, S.R. (1981), 'Organization and Control', *Administrative Science Quarterly*, Vol. 6, pp.545–62.

Dodgson, M. (1993), 'Learning, Trust and Technological Collaboration', *Human Relations*, Vol.46, No.1, pp.77–95.

Ebers, M. (1997), *The Formation of Inter-Organizational Networks*. Oxford: Oxford University Press.

Faulkner, D. (1995a), *International Strategic Alliances: Co-operating to Compete*. London: McGraw-Hill.

Faulkner, D. (1995b), 'Strategic Alliance Evolution through Learning: The Rover/Honda Alliance', in Howard Thomas, Don O'Neal and James Kelly (eds), *Strategic Renaissance and Business Transformation*. Chichester: Wiley, pp.211–35.

Fiol, C.M. and Lyles, M.A. (1985), 'Organizational Learning', *Academy of Management Review*, Vol.10, No.4, pp.803–13.

Geringer, J.M. and Hébert, L. (1989), 'Control and Performance of International Joint Ventures', *Journal of International Business Studies*, Vol.20, No.2, pp.235–54.

Geringer, J.M. and Woodcock, P. (1989), 'Ownership and Control of Canadian Joint Venture', *Journal of International Business Studies*, Vol.20, No.1, pp.97–101.

Gherardi, S. (1996), 'Organizational Learning', in M. Warner (ed.), *International Encyclopaedia of Management and Business*, Vol.4. London: ITBP, pp.3934–42.

Giddens, A. (1984), *The Constitution of Society*. Cambridge: Polity Press.

Hamel, G. (1991), 'Competition for Competence and Inter-Partner Learning within International Strategic Alliances', *Strategic Management Journal*, Vol.12, pp.83–103.

Hedberg, B. (1981), 'How Organizations Learn and Unlearn', in Paul C. Nystrom and William H. Starbuck (eds), *Handbook of Organizational Design*, Vol. 1. New York: Oxford University Press, pp.3–27.

Hu, M.Y. and Chen, H. (1994), 'The Performance of Hong Kong Foreign Subsidiaries in China', *Advances in Chinese Industrial Studies*, Vol.4, pp.185–98.

Huber, G.P. (1991), 'Organizational Learning: The Contributing Processes and the Literatures', *Organization Science*, Vol. , No.1, pp.88–115.

Inkpen, A.C. (1995), *The Management of International Joint Ventures: An Organisational Learning Perspective*. London: Routledge.

Janger, A.R. (1980), *Organization of International Joint Ventures*. New York: The Conference Board.

Killing, J.P. (1983), 'Options for Technology Seeking Firms: Joint Ventures as a Mechanism for Technology Transfer', in J.P. Killing (ed.), *Strategies for Joint Venture Success*. New York: Praeger.

Lecraw, Donald J. (1984), 'Bargaining Power, Ownership, and Profitability of Transnational Corporations in Developing Countires', *Journal of International Business Studies*, Voil.15, pp.27–43.

Lawrence, P.R. and Lorsch, J.W. (1967), *Organizations and Environment*. Boston: Harvard Business School Press.

Lin, J.L., Yu, C. and Seetoo, D.W. (1997), 'Motivations, Partners' Contributions, and Control of International Joint Ventures', in P.W. Beamish and J.P. Killing (eds), *Cooperative Strategies: Asian Pacific Perspectives*. San Francisco: New Lexington Press, pp.91–114.

Lindholm, N. (1997), 'Learning Processes in International Joint Ventures in China', *Advances in Chinese Industrial Studies*. Vol.5, pp.139–54.

Lovell, R.D. and Turner, B.M. (1988), 'Organizational Learning, Bureaucratic Control, Preservation of Form', *Adding to Our Basic Understanding of Research Utilization in Public Organizations, Knowledge, Creation, Diffusion, Utilization*, Vol.9, No.3, pp.404–25.

Lyles, M.A. (1996), 'The Impact of Organizational Learning on Joint Venture Formations', *International Business Review*, Vol.3, No.4, pp.459–67.

Lyles, M.A. (1988), 'Learning among Joint Venture-Sophisticated Firms', in Ferok J. Contractor and Peter Lorange (eds), New York: Lexington Books.

Lyles, M.A. and Salk, J.E. (1996), 'Knowledge Acquisition from Foreign Parents in International Joint Ventures: An empirical examination in the Hungarian Context', *Journal of International Business Studies*, Vol.27, No.5, pp.877–904.

Machin, J. and Lowe, T. (1983), 'Introduction', in J. Machin and T. Lowe (eds), *New Perspectives in Management Control*. New York: St Martin's Press.

Mjoen, H. and Tallman, S. (1997), 'Control and Performance in International Joint Ventures', *Organization Science*, No.8, pp.257–74.

Moingeon, S.A. and Edmondson, A. (1996), *Organizational Learning and Competitive Advantage*. London: Sage.

Mumby, D.K. and Stohl, C. (1991), 'Power and Discourse in Organizational Studies: Absence and the Dialectic of Control', *Discourse and Society*, No.2, pp.313–32.

Nonaka, I. (1991), 'The Knowledge-Creating Company', *Harvard Business Review*, No.69.

Ouchi, W.G. and Wilkins, A.L. (1983), 'Efficient Cultures: Exploring the Relationship between Culture and Organizational Performance', *Administrative Science Quarterly*, Vol.28, No.3, pp.468–81.

Parkhe, A. (1991), 'Interfirm Diversity, Organizational Learning and Longevity in Global Strategic Alliances', *Journal of International Business Studies*, Vol.22, No.4, pp.579–601.

Pfeffer, J. and Salancik, G.R. (1978), *The External Control of Organizations: A Resource Dependence Perspective*. New York: Harper & Row.

Pucik, V. (1988), 'Strategic Alliances, Organizational Learning, and Competitive Advantage: The HRM Agenda', *Human Resource Management*, Vol.10, No.1, pp.77–93.

Reynolds, M. (1997), 'Learning Styles: A Critique', *Management Learning*, Vol.28, No.2, pp.115–33.

Schon, A.A. (1975), 'Deutero-learning in Organizations: Learning for Increased Effectiveness', *Organizational Dynamics*, Vol.4, No.1, pp.2–16.

Senge, P.M. (1991), 'The Learning Organization Made Plain', *Training and Development*, Vol.45, No.1, pp.37–44.

Senge, P.M. and Sterman, J.D. (1992), 'Systems Thinking and Organizational Learning – Acting Locally and Thinking Globally in the Organization of the Future', *European Journal of Operational Research*, Vol.59, No.1, pp.137–50.

Simon, H.A. (1947), *Administrative Behavior: A Study of Decision-making Process in Administrative Organization*. New York, Free Press.

Simon, H.A. (1991), 'Bounded Rationality and Organizational Learning', *Organization Science*, Vol.2, No.1, pp.125–34.

United Nations (1997), *World Investment Report 1997*. New York: United Nations Conference on Trade and Development.

Vanhonacker, W. (1997), 'Enterprising China: An Unconventional Approach', *Harvard Business Review*, Vol.75, No.2, pp.130–40.

Vosniadou, S. (1996), 'Towards a Revised Cognitive Psychology for New Advances in Learning and Instruction', *Learning and Instruction*, Vol.6, No.2, pp.95–109.

Warner, M. (1995), *The Management of Human Resources in Chinese Industry*. New York: St Martin's Press.

Willmott, H. (1984), 'Organizational Control and the Problem of Order', *Social Science Information*, Vol.16, pp.169–89.

Yan, A. and Gray, B. (1996), 'Linking Management Control and Interpartner Relationships with Performance in US–Chinese Joint Ventures', in J. Child and Y. Lu (eds), *Management Issues in China: International Enterprises*. London: Routledge, pp.106–27.

Yan, Y. (1997), 'The Effect of Ownership on Performance in Sino-Foreign Joint Ventures', in S. Stewart and N. Campbell (eds), *Advances in Chinese Industrial Studies*, Vol.5. JAI Press, pp.219–47.

Yan, Y. Child, J. and Lu, Y. (1995), 'Ownership and Control in International Business: An Examination of Sino-foreign International Joint Ventures'. Paper presented to Academy of Management Annual Meetings, Vancouver.

10

Motivation to Manage in China: Implications for Strategic HRM

BAHMAN P. EBRAHIMI

Since 1979, the People's Republic of China (PRC) has made tremendous economic progress. As a result, China and its management practices have received increasing research attention. Human resource management practices in China have been extensively explored elsewhere (see Rowley, 1997). Unfortunately, little research has dealt with the concept of hierarchical role motivation theory; its main construct, motivation to manage; and its potential implications for strategic human resource practices in the PRC. The study reported here is an attempt to fill this void.

Motivation to manage refers to a set of motives that match the role requirements of different organizational forms. There are four role motivation theories related to four organizational forms: hierarchical, entrepreneurial, group, and professional (Miner, 1980; Oliver, 1982).

The focus of the present research is on role motivation theory in hierarchical organizations. Hierarchical organizations are typically large bureaucracies characterized by high degrees of centralization, division of labour, and formalization (Weber, 1968; Mintzberg, 1983). Motivation to manage or managerial motivation is defined as an internal force that leads select individuals to pursue, enjoy and succeed in management positions in relatively large hierarchical organizations (Miner *et al.*, 1995). Hierarchical role motivation theory is applicable to large organizations with three or more management layers (Miner *et al.*, 1995). Since hierarchies are still one of the most prevalent organizational forms worldwide and Chinese management is characterized as basically hierarchical (Weber, 1968; Nelson and Reader, 1985; Redding, 1990), the focus of the present research is on managerial role motivation in this organizational form.

Research on the topic of managerial motivation has been conducted in the United States for more than thirty years (Miner, 1963, 1993). A number of studies examining managerial role motivation theory have also been conducted outside the United States (Arsan *et al.*, 1983; Basuray *et al.*, 1985; Ebrahimi, 1985, 1997; Ebrahimi and Miner, 1991; Ebrahimi and Young, 1996; Ebrahimi *et al.*, 1997; Ebrahimi, Luk and Young, 1998; Ebrahimi, Young and Luk, 1998; Singleton *et al.*, 1987; Southern and Pih, 1987; Miner *et al.*, 1989; Miner *et al.*, 1995), including the two related studies in the PRC (Chen *et al.*, 1997; Miner *et al.*, 1991).

This study makes several contributions to the literature on cross-cultural applicability of managerial role motivation theory in general and in the People's Republic of China in particular. First, unlike much other cross-cultural research on managerial motivation theory which used samples of business students (such as Basuray *et al.*, 1985; Ebrahimi, 1985, 1997; Ebrahimi and Miner, 1991; Miner *et al.*, 1989; Singleton *et al.*, 1987; Southern and Pih, 1987) this study utilizes a sample of fully employed managers and non-managers in Chinese private and public sectors. Second, the ongoing research enhances the generalizability of findings and conclusions drawn by Miner *et al.* (1991) because it utilizes a more geographically and organizationally diverse sample. Finally, this research is the only cross-cultural study on the subject that incorporates multiple measures of performance in its design.

DOES ROLE MOTIVATION THEORY APPLY IN CHINA?

The Chinese culture is based on adherence to role prescriptions in both interpersonal and organizational relationships (Westwood, 1992). 'Li' and other 'moral rules' prescribe roles for occupants of different positions in Chinese society (Westwood, 1992). The Book of Filial Piety (*Xiaojing*) contains a set of these prescribed social rules instructing Chinese to abide by the duties of their assigned roles (Westwood, 1992). Clear hierarchical roles are apparent, with respect and obedience to elders serving as the model for proper behaviour in all relationships (Westwood, 1992). Chinese youth are strongly socialized into accepting prescribed role positions and relationships, and to the internalization of values and patterns of behaviour that are prescribed for them (Westwood, 1992). Thus, respect for hierarchical position and age is considered to be a primary aspect of Chinese culture (Nevis, 1983; Boisot and Child, 1988; Lockett, 1988).

Chinese culture is also influenced by *Wu Lun* or the 'Five Cardinal Relationships' identified in Confucianism. *Wu Lun* comprises the firm hierarchical relationships between prince and minister, father and son, husband and wife, older brother and younger brother, and friend and friend (Westwood, 1992). The role prescriptions and hierarchical aspects of filial piety, *Xiaojing* and *Wu Lun*, are extended beyond the natural family and transferred to Chinese organizations (Redding, 1990). This natural acceptance of hierarchy creates an inbuilt legitimacy for the relationship between superior and subordinate in the society (Redding, 1990). Subordinates accept the 'patriarchal right' of the owner/head, and of managers, and are deferential and compliant to them (Westwood and Chan, 1995).

Other research including Hofstede's seminal work (1980, 1981, 1983) and research involving Chinese samples outside the Mainland (Redding and Wong, 1986; Redding, 1990; Bond, 1991; Bond and Hwang, 1986) also supports the existence of role prescriptions and hierarchies in the Chinese culture. Generally, Chinese management has been characterized as basically hierarchical and benevolently autocratic (Nelson and Reader, 1985; Redding, 1990; Westwood and Chan, 1995).

LITERATURE REVIEW

Miner's managerial role motivation theory is based on the notion that, certain 'role requirements' occur frequently across a wide range of managerial jobs, at all levels of management, and in a variety of large hierarchical organizations (Miner, 1978). According to this theory, there are seven motivational dimensions corresponding to seven managerial role requirements, which when combined comprise motivation to manage. These dimensions include: favourable attitudes to superiors (authority figures, AF), desire to compete in competitive games (competitive games, CG), desire to compete in competitive situations (competitive situations,

CS), desire to assert oneself (assertive role, AR), desire to exercise power (imposing wishes, IW), desire to be distinct and different (standing out from group, SOFG), and desire to perform routine administrative duties responsibly (routine administrative functions, RAF) (Miner, 1985b; Miner *et al.*, 1995). These dimensions are based on the manner in which large, hierarchical organizations are structured and the roles managers need to fulfill to succeed in these structures.

Miner's hierarchical role motivation theory has been the subject of 36 validity studies in the United States (Miner, 1993). The results of these studies have led to the conclusion that motivation to manage is important for managerial success in hierarchical organizations with at least three levels of management (Miner, 1993; Miner *et al.*, 1995). To be successful, a manager must have the desire and the motivation to fulfill the hierarchical role requirements. In the absence of such motivation, a manager's performance is relatively unsatisfactory (Miner, 1973, 1977, 1978, 1985b).

Motivation to manage has implications for strategic human resource management practices and corporate and national competitiveness (Miner *et al.*, 1995). Motivation to manage can be employed as a tool in strategic resource management systems by improving recruitment, selection, management development and training, and promotion processes. We will discuss these applications in the discussion section.

In previous validity research, managerial motivation has been positively linked to different criterion measures of performance, success and career choice. For example, performance rates in various US organizations have related positively to the levels of motivation to manage (Miner, 1965, 1967, 1968; Quigley, 1979). Prior work has also established a positive link between compensation and promotion rates, and motivation to manage (Miner, 1967, 1968; Holland *et al.*, 1987).

Typically, American for-profit organizations provide higher pay and greater managerial discretion than their non-profit counterparts. As a result, for-profit organizations in the United States attract people with higher levels of motivation to manage compared with the non-profit sector (Miner, 1974, 1989). Miner *et al.* (1991) also found higher, but non-significant, levels of managerial motivation in their for-profit sample compared to the non-profit (state-owned) sample in the PRC.

Research in the United States also has indicated a positive relationship between hierarchical position level and motivation to manage (Miner, 1976; Miner and Miner, 1976). For example, managers in US hierarchical organizations have demonstrated higher levels of motivation to manage than non-managers (Dayani, 1980; Albert, 1981; Miner *et al.*, 1974). Similar findings were found in the PRC (Miner *et al.*, 1991).

Hypotheses

Based on the literature reviewed in the previous section, I postulate the following hypotheses:

Hypothesis 1. There is a positive relationship between three-year performance ratings and motivation to manage in the PRC.

Hypothesis 2. There is a positive relationship between three-year salary increases and motivation to manage in the PRC.

Hypothesis 3. There is a positive relationship between three-year promotion rates and motivation to manage in the PRC.

Hypothesis 4. There is a positive relationship between evaluation of overall performance and motivation to manage in the PRC.

Hypothesis 5. Managers in PRC for-profit organizations possess greater motivation to manage than managers in state-owned enterprises.

Hypothesis 6. Managers in the PRC possess higher levels of motivation to manage compared to non-managers.

THE FIELD STUDY

The Sample

The main data reported in this analysis relate to an empirical study of 194 managers employed in Chinese enterprises in Beijing, Shanghai, and in Guangdong province. One hundred and seventy-two managers (89 per cent) indicated that there were three or more levels of supervision in their organizations. Therefore, almost all organizations fulfill the necessary criterion for applying hierarchical role motivation theory (Miner *et al.*, 1995). This provides evidence for the arguments made earlier in this contribution for the existence of hierarchical organizations in the PRC.

The sample consisted of 8 per cent top managers, 56 per cent middle managers, 27 per cent lower managers, and 9 per cent non-managers. The majority of respondents (70 per cent) were males. The mean age was 38 years and the average formal years of education were 14. The mean experience in the same industry was 14 years (sd = 10.6). The respondents were employed for ten years in their current organization (sd = 8.5) and five years at their present position (sd = 4.8). The organizations in which the participants were employed had an average of 3,400 employees (sd = 8,945) and total annual sales of 523 million RMB (sd = 1.6 billion RMB).

Questionnaire

A three-part questionnaire was used to collect data. Part I consisted of the MSCS-H, Part II solicited personal and organizational information, and Part III contained items related to managerial performance. Motivation to manage is operationalized by a projective instrument titled 'Miner Sentence Completion Scale – Hierarchic' (MSCS-H). The MSCS-H scale contains 40 sentence completion style items, including five filler items to help hide the true purpose of the instrument (Miner, 1964, 1989). Each of the seven motivation to manage subscales is measured by five scoreable items. These items are scored as –1, 0 or +1 reflecting negative, neutral or positive motive towards the concept underlying each item. Thus, each of the seven subscale scores can vary from –5 to +5. An overall motivation to manage score is obtained by adding the seven subscale scores. Therefore, the total score can vary from –35 to +35. Strong motivation to manage is represented by higher positive MSCS-H scores, while negative scores imply weak managerial motivation. Table 1 depicts a description of motivation to manage and its subscales.

MSCS-H contains items such as ' My family doctor . . .', 'Federal judges ...', 'Running for political office ...', 'Playing golf ...' and 'Yacht racing ...', which are not culturally relevant or comprehensible in China. A culturally adapted MSCS-H scale developed by Ebrahimi (1997) was used in this study because of

TABLE 1
MINER SENTENCE COMPLETION SCALE (MSCS-H FOR HIERARCHIC) AND ITS SUBSCALES

Favourable Attitude to Supervisors (Authority Figures, AF)	Positive relationship with supervisors, indicating an attitude of respect and deferring to one's superiors.
Desire to Compete in Competitive Games (CG)	Competition with peers and other managers at the same level involving games or sports.
Desire to Compete in Competitive Siutuations (CS)	Engaging in competition with peers and other managers at the same level involving occupational or work-related activities.
Desire to Assert (Assertive Role, AR)	Being active and assertive in activities that are often viewed as predominantly masculine.
Desire to Exercise Power (Imposing Wishes, IW)	Telling subordinated what to do and using sanctions to influence their behaviours.
Desire to be Distinct (Standing Out from Group, SOFG)	Fulfilling the roles of a distinctive position of unique and highly visible manner.
Desire to Perform Routine Administrative Functions (RAF)	Performing managerial work of routine day-to-day administrative nature.
Motivation to Manage (MSCS-H) Total Score	The sum of the above seven subscale scores which is an indication of the individual's level of managerial motivation.

good reported test–retest reliability scores between the original and the modified scale in studies involving Chinese samples.

Part II of the questionnaire asked the respondents to provide personal information including demographics (age, gender) and educational background (degree, total number of education years). Based on earlier research and the underlying theory (Ebrahimi and Miner, 1991; Miner *et al.*, 1985), these variables should have no effect on motivation to manage. Responses were also sought regarding position title and type (top, middle, lower management, and non-management); functional area; organization type (state-owned *vs* for-profit); organization size (number of employees and total revenues); years of industry experience, and tenure in the present organization and the current position.

In Part III, participants were asked to assess their managerial performance by responding to a number of 10-point Likert-type items anchored from 'unsatisfactory' to 'outstanding'. This self-appraisal scale of managerial performance included the following items:

1. Assessment of three-year performance evaluations received relative to employees of the same rank (PERFEVL3).
2. Assessment of three-year promotions received relative to employees of the same rank (PROMOT3).
3. Assessment of three-year salary increases received relative to employees of the same rank (SALINC3).
4. Assessment of one's overall job performance (PERFOVAL).

The research instrument was translated into Chinese by a professional translation team and then translated back into English by another professional translation group. Inconsistencies were resolved through subsequent discussions aimed at maintaining the equivalency of the two questionnaires (Sekaran, 1983; Nasif *et al.*, 1991). Equivalencies of the questionnaires were assessed by administration of the English and Chinese translated instruments one month apart to a sample of undergraduate business students in Hong Kong. Significant correlations of greater than 0.80 were obtained between the two administrations ($p < .01$). No significant differences between the total or subscale scores were detected between the Chinese and English versions of the questionnaire ($p < .05$). These analyses clearly indicated the equivalency of the original English and the translated Chinese questionnaires.

Limitations

Before proceeding with the analyses of the data, limitations of the study should be addressed. First, the results of this study are based on scores derived from a projective sentence completion scale, which could be susceptible to potential scorer subjectivity. Although it is possible that this subjectivity may have influenced the results, there are a number of reasons to believe that this is not the case. First, the author has more than fifteen years of experience scoring MSCS-H scales. Second, reliability of scoring between the author and Miner were assessed in two trials. Inter-rater reliability scores of greater than 0.88 ($p < .01$) were obtained with no significant differences between the total and subscales scores ($p < .05$). Third, there is great similarity between the total MSCS-H and subscale scores obtained in this research and those reported by Miner *et al.*'s (1991) study of Mainland Chinese middle managers.

Second, we could not use a random sampling procedure or calculate non-response bias given the difficult conditions for collecting research data in the PRC. Third, because of geographical limitations, the sample in this study may not be representative of all Mainland Chinese organizations or their employees.

Fourth, the reliance on self-report measures may raise concerns about the accuracy of respondents' perceptions and their honesty in responding to the questions. Self-appraisals can be problematic because of potential self-serving biases. Given the difficult data collection conditions present in the PRC, we had no other means of assessing managerial performance. Use of similar self-appraisal scales is abundant in the literature (for example, Judge and Bretz, 1994; Ashford and Saks, 1996; Korsgaard, 1996; Furnham and Stringfield, 1998).

There are mixed reports of leniency or modesty bias in self-appraisals. For example, US studies indicate that self-appraisals of performance are more lenient than either peer or supervisory ratings (for example, Thornton, 1980; Shore and Thornton, 1986; Fox and Dinur, 1988). A study involving Chinese employees, however, asserts that these employees exhibit a modesty bias, reporting lower job performance than their supervisors (Farh *et al.*, 1991). Another study states that employees in the PRC exhibit a leniency bias similar to that shown in the United States (Yu and Murphy, 1993).

The leniency bias appears to be more profound when self-appraisals are used for granting rewards (Farh and Werbel, 1986). Because self-appraisals in this study are used for non-reward purposes, participants have nothing to gain or lose by being either lenient or modest. Furthermore, even if a leniency bias exists in the responses from our managers, it should operate consistently across the entire sample and should not impact these results.

The fact that motivation to manage scores obtained in this study are very similar to those reported by Miner *et al.*'s (1991) research involving PRC middle managers, however, may alleviate some of the concerns about the inherent limitations of this study. The results of the study follow.

RESULTS

Analysis of variance (ANOVA) was utilized to examine the influence of age, gender, educational background, and location in which the data were collected on motivation to manage. The results indicated no statistically significant influence exerted by demographic variables, educational background, or location on motivation to manage scores.

Table 2 depicts the means and standard deviations for subscale and total MSCS-H scores for the Chinese sample. Correlation analyses were used to test the hypotheses. Except for the self-reported salary increases received over the past three-year period, all the other self-appraisal measures of performance were significantly related to the MSCS-H total score. Total MSCS-H scores were also significantly and positively related to measures of position type (management *vs* non-management). These significant correlations indicated higher levels of motivation to manage for managers as compared to non-managers. All relationships were in the expected direction.

Contrary to expectations, there was no significant relation between MSCS-H total score and employment in state-owned relative to for-profit organizations. Based on the results of the correlation analyses, Hypotheses 1, 3, 4 and 6 received support. Hypotheses 2 and 5, however, were not supported. Overall, the correlation matrix results moderately support the theory.

The research further tested Hypotheses 5 and 6 using analysis of variance. These hypotheses posited higher levels of motivation to manage in for-profit organizations and for managers. ANOVA results are presented in Table 3. Except for one subscale score, there were no significant differences between other subscales of motivation to manage of individuals employed by state-owned enterprises and for-profit firms. There were also no significant differences in the overall motivation to manage of managers of these two organization types. Similar to the results obtained in the correlation analyses, Hypothesis 5 was rejected.

Hypothesis 6 posited higher motivation to manage for managers relative to non-managers. Results indicated that managers possessed higher levels of MSCS-H total scores, imposing wishes, and routine administrative function dimensions than non-managers did. Hypothesis 6, therefore, was supported.

TABLE 2
MSCS-H TOTAL AND SUBSCALE SCORES FOR THE TOTAL SAMPLE (n = 194)

MSCS-H and subscales	Mean score (standard deviation)
Total score	4.25 (5.23)
Authority Figures (AF)	0.98 (1.32)
Competitive Games (CG)	1.05 (1.80)
Competitive Situations (CS)	0.14 (1.40)
Assertive Role (AR)	0.79 (1.54)
Imposing Wishes (IW)	0.01 (1.18)
Standing Out from Group (SOFG)	0.82 (1.26)
Routine Administrative Functions (RAF)	0.45 (1.17)

TABLE 3
MSCS-H TOTAL AND SUBSCALE SCORES FOR THE TOTAL SAMPLE (n = 194) AND ANOVA RESULTS COMPARING MANAGERS AND NON-MANAGERS AND FOR-PROFIT AND STATE-OWNED

MSCS-H and Subscales	Mean (SD) Total Sample (*n* = 194)	Mean scores			Mean scores		
		M (*n* = 176)	N (*n* = 18)	F (*df* = 1,192)	FP (*n* = 107)	SOE (*n* = 87)	F (*df* = 1,192)
Total Score	4.25 (5.23)	4.50	1.78	4.50*	4.12	4.40	0.14
AF	0.98 (1.32)	0.97	1.11	0.20	0.97	0.99	0.01
CG	1.05 (1.80)	1.10	0.50	1.83	1.02	1.08	0.06
CS	0.14 (1.40)	0.19	–0.33	2.34	0.20	0.08	0.33
AR	0.79 (1.54)	0.81	0.61	0.28	0.79	0.79	0.00
IW	0.01 (1.18)	0.06	–0.50	3.77*	–0.01	0.03	0.07
SOFG	0.82 (1.26)	0.86	0.44	1.82	0.59	1.10	8.01**
RAF	0.45 (1.17)	0.50	–0.06	3.77*	0.55	0.32	1.87

Key
M: managers; NM: non-managers; FP: for-profit; SOE: state-owned enterprises

Note: * $p < .05$; ** $p < .01$.

DISCUSSION

Theoretical Implications

The purpose of this research was to test the applicability of motivation to manage in the People's Republic of China. Given the difficult conditions under which the data collection was conducted, this study achieves its stated objectives. Although two of the hypotheses were not supported, the majority of findings are consistent with the theory and supportive of the postulated hypotheses. Contrary to expectations, there are no differences between motivation to manage of employees of state-owned and for-profit organizations. There are a number of possible explanations for this finding. First, until recently most Mainland Chinese for-profit organizations were state-owned enterprises and, thus, major differences between the two sectors may not be apparent. Second, the slower job mobility that exists in the PRC may lead to a delay in the movement of higher motivated managers from the state-owned enterprises to the newly formed private enterprises. Finally, these findings are consistent with prior research by Miner and his colleagues (1991) which found minimal but non-significant differences between the managers in these two sectors.

Other findings consistent with our expectations compensate for the lack of significant differences between motivation to manage of managers in the state-owned and for-profit sectors. Consistent with expectations, managers score higher on MSCS-H than non-managers. This finding is substantiated using both correlation analysis and analysis of variance.

Positive and mostly significant relationships between motivation to manage and multiple self-appraisal measures of performance exist. Motivation to manage consistently exerts a great influence on self-appraisals such as assessment of overall performance, three-year performance and promotions.

Managerial Implications

Based on the evidence provided in this study, motivation to manage and its main construct, MSCS-H, are applicable in the PRC. Therefore, similar to the US case, motivation to manage is an appropriate construct to be utilized in the strategic human resource management of Chinese organizations (Miner, 1993; Miner *et al.*,

1995). In other words, Chinese organizations can use motivation to manage to increase the effectiveness of their strategic human resource management (Butler *et al.*, 1991). Through improved recruitment, selection, management training and development, and promotion processes, motivation to manage can increase the effectiveness of strategic human resource management system in Chinese organizations.

An effective recruitment system draws upon the largest possible pool of managerial talent. Research in the United States with American and non-American samples (Miner *et al.*, 1995) and in Hong Kong and China (Ebrahimi, 1996; Ebrahimi, Young, and Luk, 1998; Chen *et al.*, 1997) indicate no significant differences between motivation to manage of females and males. Therefore, Chinese organizations are advised to provide equal opportunities to women in their managerial recruitment and selection processes. The recruitment net should be as wide as possible to attract the largest number of qualified and managerial motivated individuals.

Insofar as selection is concerned, the objective is to sort through the pool of potential candidates and identify the ones with highest motivation to manage who possess other needed qualifications. This search may be implemented by using the modified MSCS-H used in this study or other similar selection instruments. In addition, an assessment of prior managerial performance or interviews designed to probe into motivation to manage of the candidates may be utilized.

During the selection process, a company should hire a large number of highly motivated candidates, put them into fast tracks so their performance can be monitored and evaluated, and promote the best performers into higher managerial positions. The ideal system will provide the best opportunities to individuals with the highest motivation to manage. Comprehensive psychological assessments as part of the tracking and evaluation process can serve a very useful purpose (Hansen and Conrad, 1991). Managerial promotion based on seniority and other non-performance criteria such as family or *guanxi* connections (Leung *et al.*, 1996; Xin and Pearce, 1996; Luo, 1997) would hinder organizational as well as national competitiveness and should ideally be discarded (Miner *et al.*, 1995).

Motivation to manage training can also be used to improve managerial motivation levels in Chinese organizations. Miner

(1985a) and Miner and his colleagues (1995) outline a summary of management development programmes designed to increase motivation to manage (Miner, 1965, 1977, 1985a, 1986). These management development programmes usually require participants to receive between 15 and 30 hours of motivation to manage training. The training usually focuses on demonstrating the challenges and satisfactions, and some of the pitfalls inherent in managerial careers (Miner *et al.*, 1995). The training can increase the levels of motivation to manage of the participants and make them more effective managers for hierarchical organizations. Not everyone, however, benefits equally from participation in this training programme. Generally, the training appears most effective for individuals already identified by companies as potential managers. The training programme is fully outlined in Miner's (1985a) book *People Problems: The Executive Answer Book*.

Similarly, promotion practices in Chinese organizations need to be congruent with their strategic human resource management requirements (Butler *et al.*, 1991). The objective is to promote the most able, yet managerially motivated, individuals to the top of Chinese organizations as fast as possible.

In sum, the applicability of motivation to manage and MSCS-H in China as supported by the research outlined in this article and elsewhere (Miner *et al.*, 1991; Ebrahimi, 1997; Ebrahimi *et al.*, 1998) provides a new tool for more effective strategic human resource management practices in Chinese organizations. As a result of using the motivation to manage construct, Chinese organizations can improve their recruitment, selection, management development and training, and promotion and ultimately their strategic human resource management systems.

Directions for Future Research

Future research should utilize supplemental data from other sources such as company records, peers and supervisors. Research also should expand the geographic representation and be more rigorous in sampling procedures. Furthermore, future studies should use other constructs of managerial effectiveness in conjunction with Miner's Sentence Completion Scale – Hierarchic to assess concurrent validity of the scale. Finally, research should incorporate individual measures of job-related abilities and skills and leadership as well as organizational measures such as culture in their design.

CONCLUSIONS

The main purpose of this study was to extend previous research to test the applicability of hierarchical role motivation theory and its main construct (MSCS-H) in China. A culturally modified MSCS-H was completed by a sample of 194 Chinese full-time employees. A prerequisite for the applicability of the hierarchical role motivation theory is the existence of hierarchies with three or more levels of management. Although I did not set a priori this required number of managerial levels in the sampling process, more than 89 per cent of the respondents indicated the existence of three or more managerial levels in their organizations.

This research advances the hierarchical role motivation theory and its applicability under 'adverse conditions' in the People's Republic of China. The findings of this empirical study seem to be supportive of the descriptive arguments presented earlier indicating the existence of the hierarchical form of organizations and the applicability of the managerial role motivation theory and its main construct (MSCS-H) in the People's Republic of China.

Chinese organizations are 'witnessing the emergence of a more complex, *hybrid* management model' (Warner, 1997: 31). As Chinese enterprises slowly begin to abandon 'iron rice bowl' practices involving 'jobs for life' and 'cradle-to-grave' systems of treating their employees and managers (Warner, 1995, 1997), new strategic human resource management systems are required. Chinese enterprises need to adopt new recruitment, selection, management training and development, and promotion policies that are based on managerial abilities, motivation and performance. As in the West, hierarchical role motivation theory and its main construct MSCS-H may prove a valuable tool in the selection and promotion of motivated and potentially effective managers. The progress towards utilization of such practices, similar to other HRM systems (Warner, 1997), may remain slow.

Motivation to manage is repeatedly shown to be a major cause of managerial effectiveness in the United States (Miner, 1993; Miner *et al.*, 1995) and in China (Miner *et al.*, 1991; Ebrahimi *et al.*, 1998; the present study). Miner and his colleagues (1995) have argued that motivation to manage ultimately defines the competitiveness of organizations and nations. This is because management talent is a core ingredient of organizational effectiveness which in turn is crucial in establishing competitiveness of nations in an increasingly global marketplace. Accordingly, Chinese organizations in their quest in global competitiveness need to enhance their strategic human resource management systems. Motivation to manage may prove invaluable in the ultimate quest for China's corporate and national competitiveness.

ACKNOWLEDGEMENTS

The collaboration of Vivienne W. M. Luk and the financial support of a grant from Hong Kong Baptist University (FRG/95-96/II88) in the collection of data on which this research is based is acknowledged and greatly appreciated. The contributions of John B. Miner to the development of the underlying theory and Sandra A. Young's help during various stages of this project are appreciated. The usual disclaimer applies.

REFERENCES

Albert, M. (1981), 'A Comparison of the Managerial Motivation of Creative vs. Managerial Personnel', *Proceedings, Southern Management Association*, Vol.20, pp.40–42.

Arsan, N., Hunsicker, F.R. and Southern, L.J.F. (1983), 'A Comparative Study of the Motivation to Manage of Turkish, South African and US Managers', *Southern Management Association Proceedings*, Vol.22, pp.114–16.

Ashford, B.E. and Saks, A.M. (1996), 'Socialization Tactics: Longitudinal Effects on Newcomer Adjustment', *Academy of Management Journal*, Vol.39, No.1, pp.149–78.

Basuray, M.T., Eberhardt, B.J. and Scherling, S.A. (1985), 'Comparative Analysis of Need Structures and Managerial Motive Patterns in Chinese and American Business Students: Implications for Management Development in Cultural Contexts'. Paper Presented at the Second Pan-Pacific Conference on Business, Economic and Technological Exchange, Seoul, Korea, May 1985.

Boisot, M. and Child, J. (1988), 'The Iron Law of Fiefs: Bureaucratic Failure and the Problem of Governance in the Chinese Economic Reforms', *Administrative Science Quarterly*, Vol.33, No.4, pp.507–27.

Bond, M.H. (1991), *Beyond the Chinese Face: Insights From Psychology*. New York: Oxford University Press.

Bond, M.H. and Hwang, K.K. (1986), 'The Social Psychology of the Chinese People', in M.H. Bond (ed.), *The Psychology of Chinese People*. Hong Kong: Oxford University Press, pp.213–66.

Butler, J.E., Ferris, G.R. and Napier, N.K. (1991), *Strategy and Human Resource Management*. Cincinnati, OH: South-western.

Chen, C.C., Yu, K.C. and Miner, J.B. (1997), 'Motivation to Manage: A Study of Women in Chinese State-owned Enterprises', *Journal of Applied Behavioral Science*, Vol.33, No.2, pp.160–73.

Dayani, M.H. (1980), 'Academic Library Managers and Their Motivation to Manage'. Unpublished Ph.D. Dissertation, Rutgers, The State University of New Jersey, New Brunswick, NJ.

Ebrahimi, B. (1985), 'Measuring the Effects of Cultural and Other Explanatory Variables on Motivation to Manage of Potential Managers from Five Countries: A Case of Theory Building and Theory Testing in Cross-cultural Research'. Unpublished Ph.D. Dissertation, Georgia State University, Atlanta, GA.

Ebrahimi, B.P. (1996), 'Managerial Motivation and Sex Roles in Hong Kong'. Paper Presented at the Academy of Management Meetings, Boston, MA, 8–13 August.

Ebrahimi, B.P. (1997), 'Motivation to Manage in Hong Kong: Modification and Test of Miner Sentence Completion Scale-H', *Journal of Managerial Psychology*, Vol.12, No.6, pp.401–14.

Ebrahimi, B. and Miner, J.B. (1991), 'The Cultural Dynamics of Managerial Motivation among Students from Pan-Pacific Basin Countries', *Journal of Global Business*, Vol.2, No.1, pp.87–98.

Ebrahimi, B. and Young, S. (1996), 'Managerial Motivation: A Cross-cultural Validity Study of Miner Sentence Completion Scale (MSCS)', *Research in International Business Disciplines*, Vol.2, pp.15–30.

Ebrahimi, B.P., Young, S.A. and Parsa, F. (1997), 'A Comparative Study of Motivation to Manage of Business Students in Hong Kong and the United States', *Proceedings of the Southeast Decision Sciences Institute Twenty-seven Annual Meetings*. Atlanta, GA, 26–28 February.

Ebrahimi, B.P., Luk, V.W.M and Young, S.A. (1998), 'Motivation to Manage in the People's Republic of China', *Proceedings of the International Conference of Pacific Rim Management*. Vancouver, Canada, 15–16 August, pp.114–19.

Ebrahimi, B.P., Young, S.A., Luk, V.W.M. (1998), 'Motivation to Manage of Female and Male Managers: A Hong Kong Perspective'. Paper Presented at the Inaugural Asia Academy of Management, Hong Kong, SARPRC, 29 December.

Farh, J.L. and Werbel, J.D. (1986), 'The Effects of Purpose of the Appraisal and Expectation of Validation on Self-appraisals Leniency', *Journal of Applied Psychology*, Vol.71, pp.527–9.

Farh, J.L., Dobbins, G.H. and Cheng, B.S. (1991), 'Cultural Relativity in Action: A Comparison of Self-ratings Made by Chinese and US Workers', *Personnel Psychology*, Vol.44, No.1, pp.129–47.

Fox, S. and Dinur, Y. (1988), 'Validation of Self-assessment: A Field Evaluation', *Personnel Psychology*, Vol.41, No.4, pp.581–92.

Furnham, A. and Stringfield, P. (1998), 'Congruence in Job-performance Ratings: A Study of 360° Feedback Examining Self, Manager, Peers and Consultant Rating', *Human Relations*, Vol.51, No.4, pp.517–30.

Hansen, C.P. and Conrad, K.A. 1991. A H*andbook of Psychological Assessment in Business.* New York: Quorum.

Hofstede, G. (1980), *Culture's Consequences: International Differences in Work-related Values.* Beverly Hills, CA: Sage.

Hofstede, G. (1981), 'Culture and Organizations', *International Studies of Management and Organization*, Vol.10, No.4, pp.15–41.

Hofstede, G. (1983), 'The Cultural Relativity of Organizational Practices and Theories', *Journal of International Business Studies*, Vol.14, No.3, pp.75–89.

Holland, M.G., Black, C.H. and Miner, J.B. (1987), 'Using Managerial Role Motivation Theory to Predict Career Success', *Health Care Management Review*, Vol.12, No.4, pp.57–64.

Judge, T.A. and Bretz, R.D. (1994), 'Political Influence Behaviour and Career Success', *Journal of Management*, Vol.20, No.1, pp.43–65.

Korsgaard, M.A. (1996), 'The Impact of Self-appraisals on Reactions to Feedback from Others: The Role of Self-enhancement and Self-consistency Concerns', *Journal of Organizational Behaviour*, Vol.17, No.2, pp.301–11.

Leung, T.K.P., Wong, Y.H. and Wong, S. (1996), 'A Study of Hong Kong Businessmen's Perceptions of the Role of 'Guanxi' in the People's Republic of China', *Journal of Business Ethics*, Vol.15, No.4, pp.749–58.

Lockett, M. (1988), 'Culture and Problems of Chinese Management', *Organization Studies*, Vol.9, No.4, pp.475–96.

Luo, Y. (1997), 'Guanxi and Performance of Foreign Investment Enterprises in China: An Empirical Inquiry', *Management International Review*, Vol.37, No.1, pp.57–70.

Miner, J.B. (1963), *The Management of Ineffective Performance.* New York: McGraw Hill.

Miner, J.B. (1964), *Scoring Guide for the Miner Sentence Completion Scale.* Eugene, OR: Organizational Measurement Systems Press (originally published by Springer Publishing Company).

Miner, J.B. (1965), *Studies in Management Education.* Eugene, OR: Organizational Measurement Systems Press (originally published by Springer Publishing Company).

Miner, J.B. (1967), *The School Administrator and Organizational Character.* Eugene, OR: University of Oregon Press.

Miner, J.B. (1968), 'The Managerial Motivation of School Administrators', *Educational Administrative Quarterly*, Vol.4, No.1, pp.55–71.

Miner, J.B. (1973), 'The Real Crunch in Managerial Manpower', *Harvard Business Review*, Vol.51, No.6, pp.146–58.

Miner, J.B. (1974), 'The Organization for Motivation', in J. W. McGuire (ed.), *Contemporary Management: Issues and Viewpoints.* Englewood Cliffs, NJ: Prentice-Hall, pp.575–8.

Miner, J.B. (1976), 'Levels of Motivation to Manage among Personnel and Industrial Relations Managers', *Journal of Applied Psychology*, Vol.61, No.4, pp.419–27.

Miner, J.B. (1977), *Motivation to Manage: A Ten Year Update on the 'Studies in Management Education' Research.* Eugene, OR: Organizational Measurement Systems Press.

Miner, J.B. (1978), 'Twenty Years of Research on Role Motivation Theory of Managerial Effectiveness', *Personnel Psychology*, Vol.31, No.4, pp.739–60.

Miner, J.B. (1980), 'A Rationale for the Limited Domain Approach to the Study of Motivation', in C.C. Pinder and L.F. Moore (eds), *Middle Range Theory and the Study of Organizations.* Boston: Martinus Nijhoff, pp.334–6.

Miner, J.B. (1985a), *People Problems: The Executive Answer Book.* Buffalo, NY: Organizational Measurement Systems Press (originally published by Random House).

Miner, J.B. (1985b), 'Sentence Completion Measures in Personnel Research: The Development and Validation of the Miner Sentence Completion Scales', in H.J. Bernardin and D.A. Bownas (eds), *Personality Assessments in Organizations.* New York: Praeger, pp.145–76.

Miner, J.B. (1986), 'Managerial Role Motivation Training', *Journal of Managerial Psychology.* Vol.1, No.1, pp.25–30.

Miner, J.B. (1989), *Scoring Guide for the Miner Sentence Completion Scale – Form H – 1989 Supplement.* Eugene, OR: Organizational Measurement Systems Press.

Miner, J.B. (1993), *Role Motivation Theories.* London: Routledge.

Miner, J.B. and Miner, M.G. (1976), 'Managerial Characteristics of Personnel Managers', *Industrial Relations*, Vol.15, No.2, pp.225–34.

Miner, J.B., Chen, C.C. and Yu, K.C. (1991), 'Theory Testing under Adverse Conditions: Motivation to Manage in the People's Republic of China', *Journal of Applied Psychology*, Vol.76, pp.343–9.

Miner, J.B., Ebrahimi, B. and Wachtel, J.M. (1995), 'How Deficiencies in Motivation to Manage Contribute to America's Competitiveness Problem (and What Can Be Done about It)', *Human Resource Management*, Vol.34, No.3, pp.363–87.

Miner, J.B., Smith, N.R. and Ebrahimi, B. (1985), 'Further Considerations in the Decline and Stabilization of Managerial Motivation: A Rejoinder to Bartol, Anderson and Schneier (1980)', *Journal of Vocational Behavior*, Vol.26, No.2, pp.290–8.

Miner, J.B., Wachtel, J.M. and Ebrahimi, B. (1989), 'The Managerial Motivation of Potential Managers in the United States and Other Countries of the World: Implications for National Competitiveness and the Productivity Problem', *Advances in International Comparative Management*, Vol.4, pp.147–70.

Miner, J.B., Rizzo, J.R., Harlow, D.N. and Hill, J.W. (1974), 'Role Motivation Theory of Managerial Effectiveness in Simulated Organizations of Varying Degrees of Structure', *Journal of Applied Psychology*, Vol.59, No.1, pp.31–7.

Mintzberg, H. (1983), *Power in and around Organizations.* Englewood Cliffs, NJ: Prentice-Hall.

Nasif, E.G., Al-Daeaj, H.S., Ebrahimi, B. and Thibodeaux, M.S. (1991), 'Methodological Problems in Cross–cultural Research: An Updated Review', *Management International Review*, Vol.31, No.1, pp.79–91.

Nelson, J.A. and Reader, J.A. (1985), 'Labour Relations in China', *California Management Review*, Vol.27, No.4, pp.13–32.

Nevis, E.C. (1983), 'Cultural Assumptions and Productivity: the United States and China',

Sloan Management Review, Vol.24, No.3, pp.17–29.

Oliver, J.E. (1982), 'An Instrument for Classifying Organizations', *Academy of Management Journal*, Vol.25, No.4, pp.855–66.

Quigley, J.V. (1979), 'Predicting Managerial Success in the Public Sector: Concurrent Validation of Biodata and the Miner Sentence Completion Scale in the Georgia Department of Human Resources'. Unpublished Ph.D. Dissertation. Georgia State University, Atlanta, GA.

Redding, S.G. (1990), *The Spirit of Chinese Capitalism*. Berlin: De Gruyter.

Redding, S.G. and Wong, G.Y.Y. (1986), 'The Psychology of Chinese People and its Varying Relevance in Hong Kong and Singapore', *Asia Pacific Journal of Management*, Vol.3, pp.76–98.

Rowley, Chris. (1997), 'Introduction: Comparisons and Perspectives on HRM in the Asia Pacific', *Asia Pacific Business Review*, Vol.3, No.4, pp.1–18.

Sekaran, U. (1983), 'Methodological and Theoretical Issues and Advancements in Cross-cultural Research', *Journal of International Business Studies*, Vol.14, No.2, pp.61–74.

Shore, L.M. and Thornton, G.C., III (1986), 'Effects of Gender on Self- and Supervisory-ratings', *Academy of Management*, Vol.29, No.2, pp.115–29.

Singleton, T.M., Kelley, A., Yao, E. and White, L.P. (1987), 'Motivation to Manage: People's Republic of China and Hong Kong', *Southern Management Association Proceedings*, Vol.25, pp.34–6.

Southern, L.J.F. and Pih, P. (1987), 'A Comparative Study of the Motivation to Manage of Taiwanese, Turkish and US Business Students'. Paper presented at the 26th Southern Management Association Meetings, New Orleans, LA, November 1987.

Thornton, G.C. (1980), 'Psychometric Properties of Self–appraisals of Job Performance', *Personnel Psychology*, Vol.33, pp.263–71.

Warner, M. (1995), *The Management of Human Resources in Chinese Industry*. London, Macmillan.

Warner, M. (1997), 'China's HRM in Transition: Towards Relative Convergence?', *Asia Pacific Business Review*, Vol.3, No.3, pp.19–33.

Weber, M. (1968), *Economy and Society*. New York: Bedminster Press.

Westwood, R.I. (1992), 'Culture, Cultural Differences and Organizational Behaviour', in R.I. Westwood (ed.), *Organizational Behaviour: Southeast Asian Perspectives*. Hong Kong: Longman Group (Far East) Ltd, pp.27–62.

Westwood, R.I. and Chan, A. (1995), 'The Transferability of Leadership Training in the East Asian Context', *Asia Pacific Business Review*, Vol.2, No.1, pp.68–92.

Xin, K.R. and Pearce, J.C. (1996), 'Connections as Substitutes for Formal Institutional Support', *Academy of Management Journal*, Vol.39, No.4, pp.1641–58.

Yu, J. and Murphy, K.R. (1993), 'Modesty Bias in Self-ratings of Performance: A Test of the Cultural Sensitivity Hypothesis', *Personnel Psychology*, Vol.46, No.3, pp.357–63.

11

The 'Myth' of Human Resource Management in Chinese Enterprises

MALCOLM WARNER, KEITH GOODALL and DANIEL Z. DING

China has undergone many far-reaching changes since Deng Xiaoping introduced the 'Four Modernizations' (of Agriculture, Industry, Science and Technology, and Defence) and 'Open Door' policies at the end of the 1970s. After Mao Zedong's death, Deng initiated the move from a 'command' towards a 'socialist market' economy, albeit 'with Chinese characteristics' (Naughton, 1996).

State-owned enterprises (SOEs) once dominated industrial production. Such work-units (*danwei*, as they were called), embodied the so-called 'iron rice-bowl' (*tie fan wan*) which ensured 'jobs for life' and 'cradle-to-grave' welfare for mostly urban industrial SOE employees (Lu and Perry, 1997). Now, a wider range of ownership has been introduced, most notably joint-venture firms (JVs) whereby state enterprises have linked up with foreign business partners. Joint venture collaborations were introduced from the early 1980s in order for China to obtain the transfer of both technical 'hardware' and managerial 'software'. Deng believed such firms would also produce goods on a substantial scale for export (Naughton, 1996).

The PRC received a vast flood of inward investment after 1979; China now has over 315,000 agreed foreign investments, of which about half have been implemented. State firms, having contributed two-thirds of China's industrial production, now account for less than a third (Lardy, 1998). A central feature of the reforms has been the development of equity joint ventures, though many fully foreign-funded enterprises have been set up (Vanhonacker, 1997). The country has been the largest recipient of such funds amongst developing countries. Some JVs have involved taking over existing state-owned plant and equipment, while others have been developed on 'greenfield sites' (Tsang, 1998). China has increasingly opened its door to foreign funds (and continues to do so), though this has mostly been in manufacturing. Only recently, service industries have been opened up to foreign investors. However, a disproportionate amount of investment has gone to the coastal areas and much less inland. Multinational corporations from the West and Japan have been prominent in setting up the larger JVs and have in important ways facilitated 'hard' technology transfer. Many of the wholly owned foreign funded enterprises (FFEs), on the other hand, have been on a smaller scale and mainly founded by overseas Chinese investors, especially from Hong Kong and Taiwan. Above all, the JVs and FFEs were intended to foster 'soft' technology transfer, such as the introduction of Western (and Japanese) modern management methods. The goal was to have 'role-model' enterprises for Chinese management in SOEs to emulate. State-of-the-art JVs and FFEs would provide 'bench-mark' exemplars. Reform of SOE human resource management was a major aim of this exercise, and this contribution attempts to see how far significant change has been achieved and how far reform has been 'mythical'.

The enterprise reforms that occurred in the 1980s and early1990s were aimed at phasing out the 'iron rice bowl'. Managers were given more autonomy, particularly to hire and fire, and decision making was decentralized with regard not only to personnel but also to marketing and purchasing issues (Child, 1994). Many, though not all, JVs had already incorporated such practices in their management systems (Goodall and Warner, 1997). Personnel reforms involving the introduction of labour contracts, performance-related rewards systems and contributory social insurance were also introduced (see Ng and Warner, 1998). Initially, separate sets of government regulations governed the JVs and FFEs, but later reforms applied to both state and non-state enterprises.

We have attempted in this investigation to see what the differential effects of ownership forms have been on changes in labour management in industrial enterprises. If the general thrust of the government's reforms was to use foreign firms as exemplars, then we would expect the effects of the reforms to have been most visible in JVs rather than SOEs, since many of the management reforms were first implemented in the former rather than in the latter.

METHODOLOGY

This study basically adopted a case-study approach for data collection. Hence, in-depth interviews were conducted in 62 Chinese firms, both JVs and SOEs, with managers, technicians, trade union representatives and workers. A semi-structured questionnaire was used during the interview for gathering both quantitative and qualitative information (see Goodall and Warner, 1998). The sample firms were located in seven major Chinese cities: Beijing, Dalian, Jin'an, Nanjing, Shanghai, Guangzhou and Zhongqing. These cities are located in the north and north east, the central east coast areas, the south, and also the inland regions, and therefore approximate to a nationwide coverage. The firms can be broadly classified into the following industrial sectors: engineering, electrical engineering, electronics, chemicals, and pharmaceuticals. The size of the firms ranges from small to medium to very large. In each location, we attempted, whenever possible, to match JVs with corresponding SOEs in the same industry. This effort was constrained by the distribution of firms in each sector, and difficulties of access to Chinese firms. The degree of matching was thus relative rather than absolute. The major characteristics of the firms are summarized in Table 1.

MAJOR FINDINGS

The Employment System

The reform of the employment system in SOEs is focused on attempts to break the so-called 'iron rice bowl', a system of unified job allocation, guaranteed lifelong employment, and cradle-to-grave welfare (Warner, 1996; Yip, 1996). This rigid employment model existed for several decades before economic reform, and resulted in low productivity and the need for dramatic reductions in staffing. In the early 1980s, a labour contract system emerged and was tried on an experimental basis in eight regions, representing a major departure from the traditional centralized allocation of labour (Korzec, 1992; Zhuang, 1994). During this experimental phase, increasing numbers of SOEs were granted greater degrees of autonomy in running business operations, and were also held accountable for their own profits or losses. The

TABLE 1
CHARACTERISTICS OF CHINESE ENTERPRISES SAMPLED (N = 62)*

	Number of JVs	Number of SOEs
Location		
Dalian	6	5
Beijing	3	3
Jinan	6	6
Shanghai	10	12
Guangzhou	5	6
Number of employees		
Less than 200	2	0
200–499	12	4
500–1,499	10	6
Above 1,500	6	22
Turnover in 1996		
Less than 10m (RMB yuan)	1	0
10m–100m	11	7
100m–1,000m	12	16
Above 1,000m	4	5

* Casing of missing data are mainly due to confidentiality of responses in a limited number of firms.

1994 Labour Law, which came into effect on 1 January 1995, eventually formalized the labour contract system. The new law required all employees, regardless of the types of ownership of their employers, to be hired on labour contracts. Thus, a formerly centrally planned employment system has been gradually transformed into a more market-orientated, extensive labour contract system.

Foreign-invested enterprises were allowed to operate in a market-orientated fashion after China opened its door to foreign investment in 1978. However, although they were free to determine the size of their staff and recruit workers and senior managerial personnel according to their business needs, their employment practices were constrained by the emergent nature of the labour market and the organizational inheritance of practices from their Chinese JV partners.

Our study investigated the differences in recruitment practices and employment contracts used by JVs *vis-à-vis* SOEs. As illustrated in Table 2, a larger number of JVs adopted market-orientated recruitment than SOEs, while the majority of SOEs adopted 'hybrid' practices in recruiting new employees. Individual contracts were much more extensively used in JVs than collective contracts. Interviews with senior managers and personnel directors in the firms studied revealed that, in joint venture companies, the external labour market (for example, various job fairs), advertising in the local media, and campus recruiting for university and college graduates are the three most frequently used channels in recruiting new employees. A nascent labour market has emerged in China in recent years, which offers JVs a greater degree of freedom in choosing production workers. Advertisements by reputable JVs, especially prestigious multinational corporations, attract numerous applicants. Graduates from leading universities and colleges are seen as the best candidates for JVs in high-tech industries. University-based recruiting has become increasingly popular. Few major JVs simply took employees transferred from their Chinese partner's parent company, or accepted new ones assigned by labour bureaux (Goodall and Warner, 1998).

Our study found that recruitment practices were clearly less market-orientated in SOEs compared with JVs. The two major sources of new employees for SOEs in the sample are workers recommended by the labour bureaux, and recruits from company-affiliated vocational schools. Since the beginning of the labour reforms, the role of labour bureaux has gradually changed from directly assigning new workers to enterprises to recommending job applicants. However, due to lack of experience in the labour market, many SOEs still depend on labour bureaux for hiring new employees, making only limited attempts to recruit workers through market channels. Many large, long-established SOEs have their own affiliated vocational schools to provide technical training for their workers. These schools also enrolled a large number of children of employees and offered them jobs after they graduated as part of their employees' welfare programme.

In spite of significant disparities in recruitment channels, JVs and SOEs shared some similarities in selection criteria. All firms in the sample considered previous work experience and personal ability the most important criteria in selecting new recruits. Job interviews and oral and written tests were used by JVs and SOEs alike as the primary methods for choosing qualified employees.

Reward Systems

Before the economic reforms, China adopted a centrally administered reward system, characterized by a flat structure which reflected an egalitarian mentality (Warner, 1995). Wages were not closely linked to individual or corporate performance. The reform of the reward system was first attempted in the late 1970s and early 1980s by incorporating flexible, performance-based elements into the wage system. In addition to the basic wage, a variety of incentives were introduced, such as the functional wage (based on status or seniority), and the floating wage (based on performance). Piece rates and daily rates were restored, especially in labour-intensive industries. Decentralization in the state sector gave the SOEs greater authority in designing their wage and bonus schemes. The 1994 Labour Law further legitimized the rights of the employer in determining the form and level of reward according to the characteristics of business operations and profitability. The law tries to enforce minimum wage requirements across the country to guarantee the basic needs of employees.

Our survey examined the reward systems in the 62 sampled firms. Table 2 shows that employees, in general, were paid more in JVs than in SOEs. For example, in 1996, workers in JVs, on average, earned RMB 1,004 yuan per month, compared with the RMB 755 yuan per month earned by workers in SOEs. Interviews in the surveyed firms revealed that senior managers in many JVs earned nearly three times as much as their counterparts in SOEs. It was also found that the wage structure in JVs was much steeper than in SOEs, as the wage differentials between a production worker and a senior manager in a joint venture could be as high as RMB 5,000, while in SOEs it was (nominally at least) no more than RMB 600. The relatively flat wage structure in the SOEs clearly reflected a persistent egalitarian mentality.

Forms of reward were found to be similar in both JVs and SOEs, with both using basic salary plus bonus, and an array of allowances, though we found that the details varied. In most cases, the differentials in income were determined not by basic salary, but by the performance-based bonuses and allowances based on position, seniority, skills. JVs for the most part designed their own wage systems and defined the scales of bonus and other rewards (though see Goodall and Warner (1997) for an example of an American JV with multiple Chinese partners which simply took on the SOE reward system). Although some SOEs asserted that they were still using the traditional eight-grade system, they had nonetheless introduced performance-related bonuses. Performance, corporate profit, ability and position were the most important elements used by the majority of sampled firms, both JVs and SOEs, as criteria for determining rewards.

Social Insurance System

Prior to the economic reforms, the fully company-funded 'iron rice bowl' comprehensive welfare benefits, covering illness, injury, pregnancy, death or retirement, were an increasingly heavy financial burden for SOEs in the Chinese economy. The overall costs of welfare and labour insurance, as a percentage of the total wage bill, rose steadily, from 14 per cent in 1978 to 33 per cent in 1996 (State Statistical Year Book, 1997), generating a mounting pressure for reform. The overall objective of reform was to establish a nationwide social insurance system, the costs of which would be shared by three parties: the state, the enterprise and the individual employee. The new labour law thus requires both employers and employees to make contributions to five separate funds: pension, accident and injury, maternity, unemployment, and medical funds. Managed by local government agencies, the new social insurance system provides a safety-net for employees in both JVs and SOEs in the event of their employers going bankrupt.

Our investigation found that both SOEs and JVs are respectively conforming to the current legal requirements of the new social insurance system. Certain SOEs, however, have been unable or unwilling to fully modify their welfare arrangements, and continue to take the lion's share of the responsibility, with employees making only nominal contributions. On the contrary, most JVs demand and achieve increased employees' contributions for their own welfare and benefits. One Shanghai-based joint venture, however, was paying employee contributions to social security funds as an explicit part of their recruitment and retention strategy (see Goodall and Warner, 1997). Naughton (1997) similarly suggests that certain Chinese enterprises in the hi-tech sector, which have a requirement to recruit and retain highly qualified employees, continue to offer traditional work-unit *(danwei)* benefits in order to support this need.

Labour Turnover

With the demise of 'iron rice bowl' employment practices and the development of a nascent labour market, labour mobility –

facilitated by reforms in the urban registration (*hukou*) system – has become much greater. Our study found that both SOEs and JVs reported substantially increased labour mobility. Interviews with SOE personnel directors revealed that in the course of large scale downsizing, some workers had voluntarily resigned and opened their own businesses (*cai hai*), or moved to foreign-invested sectors. A higher turnover rate for workers was observed in SOEs than in JVs for this reason.

Role of Personnel Directors

Our study found a limited degree of change in the roles of personnel directors in SOEs, who were much less market-orientated than those in JVs (see Table 2). Before the economic reforms, their role was limited to job assignment, record-keeping, and provision of welfare benefits (Child, 1994). The framework of personnel management in Chinese enterprises has been changing since the economic reforms were set in place. Personnel directors in SOEs were increasingly involved in making decisions related to recruitment and selection, dismissal, promotion, reward and punishment; and in both JVs and SOEs, personnel managers were extensively involved in arranging vocational training programmes. However, our interviews showed that personnel management in JVs had more elements of HRM than in the SOEs. Moreover, personnel directors in JVs had greater autonomy with regard to their input to recruitment, promotion, and the determining of reward and punishment systems.

Trades Union and Workers' Congress

The two challenges facing trades unions in the years of economic reform are to promote economic development, and at same time help maintain social stability (White, 1996; Ng and Warner, 1998). The 1994 Labour Law further empowered the trade union in an enterprise to sign collective employment contracts with the employer on behalf of the employees. In cases of inappropriate termination of labour contracts and labour disputes, the trade union has the right to intervene to protect the interests of employees. The trade union is the executive agency of the workers' congress, which is, in theory, empowered to supervise the management of the enterprise and represent the voices of the workforce.

TABLE 2
HRM PRACTICES IN CHINESE ENTERPRISES (N=62)*

	Number of JVs	Number of SOEs
Recruitment		
Old	2	2
Hybrid	8	18
Market-orientated	19	11
Employment contract		
Individual contract only	20	17
Individual and collective contracts	9	15
Average monthly wage (RMB yuan)		
Less than 500	2	6
501–750	6	14
751–1,000	13	8
1,001–1,500	5	3
1,501–2,500	3	1
Social insurance		
Old	0	0
Hybrid	7	18
Market-orientated	23	14
Role of personnel manager		
Old	5	27
Hybrid	25	5
Labour turnover		
Less than 1%	3	7
1–3%	12	17
3.3–5%	5	5
5.1–10%	7	2
Above 10%	3	1
Union participation		
Less than 25%	8	3
26 – 50%	0	0
50 – 75%	0	0
75 – 95%	2	4
Above 95%	20	25
Workers' congress		
0 = do not meet	16	2
1 = meet once yearly	6	9
2 = meet twice yearly	8	12
3 = meet thrice yearly	0	7
4 = meet more often	0	2

* Casing of missing data are mainly due to confidentiality in a limited number of firms.

Our survey data (see Table 2) showed that trades union participation was less extensive in JVs than in SOEs. Although trades unions in both forms of organization were involved in housing allocation, organizing leisure activities, providing assistance in labour disputes, and in individual and family problems, trades unions in SOEs participated to a larger extent in the business decision making process than in JVs. The presence of the Workers' Congress was, overall, substantially less significant in JVs (Goodall and Warner, 1997).

FURTHER ANALYSIS

The data collected in the survey were further analysed, using SPSS, to explore the extent to which type of ownership, size of the firm, and location have impacts on HRM practices.

We hypothesized that:

1. Foreign direct investment will have a positive impact on HRM practices in Chinese enterprises.
2. The size of the firm (employee numbers) will have a bearing on organizational inertia influencing the speed and extent of change.
3. The location of the firm, reflecting the openness of the business environment, will affect the general pattern of HRM prevailing in firms in that region.

In the course of our preliminary statistical analysis, our main concern at this stage, given the limitations of space, is the direction of the Pearson correlations only; a further, more extended publication will discuss the detail of the relationships. A number of interesting significant correlations (significant at $< .05$ or above using two-tailed tests) were revealed. We found that:

1. *Sales turnover* was positively related to employee numbers (.68).
2. *Employee numbers* were negatively related to year of establishment (.47), ownership type (.67), social insurance (.37), and the role of personnel directors (.48).
3. *Year of establishment* was positively related to ownership type (.67), social insurance (.33), and the role of personnel directors (.66).

4. *Ownership type* was positively related to social insurance (.33), role of personnel directors (.66), and labour turnover (.28).
5. *Location of the firm* was positively related to social insurance (.37).
6. *Labour turnover* was, as seen above, was positively related to ownership type (.28).

Test of Hypotheses

The results showed that *ownership type* was significantly and positively correlated with the following variables:

- the role of personnel directors (significant at < .001),
- social insurance (significant at < .01), and
- labour turnover rate (significant at < .05).

at the levels noted above.

This confirms our hypothesis regarding the positive impact of foreign direct investment on HRM practices. Joint venture firms in general adopted more market-orientated approaches in managing human resources and in designing social insurance schemes. The employees in JVs tended to have a higher labour turnover rate than in SOEs.

It is also noted that *ownership type* is significantly but negatively correlated with the following variables:

- participation in the trade union (–.25) (significant at < .05), and the presence of workers' congresses (–.54) (significant at < .001).

This is consistent with our observation that joint venture firms were less supportive of trades union activities than SOEs, and that trades unions and workers' congresses there played a less active role in enterprise management.

The *number of employees* was used as a proxy for the *size of the firm*. Nearly three-quarters of SOEs in the sample were large sized enterprises with over 1,500 employees. Our results showed that the number of employees was negatively related to the following variables:

- social insurance (.47, significant at < .001 level), and
- role of personnel directors (.28, significant at < .05 respectively).

Large SOEs tended to retain old-style social insurance schemes, in which the company absorbed the bulk of the cost of welfare, with negligible contributions from employees. Changes in the role of personnel managers tended to be limited in these enterprises, because of the difficulty in implementing a new HRM system due to, amongst other considerations, organizational inertia.

The variable *location* was used to code cities on a north–south axis. Our results showed that the *location of the firm* was positively associated with the following variables:

- social insurance reforms (.37), but negatively related to
- trade union participation (–.38), (both significant at < .01).

The further south you go, therefore, the less trades unions count. This finding reflects the greater openness of cities in coastal and southern regions. The finding here might also mirror the greater number of JVs, which were more heavily concentrated in the southern region, where trades unions play a relatively less important role. Trades unions are generally not welcomed by Hong Kong and Macao investors, and most foreign-invested firms there have neither unions nor workers' congresses (Ng and Warner, 1998).

DISCUSSION

The results of this study provide evidence that human resource management practices have undergone fundamental changes in Chinese enterprises in the last two decades of economic reforms, but this was most evidently the case in the foreign-funded sector. The old 'iron rice bowl' employment system is now being phased out as China steadily moves toward a market-orientated economy, and foreign direct investment has brought into China both the 'hardware' – the production facilities – and the 'software' – including human resource management practices and systems. Yet it is clear that even in the case of JVs, the grafting of new managerial and organizational forms onto older SOE structures has hindered the advent of HR practices. The degree of organizational inertia has, as our earlier research has suggested, been noteworthy.

Equity JVs have been the channel most preferred by the Chinese government for absorbing foreign technology (Tsang, 1994). Our data revealed the positive impact of ownership type on HRM practices. This is due to the efforts made by the foreign partners in JVs to transfer Western HRM techniques and systems into JVs. Although problems and impediments have been reported (Verburg, 1996; Fan, 1998; Von Glinow and Teagarden, 1988), JVs have frequently played a leading role in diffusing changes in HRM practices into Chinese enterprises, although in varying degrees, as we have seen.

With regard to location, our study found a significant correlation between location and the pattern of HRM practices. This is due to the differences in the level of economic development and degree of openness to FDI between the inland regions and the 'gold coast' provinces such as Guangdong, Fujian and Zhejiang. There must be some concern about the degree to which these 'wealthy, outward-looking and cosmopolitan' areas remain distinct from much poorer inland areas (*The Economist*, 24 October 1998: 24). Child (1994: 149) similarly offers some evidence that in the southern province of Guangdong managers spent less time than their counterparts in Beijing or Shanghai on political, administrative or personnel issues and more time focused on business issues. The effect of location on human resource practices was also evidenced by Ding and Warner (1999).

Broadly, in the present sample, we can conclude the following:

- The more northerly the location and the more distant from the coast, the greater the organizational inertia; and
- the more likely it is, therefore, that traditional attitudes and practices will still be in place in SOEs.
- The greater pace of economic reform in the south appears to be reflected in differences in many human resource practices, notably with regard to social insurance commitments, weaker trades union participation, and higher staff turnover rates.

China's emphasis on revitalizing SOEs in recent years has also provided a momentum for human resource management reforms in the state sector, but it is not necessarily referred to as such; the term 'personnel management' (*renshi guanli*) is still widely used. SOEs are under pressure to compete profitably with foreign invested firms, and the downsizing of their workforces is a prerequisite for an improvement in their competitiveness. The reduction in the size of the workforce has been even more widely encouraged in the last few years as the government has tried to reduce the burden of loss-making SOEs.

CONCLUSIONS

Modern HRM techniques and more market-orientated HRM practices are expected to become more common in Chinese enterprises, but this will take time. Human resources development, for example, will unquestionably increase over the coming years (see Zhu, 1999), but may be more narrowly defined than in Western or Japanese models. However, the concern for social stability (one reason for the growing political opposition to Premier Zhu Rongji's policies), as well as the persistence of organizational inertia in SOEs, has served as a brake on rapid change. In this regard, we would predict growing attempts at innovation in the area of HRM as China deepens its reform of the SOEs; however, regional and sectoral differences in levels of development are likely to remain as constraints for some years to come.

ACKNOWLEDGEMENTS

We would like to thank the following institutions that have helped us with this research investigation: the British Council; the China–Europe International Business School, Shanghai; the Marketing Department, City University, Hong Kong; the Judge Institute of Management Studies, University of Cambridge; and the Economics and Management Department, Tsinghua University, Beijing. We also gratefully acknowledge the assistance with field work of Zhang Qiang, of CEIBS.

REFERENCES

Child, J. (1994), *Management in China during the Age of Reform*. Cambridge: CUP.

Ding, D.Z. and Warner, M. (1999), 'Re-inventing China's Industrial Relations at Enterprise Level: An Empirical Field-Study in Four Major Cities', *Industrial Relations Journal*, in press.

Fan, Y. (1998), 'The Transfer of Western Management to China', *Management Learning*, Vol.29, No.2, pp.201–21.

Goodall, K.W. and Warner, M. (1997), 'Human Resources in Sino-Foreign Joint Ventures:

Selected Case Studies in Shanghai Compared with Beijing', *International Journal of Human Resource Management*, Vol.8, No.5, pp.569–94.

Goodall, K.W. and Warner, M. (1998), 'HRM Dilemmas in China: The Case of Foreign-Invested Enterprises in Shanghai', *Asia Pacific Business Review*, Vol.4, No.4, pp.1–21.

Korzec, M. (1992), *Labour and the Failure of Reform in China*. London: Macmillan and New York: St Martin's Press.

Lardy, N. (1998), *China's Unfinished Revolution*. Washington, DC: Brookings.

Lu, X. (1997), 'Minor Public Economy: The Revolutionary Origins of the Danwei', in X. Lu and E. Perry (eds), *Danwei: the Changing Chinese Workplace in Historical and Comparative Perspective*. New York: M.E. Sharpe, pp.21–41.

Lu, X. and Perry, E. (eds) (1997), *Danwei: The Changing Chinese Workplace in Historical and Comparative Perspective*. New York: M.E. Sharpe.

Naughton, B. (1996), *Growing out of the Plan: Chinese Economic Reform, 1978–1993*. Cambridge: CUP.

Naughton, B. (1997), 'Danwei: The Economic Foundations of a Unique Institution', in X. Lu and E. Perry (eds), *Danwei: The Changing Chinese Workplace in Historical and Comparative Perspective*. New York: M.E. Sharpe, pp.169–94.

Ng, S.H. and Warner, M. (1998), *China's Trade Unions and Management*. London: Macmillan / New York: St Martin's Press.

Perry, E. (1997), 'From Native Place to Workplace: Labor Origins and Outcomes of China's Danwei System', in X. Lu and E. Perry (eds), *Danwei: The Changing Chinese Workplace in Historical and Comparative Perspective*. New York: M.E. Sharpe, pp.42–59.

Tsang, E.K.W. (1994), 'Human Resource Management Problems in Sino-Foreign Joint Ventures', *International Journal of Manpower*, Vol.9, No.10, pp.4–21.

Tsang, E.K.W (1998), 'Foreign Direct Investment in China: A Consideration of Some Strategic Options', *Journal of General Management*, Vol. 24, No. 1, Autumn, pp.15–35.

Vanhonacker, W. (1997), 'Entering China: An Unconventional Approach', *Harvard Business Review*, March/April, pp.130–40.

Verburg, R. (1996), 'Developing HRM in Foreign–Chinese Joint Ventures', *European Management Journal*, Vol.14, No.5, pp.518–26.

Von Glinow, M.A. and Teagarden, M.B. (1988), 'The Transfer of Human Resource Management Technology in Sino-US Cooperative Ventures: Problems and Solutions', *Human Resource Management*, Vol.27, No.2, pp.201–29.

Wang, Z.M. (1993), 'Culture, Economic Reform and the Role of Industrial and Organizational Psychology in China', in H.C. Triandis, M.D. Dunette and L.M. Hough (eds), *Handbook of Industrial and Organizational Psychology*, Vol.4. New York: Consulting Psychologists Press, pp.689–725.

White, G. (1996), Chinese Trade Unions in the Transition from Socialism: Towards Corporatism or Civil Society? *British Journal of Industrial Relations*, Vol.34, pp.433–57.

Warner, M. (1995), *The Management of Human Resources in Chinese Industry*. London: Macmillan/New York: St. Martin's Press.

Warner, M. (1996), 'Economic Reforms, Industrial Relations and Human Resources in the People's Republic of China: An Overview', *Industrial Relations Journal*, Vol.27, No.3, pp.195–210.

Yip, G.K.B. (1996), 'Labour Management in Domestic and Foreign Investment Enterprises', in J. Smith and M. McFadden (eds), *Employment in China*. Hong Kong: THC Press.

Zhu, C.J. (1999), 'Major Emerging issues in Human Resource Management', in L. Kelley and Y. Luo (eds), *China 2000: Emerging Business Issues*. Thousand Oaks, CA and London: Sage, pp.333–63.

Zhu, L.X. (1997), 'The Emergence and Development of China's Labour Market', *Reference Materials for Economic Practitioners (Jingji Gongzuozhe Cankao Xuexi Ziliao)*, No.46, pp.3–13.

Zhuang, Q.D. (1994), 'Employment, Wage Distribution and Social Insurance', in G.M. Luo (ed.), *Ten Research Projects: Speeding up Reforms and Promoting Socialist Economic Construction in China (Shige Zhuanti Diaocha Yanjiu)*. Dalian: Press of Northeast University of Finance and Economics.

12

Conclusions: Implications for Employment, Organization and Society

MALCOLM WARNER

It is clear that a 'managerial revolution' has been achieved in China, at the expense of older ways of managing and organizing. To sum up, not only have the state-sector enterprises been reformed in varying degrees but also new forms of organization and ownership have been encouraged. There are now agreements regarding well over 315,000 foreign-invested firms. Joint ventures, once a novelty, are now very common, as we noted in the introduction to this volume. There are tens of thousands of these in large cities like Beijing and Shanghai. They provide both employment and exports. The larger ones, arising out of agreements between Chinese firms and Western or Asian MNCs, enable technological transfer to take place both at the level of production 'know-how' as well as managerial 'software' (Child, 1994).

CHANGING MANAGERIAL AND ORGANIZATIONAL OPTIONS

The classical model of the *danwei* is still the state-owned enterprise in many ways, yet it has not only experienced a 'managerial revolution' but is now being pushed one step beyond the 'iron rice bowl' (see Ng and Warner, 1998; Warner, 1999). The SOEs still, of course, play a key, if reduced, role in the economy; they produce well over half of the state's tax revenues and employed a significant share of workers in many cities until the mid 1990s.

'Downsizing' on a widespread scale could soon greatly fuel discontent. Strike protests such as the ones in Zigong, in Sichuan province, for example, have resulted from cut-backs in employment and unpaid wages. Large crowds of people were involved here, which is unusual for the PRC. There have been protests in the 'rust-belt' of China in the north east, such as those in Shenyang. Nearer to Hong Kong, many demonstrated in Nanhai, in Guangdong province, with similar grievances. In January 1998, over 1,000 workers demonstrated in Wuhan in a similar vein, with allegedly 30,000 onlookers. Further, sizeable disputes continued into 1999. The *China Labour Bulletin*, a labour dissident journal published in Hong Kong, regularly chronicles these occurences. Estimates of 20 million or more unemployed state-owned enterprise workers are mooted as these industrial dinosaurs shed labour. The national railways are said to be ready to shed one million or more jobs. Already, the ranks of the urban footloose are swollen by the economic migrants (or *mingong*) from the rural areas, who may well number 100 million or more (see Solinger, 1999: 18).

The truth is that nobody really knows how many there are in the shadow labour market. Many workers are laid off by their firms with a pittance to survive on, and are dubbed *xiagang*; they are not officially classified as unemployed and thus do not enter the (dubious) national statistics. According to the *Far Eastern Economic Review* (30 November 1997), the true unemployment rate was predicted to rise to between 15 and 20 per cent of the total labour

TABLE 1
CHINESE LABOUR MARKET STATISTICS

Total workforce 1997	696 million
Jobs needed in urban areas*	54 million
Jobs available in urban areas*	38 million
Surplus in cities and towns*	16 million
Jobs needed in rural towns/villages*	77 million
Surplus in agriculture*	*c*. 240 million
Downsized workforce, SOEs, 1997	6.3 million
Official urban unemployment rate, 1997	3.1 per cent
Official urban unemployment rate, 1998	3.5 per cent
FEER estimated unemployment rate, 1998	15.0–20.0 per cent

* Over five-year plan, 1995–2000

Sources: ACFTU; State Statistical Bureau.

force. In 1997, there were nearly 700 million workers and peasants in the labour force. In the preceding five years, an extra 35 million found work in the cities and towns. But there is a shortfall of jobs available for the new high-school leavers in the urban economy, let alone the estimated rural labour surplus of over 240 million peasants (see Table 1; and Department of General Planning, 1998).

According to interviews carried out by myself and colleagues in China in November and December 1998, we interpreted unemployment as much higher than the official estimates suggest. In 1997, it was officially 3.1 per cent; this rose in 1998 to 3.5 per cent (*Chinese Trade Unions*, June 1998: 2). Trade union officials we interviewed predicted it would rise to over 7 per cent by the year 2000. But this is a statistical fiction, as the real rate of urban unemployment may well be already nearer 10 per cent in the more prosperous cities and even higher than this in the rust-belt conurbations. The low official rate is based on the particular Chinese definition of unemployment, which does not follow the ILO measurement. In the SOEs, workers are laid-off (*xiagang*) for a period of up to three years, where they are enrolled in the 're-employment service' and not counted as jobless. They are paid the minimum wage; then they may be registered as formally 'unemployed' (*shiye*) for the next two years and go on to minimum social security payments.

The laid-off workers continue to be paid by the SOE and remain members of it, and may often retain their housing and other welfare benefits for the interim. The 'unemployed' are paid out of the unemployment contributory fund, into which firms have to pay 3 per cent of their payroll and workers 1 per cent of wages. After this, they are paid a minimum poverty level living allowance that is means-tested out of state funds. In Beijing, the minimum wage paid to the laid-off was about one-third of the median workers' wage, at about 300 RMB per month. The actual unemployment living allowance was a little lower at around 217–264 RMB per month, and the social security poverty level allowance was even lower, at 200 RMB per month (1 US$ = 8.3 RMB in late 1998).

A national welfare system has yet to be extended beyond the privileged minority of SOE workers. There is no long term 'safety net' for those who have lost their jobs, especially women workers, who form the bulk of those laid off. In one official study, 60 per cent of those who lost their work were female, though they were only around a third of those employed in the 1,230 enterprises that were included. The sexual division of labour and of employment and remuneration has built-in cost disadvantages for the *danwei* – hence managers under pressure to cut costs may cut back further on many female jobs. A speed-up in 1998 in the field of welfare reforms was advised by the State Commission for Restructuring Economic Systems, with a unified scheme replacing the fragmented one that exists at present. But others say it might take 10 to 15 years to complete. It is a priority, above all, in the large industrial conurbations of China, where the bulk of the problems are likely to ensue. However, in recent times major 'pilot' reforms of the social insurance arrangements have been launched in Beijing and Shanghai, for example. The 'social contract' that bound the rulers and ruled in the PRC together for so many years may be open to question if a new 'safety net' cannot be effectively and persuasively reformulated.

Much of what many of the Western critics of the status quo advocate has a familiar World Bank structural reform ring to it; the social consequences are another matter, however. Much of the dilemma lies in the fact that the social costs of deeper reforms will be high; the writing is already on the wall. Strikes and sit-ins already are in evidence, as the large SOEs downsize their workforces. The Gini coefficient has risen greatly in recent years, indicating greater economic inequality, and indeed has been underestimated. Poverty has grown, even in urban areas. Questions will be asked whether a reduction in living standards of many of the 'working class', some still in work and others retired, who have been the stalwarts of the post-1949 People's Republic as the 'masters' (*zhuren*), can be condoned. There will decidedly be winners and losers (see Solinger, 1999). But it is not yet clear who these are and how much 'voice' they can express in the present system. If the losers do not feel they are being listened to, they may further resort to less orthodox means, such as more unofficial strikes, demonstrations and sit-ins. The political risks are considerable; whether the reforming coalition led by Premier Zhu Rongji can hold the line is another matter.

Thus, taking the reforms one step further without careful deliberation and forethought may carry costs as well as benefits. The new leadership in China will have to ponder the risks to their regime. A slowdown in the economic growth rate normally puts the brake on the creation of new jobs. At least 9 per cent economic growth is said to be needed to absorb most of the newly jobless. It has struggled to reach 8 per cent, and had fallen below this as we moved to the end of 1998. Some critics doubt if it is anywhere near that and advise clipping 2 per cent off any official Chinese estimate of GDP growth. There could be a threat of public disorder not seen since 1989, if significant economic growth does not occur. Already, the alarm bells have sounded, and official pronouncements have alerted the party faithful to what might be in store in the political front. The tenth anniversary of the 1989 Beijing Spring events loomed large. The *People's Daily* editorials have called for 'solidarity'. The threat of independent trades unions has again led to arrests and repression. An economic crisis might intensify matters further and consequently be disastrous in terms of political repercussions for the economic reform process as a whole! The clock could be turned back a decade, at least if the worst was to ensue. At the time of writing, the recent Asian crisis had cooled down somewhat; China had to date avoided internal disruption, both economical and political, in the main apart from the anti-NATO street-level protests. Policy and financial analysts, indeed many foreign investors, remain anxious. Chinese devaluation to remain competitive *vis-à-vis* its 'little Dragon' neighbours has always been a worry. A form of Asian 'beggar my neighbour' devaluation cycle could be very destabilizing, as it was in Europe in the 1930s. Greater 'Asian contagion' could further unsettle the G8 economies and possibly many others.

As *The Economist* phrased it, 'China has not scraped by Asia's crisis, not by a long way' (14 February 1998). Increasingly, China's industrial workforce is now being linked to global markets, directly or indirectly, it is said. But China is not as directly dependent on exporting as many of its neighbours – say, South Korea and Taiwan. State-led development, mediated by the market, is still the order of the day; but a really market-driven economy is still a distant prospect. Time is, no doubt, not on the side of the Beijing leadership. Informed speculation is also not easy, given the nature of China's opaque, often secretive institutions. However, in these potentially turbulent millennial times, great caution is called for in second-guessing the future of the Chinese economy and society.

POSSIBLE POLICY DIRECTIONS

Government policies needs to be aimed in the following directions:

- to continue and deepen the economic and enterprise reforms;
- to consolidate and merge the viable state enterprises in key economic sectors;
- to allow non-state enterprises to expand in all others;
- to encourage in particular the growth of small and medium sized enterprises (SMEs) in all sectors, particularly for job creation;
- to ensure that economic growth is encouraged in the provinces in the interior as well as in the coastal ones;
- to further expand the supply of trained managers at all levels and improve its quality;
- to invest more in vocational training for the young, as well as extending re-employment agencies and retraining programmes for displaced managers and workers;
- to replace the old personnel management system with a more HRM-orientated one;
- to initiate a decentralized, non-adversarial industrial relations system, with choice of union representation;
- to set up a nationwide and effective social insurance programme;
- to implement a fair taxation system that keeps income inequalities within reasonable limits and raises revenue for helping the 'losers' to find new jobs;
- to institutionalize further the 'rule of law', notwithstanding its application to business and employment relations;
- to create a truly 'Chinese' model of the firm, with sound corporate governance.

CONCLUSIONS

After 1949, China had evolved its own development model, centred on the *danwei* model (see Lu and Perry, 1997). Although not typical of the whole workforce, as it only applied to the industrial proletariat in SOEs who were (and still are) a minority in a largely peasant economy, the 'iron rice bowl' (*tie fan wan*) employment system nonetheless epitomized the 'social contract' of

TABLE 2
TOWARDS A NEW MANAGERIAL MODEL 'WITH CHINESE CHARACTERISTICS'

Old model	New model
State ownership	Diffused ownership
Resource-constrained	Market-driven
Soft loans	Hard loans
Technical criteria	Allocative efficiency
Economic cadres	Professional managers
Iron rice bowl	Labour market
Jobs for life	Employment contracts
Work assignment	Job choice
Personnel administration	Human resource management
Enterprise-based training	Outside training
Egalitarian pay and perks	Performance-related rewards
Payment in kind	Marketized benefits
Company flats	Rented housing market
In-house social services	External social provision
Free medical care	Contributory medical insurance
Central trades union role	Weaker union influence
Workers' congress	No workers' representative body
High institutional dependency	Low institutional dependency

Source: Adapted and expanded from Warner, 1995: 50.

the time (see Table 2).

Today, the 'three old irons' are being replaced by what has been expressed in modern colloquial parlance as the 'three new irons', namely *tie mienkung* (iron face), *tie xinchang* (iron guts) and *tie showan* (iron hands), more broadly signifying a shift to 'tougher' attitudes towards social responsibilities and society itself; but this may also be interpreted more narrowly as relating to the specific realm of employment relations. China is, as we have seen earlier, decidedly moving towards a more flexible factor-market model; employee and managerial expectations are in turn changing. Although Chinese workers are faced with the harsher economic climate, recent empirical studies (for example, see Warner, 1999) suggest that they (particularly the younger ones) have a less pessimistic view than many accounts would suggest; they appear well aware that their work-unit (*danwei*) can no longer guarantee their jobs and benefits, but nonetheless retain their motivation and compliance to managerial authority. Even so, further unofficial strikes and sit-ins has been experienced in several Chinese cities where downsizing has taken place. It is estimated that 20 million or more industrial workers could be dispensed with. In many of the loss-making SOEs, wages and pensions have not been paid for months on end. Displaced workers often have no savings to live on and have limited compensation from their enterprises. Street-level protests may be inevitable, particularly if there are no effective official channels, other than the compliant state-guided official trades unions, for grievances to be aired and channelled to the authorities (see Walder, 1986; Ng and Warner 1998; Warner, 1999).

In several Chinese firms where we recently conducted interviews, we found strong evidence of restructuring. Taking three 'classic' types of case-studies we completed, we find the following. For example, in a traditional 'bench-mark' SOE steel plant, up to 10 per cent of the labour force is marked for lay-off status and displacement; in a notable automotive vehicle joint venture, a leading exemplary site of the post-1979 reforms, the figure was 28 per cent this year; even in a postmodern, fast-growing 'hi tech' computer equipment and software firm, new recruitment was frozen.

China's current economic restructuring is also affecting economic growth; people are spending less. For instance, we find private savings behaviour is affected in two ways. First, the restructuring of SOEs has heightened job insecurity and thus encouraged precautionary savings behaviour. Second, the removal of the socialist welfare safety net is forcing households to save more and more to cover education, medical care, housing and social insurance, pensions, unemployment cover and so on.

More upheavals can be expected if the economy falters. China's GDP needs to grow at around 8, even 9, per cent per annum if the cork is to be kept in the bottle. If this rate is not sustained, then the downsized, displaced and jobless will not remain quiescent (see *The Economist*, 20 March 1999). Such tensions can only increase in the immediate future as the Asian crisis begins to have economic implications for the PRC within, as well as outside. It is clear that in these circumstances China is beginning to see the emergence of a new, more market-orientated management system, as is clearly evidenced by almost all of the contributors to this volume on China's so-called 'managerial revolution', compared with the old *danwei*-related managerial model (see Table 2); however, it is not one as yet fully comparable with an exogenous, particularly Western, one. The concepts, terminology and practices of the Chinese workplace are correspondingly changing, albeit with a time-lag, particularly given the 'organizational inertia' not only of the SOE sector but also the wider 'mind set' it engendered.

REFERENCES

Chinese Trade Unions (ACFTU), June 1998.

Child, J. (1994), *Management in China in the Age of Reform*. Cambridge: Cambridge University Press.

The Economist, 20 March 1999.

Far Eastern Economic Review (FEER), 30 Nov. 1997.

Department of General Planning (1998) *Report on Human Resource Development in China*. Beijing: Ministry of Personnel.

Ng, S.H. and Warner, M. (1998), *China's Trade Unions and Management*. London: Macmillan / New York: St Martin's Press.

Lu, X. and Perry, E.J. (eds) (1997), *Danwei: The Changing Chinese Workplace in Historical and Comparative Perspective*. New York: Armonk / London: M.E. Sharpe.

Solinger, D.J. (1999), *Contesting Citizenship in Urban China: Peasant Migrants, the State and the Logic of the Market*. Berkeley, CA: University of California Press.

Walder, A.G. (1986), *Communist Neo-Traditionalism: Work and Authority in Chinese Industry*. Berkeley, CA: University of California Press.

Warner, M. (1995), *The Management of Human Resources in Chinese Industry*. London: Macmillan.

Warner, M. (1999) (ed.), *Changing Workplace Relations in the Chinese Economy: Beyond the Iron Rice Bowl*. London: Macmillan / New York: St Martin's Press (in preparation).

Notes on Contributors

Malcolm Warner is Professor and Fellow, Wolfson College and the Judge Institute of Management Studies, University of Cambridge. He is the author of many books on Asian management including *The Management of Human Resources in Chinese Industry* (1995).

Roger Bennett is a Reader in Business Studies at London Guildhall University, London and researches in international technology transfer.

John Child is Diageo Professor of Management Studies at the Judge Institute of Management Studies, University of Cambridge and is currently on secondment at the Hong Kong University. He is the author of many books including *Management in China During the Age of Reform* (1994).

Bahman P. Ebrahami was until recently Assistant Professor of Management in the School of Business at Hong Kong Baptist University. He is now on the faculty of the University of Denver. His interests include Chinese managerial behaviour and related fields.

Carolyn Erdener is Professor of Management at the Stuttgart Institute of Management and Technology, Germany, where she teaches international management courses. Her current research is on business ethics and strategic management in the emerging markets and transitional economies, particularly in China.

Daniel Z. Ding is Assistant Professor of Management at City University of Hong Kong. He has published several articles in the field of Chinese industrial relations and HRM. He originally undertook his doctoral research at UCLA.

Paul L. Forrester is Senior Lecturer in Operations Management at Aston Business School, Aston University, Birmingham. He has conducted extensive research in Chinese manufacturing companies.

Keith Goodall is a lecturer in Organisational Behaviour at the China Europe International Business School (CEIBS) in Shanghai and teaches on the MBA programme at the Judge Institute of Management Studies, University of Cambridge. He is also an active consultant in the field of International HRM.

Sally Heavens has conducted research in the Centre for International Business and Management at the Judge Institute of Management Studies, University of Cambridge. She is currently writing on trust and learning in cross-national teams.

Simonetta Ilari has a PhD from the University of Hong Kong and now works for a multi-national company in Hong Kong.

Adrienne La Grange is a Research Assistant Professor in the Department of Social Administration at City University of Hong Kong.

Ping Lan is Lecturer in the School of Marketing and International Business, Queensland University of Technology, Australia. He has previously worked as a journalist in Thailand. He is the author of *Technology Transfer to China through Foreign Direct Investment* (1996).

Robin S. Porter is Senior Lecturer in Chinese Politics and Director of the China Business and Policy Unit, Keele University, Staffordshire. In the 1980s he was Adviser to the China Trade Group of the British automotive industry.

Douglas N. Ross is a Professor of Management at the College of Business and Economics, Towson University, Maryland. His research interests cover comparative economic and management systems. He is currently co-authoring a book on Internet Banking.

Jan Selmer is Professor of Management at the Hong Kong Baptist University. He is the author of a recent book, *Vikings and Dragons: Swedish Management in Southeast Asia* (1997) as well as many other publications.

Denis F. Simon is Director of the China Strategy Group of Arthur Andersen Associates in Beijing, PRC. He was formerly a Professor of International Business at Tufts University. He is the author of many publications including an edited book, *The Emerging Technological Trajectory of the Pacific Rim* (1997).

Rosalie L. Tung is Ming and Stella Wong Professor of International Business at Simon Fraser University, British Columbia. She is the author of many books and articles including most recently editor of the *Handbook of International Business* (1998).

Verner Worm is Assistant Professor at Copenhagen Business School. He is the author of *Vikings and Mandarins: Sino-Scandinavian Business Cooperation in Cross-Cultural Settings* (1997).

Yanni Yan is Lecturer in the Department of Accounting, Finance and Management, University of Essex. She is a PRC national who was awarded her PhD from the University of Cambridge. She is the author of a recent book, *International Joint Ventures in China: Ownership, Control and Performance* (1999).

Abstracts

Introduction: China's Managerial Revolution, *by Malcolm Warner*

In recent years, the reform of Chinese management has been high on the PRC government's agenda. Since 1978, China has been moving from a command economy to a socialist market economy. As part of this process, it has had to turn its economic cadres into managers. In this edited collection, we first look at the ways in which the Dengist market-driven management model has been introduced, first at the macro level and then at the micro, enterprise level. Then we look at how old state-owned 'dinosaur' firms are being reformed, which has potentially enormous implications for managers. The 'contract responsibility' system, another theme we analyse, has, for example, increased managers' autonomy in decision making. We also look at specific examples of such reforms in the construction industry and in sales management. In addition, themes such as setting up a joint venture, managerial and organizational learning, as well as managers' motivation and HRM, are discussed.

Communitarian Capitalism: A 'Market' Model for China?, *by Douglas N. Ross*

As capitalist regimes of the global triad – American-style 'individualistic', European 'statist', and Japanese-style 'communitarian' – contend for dominance in the emerging world economic order, China is emerging as a critical battleground. This study examines the utility of the communitarian model for China's transition to market socialism. The first section presents salient features of Japanese-style capitalism; the second evaluates the model in terms of political-economic and socio-cultural institutional environments. The conclusion sets out implications for both Chinese leaders and foreign firms.

Managerial Adaptation in a Transitional Economy: China, *by Jan Selmer, Carolyn Erdener, Rosalie L. Tung, Verner Worm and Denis F. Simon*

Within the framework of an integrative overview of economic transition and reform in China, this contribution summarizes selected empirical studies that illustrate some of the wide-ranging problems managers encounter in adjusting to this new and continually changing environment. It argues that ad hoc processes of managerial adjustment in individual organizations are not merely reactions to changing environmental conditions, but also contribute to planning the direction of future systemic change. They can be seen as an essential mechanism for the incremental planning and implementation of economic transition.

The Politics of Management in People's China: From CMRS to Modern Enterprise and Beyond, *by Paul L. Forrester and Robin S. Porter*

This study reviews and analyses the changes in management systems in the People's Republic of China over the last decade. Within the wider context of the *Open Door* policy, the modernization of industry and increased enterprise autonomy, the contract management responsibility system (CMRS) and, more recently, the modern enterprise system (MES) have been introduced. These both provide enterprises (and the managers within them) with a framework within which to practise. This analysis describes the CMRS and the MES and then, on the basis of discussions and interviews with factory managers, and with officials responsible at the macro level for monitoring the implementation of policy, analyses the implications of the changes. The authors conclude that, despite the introduction of a degree of management discretion and independence, differences in opinion persist on what, precisely, are the current industrial problems, and therefore what to do to address them. There have, consequently, been mixed reports on the success or otherwise of both systems.

***Guanxi* and Salesforce Management Practices in China,** *by Roger Bennett*

Executives in 111 foreign enterprises selling within the People's Republic of China completed questionnaires examining the extents to which *guanxi* was recognized as a critical factor in salesforce marketing, and the influences of such recognition on their companies' local salesforce remuneration policies. The results suggest that businesses which did regard *guanxi* as important for Chinese salesforce marketing were more likely to employ behaviour-based than outcome-based reward systems. This finding is compatible with the proposition that the banking and recall of personal favours, network integration, willingness to rely on partners and other *guanxi*-related characteristics can lead to sales performances for which outcome-based remuneration systems may not be appropriate. Notwithstanding the influence of *guanxi* on the manners in which salespeople were paid, volatility in the business environments within which firms operated encouraged their managements to adopt more market-led approaches to remuneration. Differences in the perceptions of the role of *guanxi* held by managers in foreign firms based in Chinese commonwealth and in other countries were also investigated. It emerged that companies based in the Chinese commonwealth acknowledged the importance of *guanxi* to a greater extent than companies with headquarters in Western nations. The longer a company had operated in China the more likely it was to incorporate *guanxi* considerations into its local management systems.

Management in the Chinese Construction Industry, *by Ping Lan*

One important aim of economic reform in China is to allow state-owned enterprises to be more market driven. This contribution, based on an industry competition model and four cornerstones for indicating economy transformation, scrutinizes the major changes taking place in the Chinese construction industry. It finds that the behaviour of key stakeholders such as managers, contractors, government, suppliers, clients, and new entrants in the industry has dramatically changed. However, a contractual chain within the industry is far from complete, and relationships between the main stakeholders are problematic. Thus, further reforms are needed to maintain industry's orderly development.

Transferring Ownership-specific Advantages to a Joint Venture in China, *by Simonetta Ilari and Adrienne La Grange*

In 1994, a Sino-Italian joint venture was established in Foshan (China) to manufacture and sell motorcycles. The Italian parent company perceived important ownership-specific advantages in investing directly in China. These included its state-of-the-art production process, its marketing and distribution network, and its organizational and work concept. Indeed, it was intended to virtually 'replicate' these features of the parent company in China. This study explores problems experienced in attempting to reproduce these features of the parent company's European operation during the start-up phase of its Chinese affiliate. One problem was that core suppliers were reluctant to relocate part of their operations to China, making it difficult for the parent company to 'replicate' its production process abroad. There were also major difficulties in transferring the principles of its marketing and distribution network and its organization structure and work concept to China. While it is possible that many of these preliminary problems would be overcome and the parent company would realize its vision for its Chinese affiliate over time, this case-study not only highlights the complexity of harnessing ownership-specific advantages of foreign direct investment (FDI) in China, but also raises important issues about the expansion of FDI from low technology to medium technology enterprises in the circumstances prevailing in China.

Managing Corporate Networks from America to China, *by John Child and Sally Heavens*

Multinational corporations (MNCs) are making a major contribution to China's economic development. This analysis examines how eight prominent American MNCs are handling the process of linking the management of their China joint ventures into their global structures. It looks at how the MNCs are addressing the tensions that arise between maintaining control in terms of their worldwide standards while attempting simultaneously to adapt to the complex and dynamic environment of China. The reconciliation of these requirements depends on a relatively few focal actors, who are located at critical interfaces within the MNCs' internal networks between the China joint ventures and the corporate level.

Managerial and Organizational Learning in Chinese Firms, *by Yanni Yan*

This investigation has thrown light on ways in which international joint ventures (IJVs) are addressing the issues of balance between the need to learn the knowledge and management practices introduced by the other partners and the need for the partners to maintain that level of control which enables them to secure appropriate returns from their equity investment. The results from the investigation of 67 IJVs show equity can be used as an appropriate indicator for examining both the process and the outcome of learning embedded in the organization. They also suggest that the control leveraged from a majority equity share can be used to safeguard knowledge and competencies whilst simultaneously responding to the necessity to incorporate the knowledge and management practices of its partner. Learning achieved in an IJV may not necessarily relate only to the control mechanisms exercised as there are many other variables that may have an impact including attitudes, cultural capital building, or even government policy. This study thus highlights the relationship between the impact derived from the ways of committing the resources onto an IJV and its contribution to the learning achieved in an IJV.

Motivation to Manage in China: Implications for Strategic HRM, *by Bahman P. Ebrahimi*

Since 1979, the People's Republic of China (PRC) has made tremendous economic progress. As a result, China and its management practices have received increasing research attention. Human resource management practices in China have been extensively explored elsewhere. Unfortunately, little research has dealt with the concept of hierarchical role motivation theory; its main construct, motivation to manage; and its potential implications for strategic human resource practices in the PRC. The study reported here is an attempt to fill this void.

The 'Myth' of Human Resource Management in Chinese Enterprises, *by Malcolm Warner, Keith Goodall and Daniel Z. Ding*

This study examines changing labour-management practices in China's state-owned enterprises (SOEs) in comparison with those in joint ventures (JVs). Based on a sample of 62 firms in seven Chinese major cities, it explores the degree to which HRM practices are a 'myth'. The researchers carried out semi-structured interviews with managers and other employees at all levels. The role of trade unions and workers' congresses are also examined. The results show that the ownership type, size of the firm, and its location are important factors affecting the extent to which these enterprises have adapted to market-orientated HRM practices. The study concludes that most firms have not fully made this adaptation, and that even where it has been taken up, it has in many cases only been done so partially due to organizational inertia, amongst other factors.

Index

Other Titles in the Series

East Asian Direct Investment in Britain

Philip Garrahan, *University of Northumbria at Newcastle* and
John Ritchie, *Durham University Business School (Eds)*

This book is a highly topical study of the role of FDI and its effect on regional political economy. The North of England has claimed more inward investment from East Asia than any other region in the European Union. Specialists from business organization and management join with political economists and geographers to consider how this FDI has influenced change in the region, and plot the dynamics of this particularly British phenomenon. The contributors investigate the main indicators of change and the interaction with FDI from East Asia against the background of profound changes in the regional economy in the last decade and a half. They discuss in particular how the North has met the challenge of its long-term decline and, now that this source of FDI is levelling off and there are signs of dis-investment, the implications for the region.

168 pages 1999
0 7146 4981 3 cloth
0 7146 8044 3 paper
Volume 6

Korean Businesses

Internal and External Industrialization

Chris Rowley, *City University Business School, London* and **Johngseok Bae,** *Hanyang University, Seoul (Eds)*

This volume represents a broader and more historical perspective in order to demonstrate the determinants of Korean economic success, a more balanced view which is long overdue. Essays focus on the Korean model of industrialization and internal internationalization, organizational capabilities and management roles, and the disadvantages inherent in the model.

The subjects covered include the sources and underpinnings of economic growth and industrialization, corporate catch-up strategies, foreign investment, and the causes of the financial crisis and future possibilities. Links are made to longer-term trends and the sustainability of the Korean model.

160 pages 1998
0 7146 4924 4 cloth
0 7146 4483 8 paper
Volume 5

FRANK CASS PUBLISHERS
Newbury House, 900 Eastern Avenue, Ilford, Essex, IG2 7HH
Tel: +44 (0)181 599 8866 Fax: +44 (0)181 599 0984 E-mail: info@frankcass.com
NORTH AMERICA
5804 NE Hassalo Street, Portland, OR 97213 3644, USA
Tel: 800 944 6190 Fax: 503 280 8832 E-mail: cass@isbs.com
Website: www.frankcass.com